START YOUR OWN

RETAIL BUSINESS AND MORE

Fourth Edition

Additional titles in *Entrepreneur's* Startup Series

Start Your Own

Arts and Crafts Business

Automobile Detailing Business

Bar and Club

Bed and Breakfast

Blogging Business

Business on eBay

Car Wash

Child-Care Service

Cleaning Service

Clothing Store and More

Coaching Business

Coin-Operated Laundry

College Planning Consultant Business

Construction and Contracting Business

Consulting Business

Day Spa and More

eBusiness

Event Planning Business

Executive Recruiting Business

Fashion Accessories Business

Florist Shop and Other Floral Businesses

Food Truck Business

Freelance Writing Business and More

Freight Brokerage Business

Gift Basket Business and More

Grant-Writing Business

Graphic Design Business

Green Business

Hair Salon and Day Spa

Home Inspection Service

Import/Export Business

Information Marketing Business

Kid-Focused Business

Lawn Care or Landscaping Business

Mail Order Business

Medical Claims Billing Service

Microbrewery, Distillery, or Cidery

Net Services Business

Nonprofit Organization

Online Coupon or Daily Deal Business

Online Education Business

Personal Concierge Service

Personal Training Business

Pet Business and More

Pet-Sitting Business and More

Photography Business

Public Relations Business

Restaurant and More

Retail Business and More

Self-Publishing Business

Seminar Production Business

Senior Services Business

Staffing Service

Travel Business and More

Tutoring and Test Prep Business

Vending Business

Wedding Consultant Business

Wholesale Distribution Business

Entrepreneur
MAGAZINE'S

 STARTUP

START YOUR OWN

RETAIL BUSINESS AND MORE

Fourth Edition

BRICK-AND-MORTAR • ONLINE
MAIL-ORDER • KIOSK

The Staff of Entrepreneur Media, Inc. & Ciree Linsenman

Entrepreneur
PRESS®

Entrepreneur Press, Publisher
Cover Design: Andrew Welyczko
Production and Composition: Eliot House Productions

This publication is designed to provide accurate and authoritative information in regard to the subject matter covered. It is sold with the understanding that the publisher is not engaged in rendering legal, accounting or other professional services. If legal advice or other expert assistance is required, the services of a competent professional person should be sought.

Library of Congress Cataloging-in-Publication Data

Linsenman, Ciree.
Start your own retail business and more: brick-and-mortar stores, online, mail orders, kiosks/by the staff of Entrepreneur Media, Inc. and Ciree Linsenman.—4th Edition.
    p. cm. — (Startup series)
Revised edition of the author's Start your own retail business and more, 2011.
ISBN–13: 978-1-59918-566-8 (paperback)
ISBN–10: 1-59918-566-0
1. Retail trade—Management. 2. New business enterprises. I. Kingaard, Jan. Start your own successful retail business. II. Entrepreneur Media, Inc. III. Title.

HF5429.L527 2015
658.8'7—dc23   2015007089

Printed in the United States of America

Contents

Chapter 5

Legal and Finance Issues 67

Chapter 6

Operations 81

Chapter 9

Chapter 10

Chapter 13

Social Network Marketing

Chapter 14

Customer Service

▲

Preface

We're assuming you've picked up this retail business startup guide because:

- you've worked in someone else's business and are ready to take charge of your own;

- you're an extrovert and enjoy constant contact with people;

- you're comfortable with the unexpected and are a problem-solver;

- you enjoy sales and don't mind working long hours indoors; and

- you know where you want your retail business to be in five years.

▲

Our goal is to tell you everything you need to know to:

- decide if a retail business is right for you;
- get your doors open for business;
- limit the number of mistakes you make; and
- keep your retail enterprise running successfully.

We've tried to make this guide as user-friendly as possible. Experts across the country share their experiences and insights with you to show you what really works and to help you avoid the pitfalls they've encountered. We'll tell you retailers' stories and give you some hard-won advice and cautionary notes. We hope you'll consult the useful contacts in the Appendix as often as you need to for answers and direction.

We've broken this guide's chapters into manageable sections on every aspect of starting and operating a retail product or service business. We've even included tip boxes with go-to action steps and some brainstorming questions to ask yourself to stimulate creative solutions to the particular problems you may face.

The concept of retailing in the United States began in the 1800s through a interchange between settlers and traders in New York and Chicago. As maturation of brick-and-mortar retailing occurred major players Montgomery Ward and Sears added the mail order business to the retail scene. Macy's, J.C. Penney, Woolworth, and Walmart increasingly offered more discounts and a variety of merchandise in bigger and bigger venues and the big box concept came to be.

Today, retailing encompasses so much more—we do business with people all over the world after courting them through social media and purchase from retailers who've presented to us our future wants by studying our online behavior. Mastering the new face of retail requires combining classic methods with a new intelligence attuned to how online relationships affect the bottom line. We've organized this guide to give you the navigational tools you'll need.

Now let's get started on your adventure. Happy trails!

Introduction to Retailing

The retail industry provides an exciting way of life for the more than 42 million people who earn their livelihoods in this sector of the U.S. economy. Those retail establishments provide the goods and services you and I need—from food, auto parts, apparel, home furnishings, appliances, and electronics to advice, home improvement, and skilled labor. Let's take a look behind the scenes at the many facets of this exciting business.

Welcome to the Big Leagues

Retailing is one of the fastest-growing segments of the economy. As one of the nation's largest employers, the retail industry provides excellent business opportunities. Entrepreneurs behind these ventures risk their capital, invest their time, and make their livings by offering consumers something they need or want. You'll meet several of them in this guide and learn how they created a niche for themselves.

Most retailing involves buying merchandise or a service from a manufacturer, wholesaler, agent, importer, or other retailer and selling it to consumers for their personal use. The price charged for the goods or services covers the retailer's expenses and includes a profit. Each year, this vital sector of our economy accounts

Who Are Your Competitors?

Wto know what the world's retailing status? Deloitte's Global Powers of Retailing 2015 Report illuminates the top ten retailers by their 2013 net income:

1. Walmart Stores — $476,294,000
2. Costco Wholesale — $105,156,000
3. Carrefour S.A. (France) — $ 98,688,000
4. Schwarz Unternehmens Treuhand KG (Germany) — $ 98,622,000
5. Tesco PLC (U.K.) — $ 98,631,000
6. The Kroger Co. — $ 98,375,000
7. Metro Ag (Germany) — $ 86,393,000
8. Aldi Einkauf GmbH & Co. oHG (Germany) — $ 81,090,000
9. The Home Depot — $ 78,812,000
10. Target Corporation — $ 72,596,000

for approximately two-thirds of all economic activity. The National Retail Federation (NRF)—the world's largest retail trade association—reported that retailing currently contributes $2.6 trillion to our annual gross domestic product, giving employment to 42 million (one in four) Americans.

Storefront ventures run the gamut from clothing boutiques and health-food stores to hardware stores, coffee shops, bars, laundry mats, convenience stores, and so on. Recent arrivals include mobile and temporary "pop-up" shops that set up for months, weeks, or days. Pretty Parlor A Go Go (prettyparloragogo.com) in San Francisco is a mobile beauty shop that goes to the customer and Spirit Halloween (spirithalloween. com) in New York sets up each annually to sell nightmarish get-ups from August through November. Vacant (govacant.com) in L.A. and New York helps pop-up retailers locate space and create a presence.

The NRF says there are more than three million retail establishments in the United States. Most are store retailers, though there are other types of enterprises— such as electronic commerce (etailing), mail order, automatic-merchandising (vending) machines, direct retailing (door-to-door selling), and service providers. The service and retail sectors of the U.S. economy continue to report the largest numbers of startup companies.

What about Jobs?

Chain Store Age's 2015 Retail Forecast predicts blue skies and cool breezes for the coming year—shoppers are increasingly more willing and able to spend. Managing director of industry economics at Moody's Analytics, Sophia Koropeckyj, says "stronger job growth, record low debt service burdens, record high stock values, and rebounding house prices" foster the upswing. The current rate of unemployment is 5.5, which is classified as "full employment", an ideal balance according to mainstream economists, who say that rates as low as zero cannot control inflation. We are coming to a point of balance from years of a struggling recession state and purse strings are more relaxed. Chain Store Age reported brick-and-mortar sales of $3 trillion in 2013 within the Top 100 Retailers group, dominated by big box, discount home stores like Walmart. According the National Retail Federation's 2015 economic forecast retail sales will increase 4.1 percent through 2015, up from 3.5 percent in 2014. The market is shifting toward what millenials will buy. *Time* magazine says by 2017 millenials will have more buying power than any other generation and have much different priorities and spending habits than their forefathers. They won't spend much money on pay TV (preferring media consumption on mobile devices), mass market beer (preferring craft beer), homes (can't afford them), weddings (waiting longer to get married), children (fewer than half plan to have them), and bulk warehouse goods, which is connected to not owning a home. An impressive list put out by Stores.org, in November 2014, demonstrates the hoops retailers are jumping through to earn business. They include using extremely fast delivery options from companies like UberRUSH and Deliv, offering same day delivery for local purchases, sometimes within mere minutes. Retailers are including extensive retail management options on their websites that let lookers see every possible color and size option available and even show dressed up doll versions of an outfit.

stat fact

The NRF says the retail industry supports nearly five million logistics jobs, four million management and administration jobs, two million healthcare and service jobs, two million finance, insurance, and real estate jobs, and 800,000 technology jobs.

Basic Kinds of Retailers

Retailing is one of the most mature industries in our economy, and constantly being reinvented with the advent of new technologies. Changes in buying behavior, attitudes and buying patterns, and the restructuring of the retail industry, have all had a significant impact on small businesses. While some predict the local retailer may become a thing of the past, there is a bright future for those who can identify and respond to changing consumer needs faster and better than their larger competitors. With the internet, TV, telephone, overnight delivery, and credit and debit cards, any enterprising individual can find a niche and begin making commercial transactions right away.

To give you an overview of the competitive marketplace, we'll take a brief look at the various faces and configurations of selling to the consumer. Keep in mind that all of these enterprises began as simple concepts and grew to various proportions through popularity and perseverance. At this point in your exploration, anything is possible for you, too.

Store Retailing

The retail scene in America is a dazzling array of independent shops, department stores, discount and off-price enterprises, convenience stores, membership warehouse clubs, national and regional chains, category-killer stores (superstores like Home Depot and Staples), conventional supermarkets, and other large-scale enterprises that seem to dominate the retail sector.

Store retailers operate fixed point-of-sale locations designed to attract a high volume of walk-in customers. In general, stores have extensive merchandise displays and use mass-media advertising to attract customers. They typically sell merchandise to the general public for personal or household consumption, but some also serve business and institutional clients. These include establishments such as office supply stores, computer and software stores, building materials dealers, and plumbing and electrical supply stores. Catalog showrooms, gasoline service stations, automotive dealers, and mobile home dealers are treated as store retailers by the U.S. Census Bureau.

To understand this diverse business sector, government reporting and other information is broken down into several sectors for easier digestion and fact-finding. The sector groupings are based on one or more of the following criteria:

tip

Successful retailers do not run their business to suit themselves. Retailers must cater to the tastes and requirements of customers. This can mean keeping the doors open on holidays and weekends, and opening early or staying late on some weekdays. You marry the store when you go into business for yourself, so expect many compromises along the way to profits.

- The merchandise line or lines carried by the store: For example, specialty stores are distinguished from general-line stores.
- The usual trade designation of the establishment: This applies in cases where a store type is well-recognized by the industry and the public but is difficult to define strictly in terms of commodities offered. Examples are pharmacies, hardware stores, and department stores.
- Capital requirements in terms of display equipment: For example, food stores have unique equipment requirements.
- Human resources requirements in terms of expertise: For example, the staff of a computer store requires knowledge that's not necessary in other retail operations.

Brick-and-Mortar Stores

While shopping by mobile device and online grow stronger every day, independent brick-and-mortars (retailers with physical stores) still dominate consumer sales and are expected to remain viable for several reasons. Foremost is their real-world presence, having a location that people can drive by, call, and walk through time and time again. It serves as a customer fulfillment destination for completing orders, socializing, and human engagement activities like events and bonding over merchandise. Gathering at a store validates the lifestyle customers are buying when they fall for your products because they meet, or see other people that like the same things there.

Shared experiences and one-on-one exchanges are valued by people of all ages. The ability to look someone in the eye and ask them questions or watch a demonstration appeals to human nature. Another advantage is the ability to feel and smell the merchandise, and to try it and compare it side by side with other items. Shoppers appreciate having a selection of items at their fingertips. There's instant gratification for buyers in carrying their purchases home with them. Additionally, there are no shipping charges to deal with or minimum purchases to make. People feel more comfortable paying in person than giving out credit information to disembodied entities. Returning items to a store is more convenient than mailing something back. Personal service, community involvement and local employment are three additional aspects of storefront retailers that will continue to appeal to the public for decades to come.

David vs. Goliath

You read a lot about the power retailers like Walmart, Home Depot, and Target. They have huge physical facilities housing a broad range of merchandise. Faced with these price-oriented giants, won't the little guy get crushed? Not necessarily. Many "Davids" are learning a thing or two about efficiencies and customer focus from "Goliaths" like Walmart, and they're flexing their own muscles. In fact, the United States is primarily a nation of small, independent merchants: More stores are small, both in size and sales volume.

The typical store is run by the owner alone or by a partnership. Such small enterprises naturally lack the substantial resources, purchasing muscle, and sophisticated operations of the large-scale retailers. For the small retailer, there may be a few employees, and one or two may be part-time workers. The store's size is, of course, related to the type of establishment: Furniture outlets, for example, require much more space than shoe stores and neighborhood groceries.

Matt Murphy, a New York-based designer, began his first incarnation in the fashion business quite by accident. In the early '90s, while in school for architecture he designed a series of portable bags as part of his thesis about an "urban nomad" with bags designed to hold technology and life's daily essentials. He created a small line of unusual handbags that caught the attention of *Vogue* magazine, and buyers' attention at stores like Maxfield, Fred Segal, and department stores.

In the 20 years since that initial coverage from Vogue, Matt Murphy and his studio have grown, and their work now covers product, interior, event, and graphic design (with a focus on branding and marketing). Murphy and his team also founded and designed the gourmet food and salt blend company, Sel Magique.

Specialty Retailing

While power retailers tend to sell "needs," specialty retailers tend to sell "wants." Specialty retailers focus on neighborhood convenience, the richness of the shopping experience, and inventory that meets the needs of their target customer on a personalized basis. Small specialty stores show surprising strength and resilience in the face of competition from large-scale retailers and internet retailers. They offer the consumer a warmer atmosphere, and perhaps a broader and deeper selection of merchandise.

tip

48days.net provides low-cost business ideas and inspirational case studies. Dan Miller, President of 48 Days, also provides business and life coaching and a podcast you can tune in to for weekly encouragement.

Many stores can be owned and operated by one person with minimal assistance. Compared to manufacturing operations, specialty retail outfits are relatively easy to start, both financially and operationally. However, a number of failures are due to undercapitalization, poor location, and insufficient market analysis. This guide is intended to help you avoid startup pitfalls by providing you with tricks of the trade to help you succeed.

There is always room for the right kind of store. Geographic shifts of large numbers of consumers are characteristic of our mobile population; stores need to be wherever people live. Fashions, changing lifestyles, evolving ethics, increasing concern about health care, and technological advances all contribute to the need for new variations on old retailing themes. Finally, retail openings continue to occur as established merchants retire, sell their businesses, or close down because of poor management practices or changes in the local environment. Your small store launched today may become the next Lowe's or Starbucks within the next decade. Niche retailer Neka Pasquale already had a successful holistic acupuncture and Chinese medicine practice in Mill Valley, California, when she began offering her clients fresh, raw juice on retreats. Due to overwhelming positive feedback she found herself opening up a small juice store, which today ships raw, fresh products to the health conscious all over the United States.

Nonstore Retailing

When you look at the array of business opportunities in retailing, be sure to include the $128 million nonstore retailing sector, as reported by the National Retail Federation. These businesses are primarily engaged in the retail sale of products through TV, electronic shopping, paper and electronic catalogs, in-home demonstration, portable stalls, vending machines, and mail order. With the exception of vending, these businesses do not ordinarily maintain stock for sale on the premises. They deal in books, coins, computers and peripherals, food, fruit, jewelry, magazines, novelty merchandise, CDs and DVDs, stamps, and home-shopping ventures, among others. An interesting variation on this is Pasquale's Urban Remedy. First, shoppers may take advantage of an online customization service offered by customer service agents standing by to offer educated advice. Then juice cleanse kits are selected for delivery or pick-up in one of her three stores.

When exploring your options, consider combining one or more retail opportunities.

There are many advantages to this type of retailing—one being that the buying, maintenance, and protection of a large inventory is not necessary, as you contract with others to handle these matters. The U.S. Census Bureau says total online sales for 2012 were $225 billion and in 2014 online sales represented over six percent of all sales.

aha!

Even if you're working full time, pick up some part-time or seasonal work in a retail store to get the feel of a small business. Observe how decisions are made, how employees are trained, and what kinds of customer attitudes you encounter. How are resources allocated? See how vendors and inventory are handled. See what works and what doesn't.

Temporary Locations

In your travels down remote roads and through the countryside, you'll find roadside stands offering ripe tomatoes, fresh corn by the bushel, avocados, freshly laid eggs, and other agricultural and dairy products. You might also see handcrafted items, artwork, souvenirs, holiday gifts, regional tokens, and novelties. Many of these businesses sell year-round, though some are seasonal by nature. Carts in malls, booths at festivals, spontaneous garage sales, and seasonal farmers' markets are additional outlets for the ambitious retailer.

Direct Selling

Direct retailing means selling to the consumer in his or her home using the telephone, the internet, or direct mail. Home-shopping TV channels and infomercials have boosted the popularity of shopping from the privacy and comfort of home. TV-based home shopping was originally touted as a new era in retail, but today the sector is dominated by two main players: HSN, with an average growth rate of five percent for the last three years, reporting 2014 third quarter earnings of $837.5 million and QVC, with $584 million in U.S. sales as of 2013.

QVC reports distribution to more than 300 million homes globally. People have to watch a show in real time to order items before they disappear from the air, although both networks also have ordering capability through their websites.

The convenience of ordering from home amid fluctuating gasoline prices, crowded highways and stores, time crunches, and physical and geographic barriers works to the advantage of direct retailers. According to Statista (statista.com) in 2014, 191 million adults in the U.S. bought something online

With phone marketing, in less than two minutes you can complete a transaction—speak with your customer, exchange information, and take an order. For more than a decade, there has been an increase every year in the use of pay-per-call, toll-free numbers, and fax (and now efax), -on-demand for almost every application imaginable. Consumers can purchase advice, news and information, magazine subscriptions, telecommunication programs, investments, DVDs, health supplements, and exercise equipment over the phone. The market is endless. Using telephone technology, you can inform, educate, solicit, and satisfy the consumer and your business needs. Because sales are made by phone to one person at a time, bulk orders, higher-priced items, and contract purchases are the most cost-effective.

In this internet age, many consumers like to be able to ask a real person questions before they buy and to feel like the person cares about them. According to the Direct Selling Association sales reached 32.67 billion in 2013. Home and family-care products, such as cleaning products, cookware, cutlery, etc., and personal-care items, such as cosmetics, jewelry, skin and health care products are sold through direct sales by companies. Direct Selling News (directsellingnews.com) 2014 Top 100 Global achievers list reports the top three spots as Amway earning $11.80 billion, Avon $9.95 billion, and Herbalife $4.80 billion.

Mail Order

From glossy wish books to basic brochures, catalogs are popular with those who live far from shopping areas, the elderly, those seeking the unusual or the obscure, and those who simply hate to shop. What could be easier than calling a 24-hour, toll-free phone number to order clothing, gifts, and gadgets? With direct mail, sales materials can be sent via snail or email to thousands of potential customers at one time to either make a sale or generate a sales lead. According to the Chief Marketing Officer Council World Wide, in 2014 email marketing was cited as the most effective digital marketing channel for customer retention in the U.S. A 2015 study by MailChimp (MailChimp.com) says the open rates for companies of all sizes on email campaigns range between 21.22 and 23.57 percent. The 2015 State of Marketing Report by Sales Force Marketing Cloud shows that 68 percent of the 5,000 global marketers surveyed said email marketing produced very effective results and 23 percent rated results as somewhat effective.

Selling products and services directly to consumers by mail and email is a growing sector because it offers entrepreneurs a high return on a low initial investment.

Mail order enterprises include general merchandise businesses, companies that sell specialty goods of all kinds, novelty firms, various types of clubs (CDs, DVDs, book, and ebook), and so on. In most cases, catalogs are sent to consumers in defined niches on a regular basis. Most of the catalog companies offer some form of expedited delivery so customers can receive merchandise quickly.

The extraordinarily versatile medium of direct mail enables you to target people, groups, or organizations within your trading area, all of which may be likely prospects for your retail business. You can work out of your home, a warehouse, or a brick-and-mortar store.

An up-to-date mailing or emailing list is the key to direct-mail profits with back-end fulfillment and relational database support. Most people selling things by mail need at least a 200 percent markup to make money. You shouldn't pay more than $10 for something you sell for $30. If you think this is the retail area for you, check out *Entrepreneur Magazine's Start Your Own Mail Order Business.*

The Internet

The internet has changed the retail landscape, connecting companies, markets, and individual consumers. Currently, consumers don't pay tax on products shipped out of state from non-store retailers. If they purchase online from a non-store retailer in their own state, that sales tax applies. All that may change soon, so don't get too excited about capitalizing on the zero tax frenzy web shoppers are attracted to. The National Retail Federation is lobbying for tax fairness to level the playing field for

---

Specialty Catalogs Deliver

Mail order has evolved from general catalogs to specialty ones. Small entrepreneurs can compete with the large houses and sell at bargain-basement prices because of low operating costs. Improvements in technology and delivery speed merchandise to customers. Specialty mail order appeals to busy people, hobbyists, people located in remote areas, and collectors. Local merchants and homebased entrepreneurs can fill niches and meet special needs for one-of-a-kind and limited-production items, gifts, novelties, leather goods, and personalized products. The U.S. Census Bureau reports that total ecommerce and mail order sales for 2013 were over $348 million.

brick and mortar retailers. The nearly $25 billion in sales tax going uncollected from this every year and the fact that consumers often ditch face-to-face shopping just to avoid paying sales tax results in lost jobs and income. Economist, Arthur Laffer, estimates a $563 billion increase in gross domestic product and 122 million jobs gain by 2022, should online retailers be required to pay those taxes.

Storefront retailers of all kinds are using the internet in increasingly creative and profitable ways, and you'll hear from some entrepreneurs in this book about how they're doing that. For more information on setting up an ecommerce business, read *Entrepreneur Magazine's Start Your Own eBusiness*.

Gary Vaynerchuk's family run, New Jersey wine store is very much influenced by the web presence he's created through his many online media outlets. Wine Library TV (tv.winelibrary.com) was a wine review show and though Gary created the very last episode in 2011 it continues to draw followers and support his family's business. He has since crossed over to operate VaynerMedia.com, a brand equity service he operates with brother, A.J. Vaynerchuk. GaryVaynerchuk.com is his official, all-encompassing site, through which this social media guru can be hired for speaker events,

Reinventing Retailing

Until the late 1990s, buyers and sellers conducted trade through three channels: in person, by phone, and by mail. The internet has become the fourth way for consumers to get what they want and it is quickly becoming a favored way to shop for it's efficiency, comfort, and money saving attributes. According to Walker Sands' 2014 Future of Retail Report, the most common attributes to influence online shopping are:

Free shipping	80%
1-day shipping	66%
Free returns and exchanges	64%
Easier online returns	48%
More confidence in payment security	42%
Multiple versions shipped at once	42%
Same day shipping	41%
Easier in-store returns	39%
Visual try-on capabilities	37%

interviews, and business consulting. Additional media outlets include the countless impromptu videos he's created on wine and social media presence, which are shown all over the web and cross-posted on many venues. On GaryVanerchuk.com, fans can also get the lowdown on his non-stop flow of current media projects, such as Vayner RSE, a $25 million seed fund that will help invest in and launch the next generation of world-changing technology companies . His best selling book, *Jab, Jab, Jab, Right Hook* helps business owners be heard and recognized amongst all of the competing noise on social media.

Though Gary's deep investment in the virtual world has enhanced Wine Library's customer traffic, once in the actual store, customers are delighted by affable, connected, human interaction.

His now famous face behind the once quieter family business is recognized as a "friend" for online followers and those relationships are nurtured with sincerity and one-on-one conversations. Closing the gap between virtual and actual through conscientious use of social media, he creates a unique business model and genuinely warm presence online for those millions who'd like to meet him. When asked why his videos seem so personal, he replied, "Because of their intent. Intent is outrageously underrated and mine is to be more personal than anyone else out there. People with good emotional intelligence are able to feel that."

fun fact

According to the National Automatic Merchandising Association, vending dates to 215 B.C. in ancient Egypt. In his writings, the mathematician Hero, of Alexandria, described a device found in places of worship that would dispense holy water when a coin was deposited.

Vending Machines

Automatic merchandising—or vending machine retailing—has been a proven business concept for more than a century. Omar Khedr, industry research analyst at IBISWorld says the American vending industry will hit $7.7 billion by 2019. As with any other sales venture, having the right product in the right place at the right time is key. This business is highly appealing because of the low startup cost, low working capital, and low overhead. This is a cash business, with you collecting the money when you replenish supplies. In Europe, shoppers can use their cell phones to pay for items in vending machines by debiting their checking accounts online. This is the future for American vendors as well.

Once mostly restricted to gum, candy bars, and canned sodas, today's vending machines sell snack foods, fruit, hot drinks, soups, milk, ice cream, fresh flowers, and an array of impulse goods and necessities. The machines are usually placed in high-traffic locations, such as subway stations, railroad and bus terminals, restaurants, office buildings, and bars. *Entrepreneur Magazine's Start Your Own Vending Business* shows you how to capitalize on the billions of dollars Americans feed vending machines every year.

Service Retailers

Some retailers offer after-sales services, such as repair and installation. For example, musical instrument stores, electronics and appliance stores, pool and spa stores, and computer stores often provide repair services. Then there are stores that are dedicated to service, such as shoe repair, pool and spa water treatment, and vacuum and sewing machine service. Service organizations include those specializing in education, travel, entertainment, health care, home care, child care, physical training, space planning/organization, coaching, insurance, and countless others.

A service firm is one that derives more than 50 percent of its sales from providing services that may involve a combination of tangible and intangible offerings. Service businesses are currently the most frequently established operations. Since they usually sell a specialty or skill, credibility is very important. Startup costs are often low, and many service businesses can be operated from home.

Selling a service to consumers is usually more of a challenge than selling merchandise. Consumers can touch, handle, and examine goods; this is something they cannot do with most services. Services must be experienced. For example, hair styling and dating services have to have established a track record to be evaluated.

You may need to tell the prospective customer what you are going to do, do it, and explain why you did it that way. For example, a carpet-cleaning service that uses a deodorizing process after cleaning the carpet should tell its customers about the special care included in the price and why this extra step is beneficial. Service providers often spend more time with their customers than do merchandise providers.

Many services are essentially perishable. For example, event tickets are only good for the day and time of the event. Dentists, physicians, attorneys, consultants, and accountants cannot recover earnings lost because of an unfilled or lost appointment. In contrast, tangible goods can be held in inventory and sold over several days or months. If a hotel room is empty for an evening, the revenue is lost forever, whereas a book or roll of wallpaper can be profitable for many seasons.

Most service firms are small, single-unit operations, and small size limits service companies' ability to achieve economies of scale. Changes are occurring, however, as tangible-goods firms have established major stakes in service and have introduced tangible-goods merchandising techniques in the services area. The International

Franchise Association says that one of the newest and fastest-growing sectors is high-tech medical spas, offering noninvasive services like laser hair removal and facial treatments. In addition, meal-assembly stores, which only began franchising in 2003, are hot franchise opportunities and growing quickly. Franchises that save people time and effort are also big, such as franchised home repair services, where employees perform simple tasks, like installing a shelf or curtain rods, for a fee. Service industries are typically characterized by low barriers to entry. Consequently, competitors can quickly enter a market and challenge existing businesses.

Many service organizations are labor-intensive. The output of an attorney, florist, or tax preparer cannot easily be increased. These and other services must be personally produced and tailored to the needs of individual clients. This precludes the use of automation and other labor-saving strategies. Because of this, and the fact that many services are offered only at the point of sale, standardization in the level of service and quality is difficult to achieve.

The demand for services is often more difficult to predict than the demand for tangible goods. Demand for services can fluctuate widely by the month, day of the week, or even the hour of the day.

Consumers also seem to feel that purchasing services is a less pleasant experience than buying goods, and consumers perceive higher levels of risk in buying services than in purchasing tangible goods. To bridge the "information gap," consumers are increasingly doing their research on lawyers, mechanics, banks, and a host of service providers on the internet the same way they compare features and prices for tangible goods.

Consuming Appetite for Services

Time is becoming increasingly scarce for millions of people. The 24/7 pace that technology has brought us spells opportunity as well as challenge for retailers. New businesses have sprung up to take care of many of life's chores. Personal shoppers, mothers' helpers, after-school programs, tutors, handyworkers, maids, valets, insurance and tax preparers, home grocers, pet care professionals, and reminder services are just a few ideas entrepreneurs are cashing in on. The majority of couples are two-income families, leaving little time for preparing meals, picking up the dry cleaning, reading a software manual, remembering birthdays, standing in bank lines, and waiting for the cable installer to show up. People will pay dearly for more time, so figure out what you can sell or do to put people back in charge of their days, and you'll be

stat fact

The average fulltime wage for retail workers 25 to 54 years old is $38,376, compared to the $37,968 for non-retail workers in the same age range.

a winner. Check out *Entrepreneur Magazine's Start Your Own Green Business*; *Start Your Own Senior Services Business*; *Start Your Own Blogging Business*; *Start Your Own Event Planning Business*; *Start Your Own Wedding Consultant Business*; *Start Your Own Personal Concierge Service*, and other startup guides for details on how to fill consumers' needs.

Step Up

Whether you are interested in a store, service, or hybrid operation, the deciding factor in your success or failure will be your relationship with the consumer. Get to know your prospects. Consider testing your business concept from home to control overhead costs. After gaining encouraging sales from friends, relatives, and neighbors, you can extend your reach through catalogs, efaxes, videocalls, and phone sales. From there, you might want to sell from an online store, a cart in a local mall, or through a pop-up shop (a short rental in temporary space) to test results, walk-in traffic, and promotional efforts. Then you can determine if your sales and management skills justify startup costs and long-term commitments. With a realistic view of what you're getting into, you can examine your options for location, size, and format—that is, can you sell more, and more profitably, through one distribution channel over another? Which form would that be—catalog, physical, or virtual store, or TV and radio sales?

Retailing's Image

Understand that shoppers are usually buying into a lifestyle in choosing a product. What lifestyle are you representing? Is the quality of your product "braggable"? Ask yourself which potential customers you alienate in choosing your branding and surrounding implied associations. These facts can be as helpful as knowing who is attracted to you and how they want to see themselves. You must be concerned with the perceived risk your customer has in doing business with you, be it social risk and being viewed in a certain light, or economic risk or putting the customer in a vulnerable position if dollars spent don't add up to solving their needs.

Social Responsibility

Retailers are improving their image by assuming greater social responsibility. In doing so, they're meeting the needs of society as a whole, rather than just focusing on maximizing profits. They provide their facilities for art exhibits, forums, and community activities. Executives lead fund-raising drives that benefit their communities,

▲

underwrite programs, sponsor events, and mentor students. Being a business owner provides opportunities for you to be involved in issues that matter to you and your customers.

Some retailers choose to locate in a downtown area that has become blighted over the years. They use some of their profits to help supplement federal funds for revitalizing the area. Locating in an inner city has special challenges because of the problems of vandalism, shoplifting, and other crimes. Nonetheless, some retailers want to make a contribution to society by upgrading the inner city while looking for profits over time.

Long a leader in providing career opportunities for women, retailers have generally made an effort to match the cultural mix of their employees to the community that surrounds them. This is a combination of social responsibility and good business sense. Many retailers have also initiated internal affirmative action programs to provide minorities with equal opportunities for upward mobility. Some retailers make a special contribution by employing high school dropouts and prison parolees in an attempt to train and retain them for the good of society and the firm.

Air and water pollution, accumulation of toxic chemicals and wastes, and overflowing landfills are just some of the environmental problems of the 21st century. Retailers are also assuming greater responsibility for the products they sell. As a retailer, you will have to be educated about the products and resources you support. This involves ownership and licensing issues, labor practices, environmental concerns, and research procedures. Growing numbers of consumers prefer con-

Retailers' Call to Action

To help fight the problem of so-called "sweatshops," all members of the National Retail Federation endorse the organization's Statement of Principles on Supplier Legal Compliance and pledge that they:

- ○ are committed to legal compliance and ethical business practices
- ○ choose suppliers who share that commitment
- ○ include contractual language requiring their suppliers to comply with the law
- ○ take appropriate action if a supplier has violated the law
- ○ support and cooperate with law enforcement authorities in the proper execution of their responsibilities

scientiously made products, which are sustainable, cruelty-free, organic, and made without the use of sweatshops. Because consumers vote with their dollars, they can discourage the use of unethical practices by not supporting those companies financially. A growing concern over toxic products and materials harming people, animals, and the environment, as well as a wariness of genetically engineered foods create spending behaviors.

Retailers should be aware of the lasting imprint their business leaves on the earth and its inhabitants. Groups such as Sierra Club, People for the Ethical Treatment of Animals, and Greenpeace not only hold business owners accountable for their effects on others, but also influence the flow of consumer dollars. More and more consumers are using their retail dollars to support businesses they believe in. Cutting edge retailers are realizing that if they earn a philanthropic, humane reputation they will not only glean more business from local compassionate consumers but also online recognition from travelers looking for ethical vacation destinations, an entire industry in itself. The Fair Trade Federation is an association of fair trade retailers, wholesalers, and producers whose members adhere to social criteria and environmental principles to foster a more equitable and sustainable system of production and trade.

tip

Retailers should be personable and charismatic. But having the gift of gab and being comfortable in diverse and changing conditions are not the only traits that contribute to success. Your ability to schedule payments, people, promotions, and products requires a remarkable amount of planning, focus, and perseverance.

You may also be required to have products tested or review test documentation before selling. Not only is it important to ensure safety for the users of your products and be able to proudly stand behind your reputation, but government regulations also make it mandatory. The increasing cost of liability insurance is forcing retailers to eliminate certain items. As our world evolves to a more sustainable, compassionate future, consumers are becoming quite well informed, insisting on higher levels of safety and responsible business practices. To have confidence and pride in your products, you'll need to do some research.

Many retailers now are considering their business and life goals as one journey. Erik Ekman's Outside Van in Portland, Oregon, sprang to life as a result of his survival skills. During college he was one of the top ten snowboarders in the world, as well as being a passionate surfer. Caring less about his studies than catching the next powder wave, he decided to renovate a smashed up van to be a place to live to save money for the important things in life—waves and powder. The first Outside Van was born of intertwining necessity, creativity, and athletic drive and now pro athletes all over the nation look to him to design their ideal livable ride. Because Erik's priorities on the road are largely the same as the athletes he designs vans for, creating what he prefers makes an industry perfect product.

There are currently many likeminded industries to operate or invest in as a business or franchise, such as organic produce and herb sales, natural garden services, natural and recycled material products, and ecotourism. Charlotte Cozzetto, founder of Ethique Nouveau in Minneapolis, Minnesota (ethiquenouveau.com), is known for all of the little green business habits she practices, as well as her eco-friendly products. And it pays off. Stopping in for some fair-trade chocolate or the latest ethical children's book may be the initial motivator, but the experience doesn't stop there for her customers. From washing her windows with vinegar and newspaper to holding bake sales for hurricane victims and asking if customers "need" a bag with their purchases, Charlotte acts as a role model for her community and attracts like-types to her store.

Windows of Opportunity

Today, finding the right goods or services and creatively marketing them no longer assures that a retail firm will grow and prosper. You must run your business with a constant eye on the consumer. You must have a strategic view of your business and focus on your positioning, changing consumer lifestyles, technological advances, and competitive business concepts.

Of all the habits of highly successful businesses that sell directly to the consumer, the ability to assess relationships with the marketplace is perhaps the most crucial. The ability to harness the energy of change is what separates innovative, energetic, growing, profitable companies from obsolete, static failures.

Store retailing offers the opportunity to meet lots of people. The retail store is a cash-and-carry operation. The day you open your store to the public, you begin taking in money at your cash register. Capital requirements are characteristically lower than for either manufacturing or wholesaling. This ease of entry is very attractive and explains the large number of new stores launched every year.

Consumers 45 and older are more familiar with retail stores than with all other business types because they have shopped in stores all their lives. Younger consumers have a broader perspective on shopping, which incorporates various electronic outlets (telecommunications devices, the internet, and TV) for purchasing goods and services.

What Now?

Take a look at the demographic trends. Ask your chamber of commerce, local college or university business school, reference librarian, and newspaper marketing department for reports on demographic trends in your city. How are national trends reflected in your market area? Are you ahead of or behind what's going on? Watch what the leaders are doing. Search reputable statistical websites. What are the master plans for major educational institutions, governmental agencies, and businesses in your community? Leverage their investments to get a higher return on yours in the marketplace.

With a growing population over 50, businesses that sell medical alert necklaces, jar openers, easy-dressing clothing, large-print books, and other useful items for the elderly are promising.

Other growing businesses cater to teenagers. Tutor concepts like Sylvan Learning Systems Inc. in Baltimore, Maryland, and Huntington Learning Centers Inc. in Oradell, New Jersey, are two examples of early entrants in this growing field. Plato's Closet, a unit of Winmark Corporation, in Minneapolis, Minnesota, sells secondhand designer clothing—just the kind teens are looking for.

Do You Accept the Challenge?

The best retailers are outgoing, verbal people who like to live in the fast lane. Most retail jobs present continual variety, meeting and mixing with people, creating your own opportunities, and generally engaging in self-promoting activities. This is a dynamic field that places a high demand on responding quickly to change, bringing diverse elements and people together, working unscheduled hours, taking rejection, negotiating deals, resolving confrontations, and adjusting to periods of high and low activity.

Is this the kind of atmosphere you want to work in? Do you have the personality for retailing? If you answer yes, read on. The more you learn about retailing, the better prepared you are to make the right choices when starting your business.

In the next chapter, we'll cover more about the personality of a successful retailer and help you decide, based on your strengths and interests, what type of retail business is right for you.

Making a Plan

There are two typical startup scenarios for entrepreneurial ventures. One: An entrepreneur has an idea and turns it into a business. Two: A business idea turns someone into an entrepreneur.

Dan Dye and Mark Beckloff loved dogs. One Christmas, Beckloff's mom gave him a recipe for homemade dog biscuits and a dog bone cookie cutter. A few months later, Beckloff's neighbors and friends were clamoring for freshly baked biscuits from the budding entrepreneur's home kitchen. This unique business eventually grew into the Three Dog Bakery retail and wholesale operations and earned the entrepreneurs appearances on *Oprah* and *Good Morning America*.

"Business, by its very nature, is nothing more than a couple of people coming together and creating something where there was once nothing," says Dye. "We've seen people's lives ruined by greed and bad choices. But we have also seen lives enriched and empowered by hard work and creative visualization." Seeing is believing, as you're about to find out, even if the "seeing" is only in your mind's eye. This book will show you how to make your dream real. Neka Pasquale of Urban Remedy believes that food is medicine. She incorporated food education and the healing power of raw nutrition into her acupuncture and Chinese medicine practice on client retreats and soon they were hooked, suggesting she open a raw food business. Both of her parents are entrepreneurs and demonstrated the drive that Neka emulated growing up to bring her business to life. Neka and her mom, Gail, were running a spa together when Neka opened a small juice shop, which she quickly outgrew. Just as she was determining that she needed $200K to move into a larger facility, a friend mentioned her to a key supporter, Mike Jones at Science Inc. He was immediately interested and offered to invest in the project. "I never planned on starting Urban Remedy. It happened organically. I always tell people, if you are following your dream, it will happen." Today Pasquale operates a gargantuan food manufacturing facility appealing to the built in audience she worked with for years as a practitioner. They are the same demographic as the juice lovers she seeks and are strongly connected to her because they know her. But now 90 percent of her sales are online so a great marketing team helps stay connected to those far away.

Retail and You:
A Match Made in Heaven?

Is retail the right opportunity for you? Weighing several factors will help you answer that question. Personality, motivations, your strengths and weaknesses, money, and experience should be at the top of your checklist.

Making a good career decision involves both self-assessment and market research. Begin the self-assessment process by examining your skills and identifying what kinds of products or services you can offer. What skills do you most enjoy using? If you are artistic, merchandising a store or designing advertising may appeal to you. Or you may be mechanically inclined, enjoy solving puzzles, or helping people. Therefore an auto parts store, business consulting practice, or birthing coach business may be for you. By tying your skills to your market's wants and needs, you greatly increase the likelihood that your new business will be successful.

Christine Ward was an assistant manager at a major museum gift shop in Minneapolis when she got transferred to the accounting department and gained even more valuable experience for her future venture: Patina, a trendy home goods and gift boutique. Her husband, Rick Haase, was a buyer for a small, local specialty retail store. They both saw a chance to fill a unique gap in the Minneapolis-St. Paul market. "People in this type of climate tend to be nesters and have an appreciation for home products that are clever, unusual, and highly aesthetic." Thus, Patina was born, a shop catering to nesters with an eye for distinct creature comforts and unique treasures.

So what are retailers selling and where? The big picture is that consumer electronics and apparel are the best online product categories, according to research firm IDC. In the catalog sector, apparel, gifts, music, and computer hardware do best. Storefront retailers fare well with everything from hardware and books to food and apparel. However, the lines are blurring as brick-and-mortar stores are doing more business on the web and manufacturers exercise all their options for making a sale. Retailers are no longer limited to one way of doing business. Regardless of whether consumers buy online or not, the richness of the online experience has raised the standards for retailers in all channels. Retailers must listen carefully to customers, know what competitive channels are doing, continuously hone their unique selling propositions, and respond quickly to changes.

Personality

Many people successfully make the transition from being an employee to an employer, but many do not. Do you have what it takes to be in business for yourself? Even if you are suited to be a business owner, is a consumer-focused business for you? Are you better suited to be a wholesaler, distributor, or manufacturer? Answer the following five questions honestly. Talk to your spouse, best friend, or prospective partner about your answers as a reality check.

1. *Are you good at multitasking?* In your own business, you have to be willing and able to do everything

warning

Learn from the mistakes of others by watching how they approach growth. The dotcom bubble burst of Silicon Valley looked just like a runner getting ahead of his stride, and then tripping, and falling. So many people invested too fast without proof of returns. Most of the entrepreneurs we talked to for this book shared the same successful, conservative growth strategy: start small, focus on value, then watch your products prove themselves and invest only with profits from that proof.

▲

Old Shoppers vs. New Shoppers

Over the past 20 years, technology—specifically the internet—has transformed the "old" shopper into a "new" shopper with unprecedented control over the retail industry. These new shoppers use the internet to identify needs, search for solutions, compare prices, rely on user reviews, buy what they want, and resolve problems. Many "old" shoppers have become part of this new breed, and as their numbers increase, the entire retailing experience—online and offline—is changed.

Previous generations have only been able to buy clothing, cars, and household items by going to a store, ordering through a catalog, or responding to a direct sales solicitation. Today's consumers have a full menu of choices, including cell phones, PDAs, TV, efax, manufacturer-direct purchasing, and websites. Can you deal with these new realities?

yourself. When you work for someone else, you are usually responsible for just one thing and have limited control. You are supported by others with expertise or experience in different roles and functions. In retail, every day can be a stretch, as you encounter customers, employees, vendors, and landlords. You can't say "That's not my job." It's all yours.

2. *What is your risk tolerance?* In a startup retail business, you worry about being in the right place at the right time with the right goods and services for the right people at the right price. Do you adjust quickly to unplanned events or prefer more predictable, organized projects? Do you see risk as a threat or an opportunity?

3. *Do you count on a paycheck?* New business owners can rarely count on a regular paycheck. Startups frequently require more capital than planned. If you break out in a cold sweat if you aren't paid on the same day every month, you may want to rethink going out on your own. Most of the money you make will go right back into inventory and other costs of doing business.

4. *Are you a self-starter and comfortable being alone?* Or do you draw your energy from being around others and count on colleagues for support and advice? In your own business, you must lead, knowing what to do and when to do it, and be fully accountable for everything that happens.

5. *Do you value predictability or prize diversity?* Not only are there laws against discrimination in hiring and business practices, but America is a multicultural society. When you open your store or service company, you will be interacting with a wide spectrum of customers, vendors, advisors, and employees. Retailers need to be people-oriented, flexible, and good-natured. Can you

manage conflict, see things from your customers' points of view, and cater to their tastes, instead of your own?

Growth or Income?

What is your business goal—income or equity? The difference between a lifestyle and growth business will factor into your decision to launch or buy a company. The choice boils down to: Are you buying a job, investing in an asset, or both? Many entrepreneurs choose a business that offers both income and equity growth because they want to sell the business down the road and use the equity return as a retirement nest egg. Considering the wild swings in the consumer market, relying solely on the proceeds from selling your retail operation for your retirement is risky.

An income company is one that creates more income than value or equity, such as a single-person professional practice. When the lawyer, handyman, or other principal practitioner retires, the business shuts down with few assets to sell.

tip

"Your success as an independent retailer in the 21st century depends on your ability to provide expertise and to use it to benefit your customers. In retailing, you may be boss, but you work for everyone who walks into your store," says Michael Antoniak in his book, *How to Open Your Own Store* (Avon Books).

Strengths and Weaknesses

There has to be a compelling reason why you want to become a retailer. There needs to be an even stronger reason for the type of retail business you choose. Think about what you're good at, what you really know, and most of all, what you truly love doing.

Part of what makes a good entrepreneur is originality, not the ability to catch a ride on somebody else's coattails. Look at "unglamorous" areas for new business ideas. (Insurance billing and pest control businesses can provide a good living.) Be open to all of the possibilities. As an entrepreneur, you will need to oversee the present while planning for your next two stages of growth and development. First you must raise your awareness of what's out there. Then you must get into the habit of writing down the ideas that you hear.

Money

You may like the security of having a steady paycheck but want to be your own boss. How can you decide what's more important: job security or self-employment? In

▲

a workplace defined by constant change, there are very few people who truly have the security they're seeking. There are no guarantees you will have customers tomorrow. To help you test your resolve to be a retailer, you can develop your new business on a part-time basis. Perhaps you could see individual clients or sell your products in the evenings or on weekends. This would allow you to test the marketplace and increase your confidence in your ability to market yourself or merchandise.

How solid are your finances today, and what do you project for the future? This is not the place for rationalizing or unrealistic optimism. Most businesses fail because they are undercapitalized or because they are unable to manage the money they have. Does your proposed team have the leadership, skills, and experience to compete? An honest answer here can save you a lot of pain down the road.

Do You Have the Stuff

What's your RQ? People with high "retail quotients"—the ability to weather the ups and downs of this industry—are self-aware, decisive, patient, strategic thinkers, courageous, and good students. Answer the following questions to estimate your RQ:

- ○ Why am I entering retailing?
- ○ Which business am I starting?
- ○ What goods or services will I sell?
- ○ Where will I get my goods or talent?
- ○ What is my market and who is my consumer?
- ○ Who is my competition?
- ○ Can I compete successfully with the competition?
- ○ What is my sales strategy?
- ○ What marketing methods will I use?
- ○ How much money is required?
- ○ Where will the money come from?
- ○ What technical and management skills do I need?
- ○ Where do I want to be in five years?
- ○ Do I want equity, income, or both?

How long do you plan to be in business before you retire or sell? Will this be a family-owned and -operated business, or are you planning to go public? Whose money will be invested in the business—yours or other people's?

Experience

Another consideration is the extent of your preparation for the business. Your chances for success are significantly improved if you've had prior experience in the particular line or trade.

Before opening Stillwell House Antiques in Red Bank, New Jersey, co-owners Ron Knox and Paul Gallagher had given themselves a thorough education in French antiques. Both were longtime collectors, and Knox had managed the renowned Pierre Deux antique furniture store in New York City, where he made connections with top interior designers and worked with a number of celebrities, politicians, and notable personalities. Gallagher, in addition to being an antiques collector, had experience in online selling through eBay, which provided an important early revenue stream for the shop.

tip

Ask 20 acquaintances to participate in a custom survey that you'll create with Surveymonkey.com. Find out what products are the most needed, creative, used, and delightful to them. Ask them what kinds of products or services they wish were available, but aren't yet.

If you love to take photography, think about selling your work on sites such as Flickr.com and Shutterstock.com. Alicia Shaffer turned her talent for making homemade scarves and headbands into an $80,000 per month business on Etsy.com. Kate Rothacker thrives through her scrapbooking business, Cozy Crop House (cozycrophouse.com) and Tommy Dement also turned his hobby into a money stream by creating Vintage Vettes (vintagevettes.net) and restoring vintage Corvettes for enthusiasts. You can turn your hobby into a moneymaker, too.

Technical and Management Skills

Have your co-workers, friends, or relatives always paid you compliments about your ability to organize things, persuade people, or create beauty wherever you are? Ask people who know you what they think you're good at doing.

Take a look at your resume or news articles and memos written about you. Refer to your teachers' assessments of you on old report cards and your boss's comments on employee evaluations. What have you been given awards for? We've talked about what you enjoy; now take a hard look at what others identify as your talents. After

▲

all, you will have to rely on strangers—hundreds or thousands of them—for your livelihood. To make a profit from your retail venture, you will need to get people to pay you for what you have to offer.

Ask friends, "What duty would you entrust to me above anyone else?"

Accurate and timely record keeping, fiscal responsibility, and interpersonal skills are the basic requirements for a startup. Some store types call for technical skills or professional preparation (optical shops, photo studios, beauty salons, pharmacies, electrical supply stores, and plumbing-fixture outlets, for example). Others require special licenses (liquor stores, car dealerships, restaurants, bars, caregiving, and so forth). You will either have to have the proper license or hire someone who does.

Who do you know who could help, either in the business itself or as an advisor? Who can you rely on to give you solid information? Who can you bounce ideas off?

Business Goals

What do you want to create? Starting a business is an act of creation, an opportunity for personal expression of goals and values as well as a means to an end. Jeff Prouty, of the Prouty Project in Minneapolis, Minnesota, gives new entrepreneurs clarity and direction by asking crucial questions that intertwine life with business. "If I ask someone what their goal is and they say something like 'I want to own the Minnesota Vikings,' I ask them to account for all the steps it would take to get that to happen and see if they still want it. Would they the enjoy road taken? A lot of people like the artistry or creation element of business but are not as comfortable with the other parts, like writing invoices, budgets, and hiring procedures. After reviewing all of the steps necessary to achieve your goal, do you still want it? Hope and wishful thinking are not a strategy."

Deciding what type of retail venture is right should be viewed as a life investment. Will it be socially and environmentally responsible, a big business that you can later sell, or one that doesn't require employees? Perhaps your enterprise will provide valuable jobs for others or be one you can pass on to your family or even provide you with a glamorous lifestyle.

"I've been in the trenches since I was six," says Gary Vaynerchuk of running several mini businesses as a child from baseball card sales and lemonade stands. "I learned to deal with rejection at that age. I learned to give people what they wanted. That's very important."

Because he was too young to drink wine, under the tutelage of his father, he sampled its vast array of flavors by tasting soil, tobacco, leather, and anything related to the elements of wine. Studying the flavors connoisseurs use to describe wine and his innate, relentless business hustle helped him take the family business to gargantuan levels of success. "My dad gave me freedom to execute, allowed me to use him as a mentor, and taught me that word is bond. That's the best thing I've ever been taught," concludes Gary. Surround yourself with those who want to see you succeed.

Is There Enough Time or Demand?

tip

For retail news you can use, check out these websites: Dun & Bradstreet, dnb.com; the National Retail Federation, nrf.com; and Chain Store Age, chainstoreage.com.

Many entrepreneurs leave companies to do the same thing better on their own. Even though you've worked for someone else's successful retail operation, duplicating that store or service somewhere else is no guarantee that it will do as well as the original. (You could also run into legal problems if you signed a noncompete agreement with your former employer, so tread cautiously.) Timing, trading area, population, and other factors such as your mix of skills and experience impact the outcome of your efforts. It may have taken your former employer ten or more years to build that business up to the level you found while working there. There may no longer be a need for another of the same enterprise or sufficient reason for the customer to switch to your business. The cost of entering the market now may be too high to survive the startup and development phase of the business.

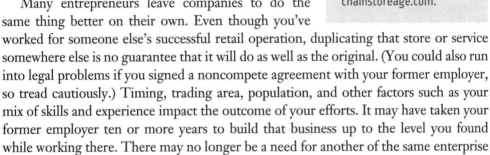

Will It Work?

Test your concept before investing heavily in starting up a business. You can gauge consumer response to your business idea by renting a booth at a flea market. Commit to several weeks at the same location and do some market research. Find out what shoppers think of your selection and what they would like that they don't already see. Do you like dealing with the public? Try a few different venues to sample a cross section of your market. Fine-tune your concept, presentation, and prices. Do people want what you're selling? The only way you can tell is if you are converting interest to sales. If you can make a profit at this point, you may want to move up to rent a cart or kiosk in a shopping district. Many shopping malls provide temporary space in empty storefronts between leases to full-time tenants. While these options are more expensive than working from home or going door to door, they expose your idea to a greater number of prospects, which will give you the facts and figures you need to make a wise decision about the future of your business.

If you want to get into retail because you want to cash in on the dollar store, specialty food, or high-end electronics crazes, beware of oversaturation. Just because it's a popular type of business does not mean the market will support one on every block. A smart approach to choosing what to sell is to look at what the market supports in your town and find a hole in the offerings. If spas, hair salons, and doggie grooming stations do well there, then you can bet if there isn't already a nail salon, it might also do well—all of the offerings support pride in appearance. In Chapter 4, we'll give you some additional information for a reality check.

At the opposite end of the spectrum from the "safety in numbers" approach is the "break out from the pack" route. Because certain retail types are few in number, advocates leap to the conclusion that there is ample room for more. Ask yourself if more are needed for a growing population, or if they are few in number because only a small segment of the total population is interested in old maps or bagpipes. Refer to the Statistical Abstract of the United States in your public library for the number of stores of a particular type in existence, and see which ones are in short supply and may spell opportunity for your area and interest.

> **fun fact**
>
> Price Waterhouse Coopers' Retailing 2015 Frontiers report states that households are getting smaller due to the aging population and fewer traditional families forming so product and service development opportunities for personalized products for just one person will abound.

Look at Industry Numbers

Operating results for retail businesses can vary considerably from one year to the next. The retail industry is in a continuous state of flux. So if you're basing your business choice on the rate of growth, businesses that yielded the highest operating profit percentages, or top sales, you still need to keep up with the financial news.

The 2014 "Top 100 Retailers" list compiled by the National Retail Federation at Stores.org reveals the current market strength of online discount marketplace competitors and also off-pricers in the areas of housewares, home improvement goods, groceries, personal care products, electronics, and clothing. Discount retailers Walmart, Kroger, Costco, Target, Home Depot, Walgreen, CVS, Lowe's, Amazon, and Safeway occupy the top spots. Amazon joined the list for the first time adding almost $10 billion in sales in 2013, competing neck and neck with Walmart. Walmart now is considered the number four online retailing performer with an increase in online sales by 30 percent. Bryan Gildenberg, chief knowledge officer for Kantar Retail says that "old dogs" like Walmart and Amazon are learning new tricks and their successes in online sales are because they are "large-scale profitable businesses well-grounded in the mechanics of retailing." He points out that "89 percent of ecommerce is 'commerce.' That's what bricks-and-mortar is good at."

Start Thinking about Your Mission

Can you explain why your business will be sustainable over time? A strong business plan begins with a statement of the mission or purpose of your business. From it, you establish the objectives that you want to achieve, and then you work on your positioning strategy and all the other details that add up to a profitable venture.

Take a moment to write down your mission statement. It will be invaluable in helping you make decisions before and after you open your business. The basic ingredients of your mission statement are definitions of products and services to be offered; customers to be served; geographic area(s) to be covered; how physical assets, financial assets, and human resources will be used to create customer satisfaction; and how the firm intends to compete in its chosen markets.

Your mission statement provides a clear sense of direction for the enterprise and distinguishes your business from all others. It also often reflects the values and philosophy by which you want to run your firm.

Dr. Leonard L. Berry, chair in retailing and marketing leadership at Texas A&M University in College Station, Texas, warns that uninteresting stores, unfocused stores, and stores with order-takers, not salespeople, won't make it. Consumers are value-minded and have high expectations for their shopping experience, including choices, fun, convenience, and service. Consider these elements when writing your mission statement.

Neka Pasquale's mission is two-fold: to educate people about health and wellness so they can be as vibrant as possible, and to help people who aren't familiar with healthy food to realize they don't have to sacrifice taste—food can be as good for you as it tastes. They can still celebrate food, eat with gusto, and enjoy all the flavors.

tip

The arrival of a superstore or national chain in a retailer's market area need not spell doom for a small retailer. Jack A. Taylor, professor of retailing at Birmingham-Southern College in Alabama, suggests you follow the advice of Jerry Garcia, the late leader of the Grateful Dead. "You don't want to be considered the best at what you do. You want to be the only one who does what you do."

Christine Ward developed this mission statement for Patina, her specialty home and gift shop in St. Paul, Minnesota: "To add inspiration and creativity to people's lives with everyday objects."

New York handbag and graphic designer, Matt Murphy's mission is: "To collaborate with, and provide outstanding creative solutions for a diverse and expanding client base."

You must clearly and simply define who you are and what you're doing. If you can't clearly state who you are, what you're doing and for whom, you are going to have trouble communicating your value to financiers, vendors, employees, and customers—and you" have trouble staying on track when there are forks in the road. Use the "Mission Statement Worksheet" on page 33 to formulate your own.

Highest Operating Profit Percentages

Operating profit percentages say a lot about the health of business opportunities. Operating profit is the amount of money remaining after subtracting operating expenses from gross profit. Here are some dramatic examples of sales growth and profitability by major sub category sampled from Sageworks 2014 Retail Report Card:

Sales Growth		Net Profit Margin
Direct selling establishments	13.3%	4.7%
Home furnishing stores	10.7%	4.1%
Specialty food stores	10.4%	2.8%
Furniture stores	6.7%	4.3%
Health and personal care stores	6.1%	4.3%
Auto dealers	7.6%	2.5%
Electronics and appliance stores	7.8%	1.7%
Jewelry, luggage, and leather goods	.1%	5.4%
Beer, wine, and liquor stores	4.9%	1.3%
Clothing stores	4.3%	3.2%
Gas stations	.9%	1.7%

Mission Statement Worksheet

Fill in your mission statement on this worksheet. Remember that the mission statement should clearly define the following:

○ *A view to the future.* How do you envision your business down the road—in one year, two years, and in ten years?

○ *An insight on your customers' perception of your company.* How do you want them to think of you?

○ *A view to the retail community at large.* How do you want the retail community to perceive your business?

Mission Statement for (your business name)

Be a Trend-Watcher

Newspaper, magazine, and reputable website articles identify trends you can take advantage of or test your idea against. Business news and programs dedicated to entrepreneurs reveal opportunities, and futurists, cultural anthropologists, and industry analysts can help you navigate what is to come. Deloitte & Touche, Ernst & Young, Dun & Bradstreet, Faith Popcorn's BrainReserve (a marketing consulting firm that specializes in identifying and applying consumer trends), and the Trends Research Institute (a trend forecasting company) publish useful information. Refer to the Appendix for more great sources.

Though the dreams of entrepreneurs have given birth to a multitude of different businesses, identifiable trends are constantly changing. Entrepreneurs' Organization has identified the top nine entrepreneurial growth industries as follows: biotechnology, health and medical services, computer services, environmental, computer software, computer consulting, communication services, education and training, and waste management. While many opportunities for need-driven startups exist, such as elderly and disabled services, it's important to assess financial and labor investment risks as well as matching yourself to what you are most suited for.

Sarah Blakely invested $5,000 to produce a slimming undergarment called Spanx and by 2014 claimed over $250 million in annual revenues, according to her interview in *Forbes* magazine. Don't have $5,000 to invest? The McKinsey Global Institute focuses on evolving global economy trends and points out that while most boomers envision themselves retiring to a life of relaxation and comfort, not all of them are financially prepared to do that. Today's nearly 74.9 million baby boomers are more active at a later age than their predecessors. They are online dating, participating in more sports (and getting more sports related injuries), and starting their own businesses due to second stage life choices and layoffs. Their online presence has increased and they have money to spend. This generation is also the "best-educated, most highly skilled aging workforce in U.S. history," according to McKinsey. Another area to follow is creative, end-of-life services. As our world focuses more on compassion and the green industry, those aging kids from the '60s—the age of peace and love—are planning their deep, spiritual legacies.

Paco Underhill, founder and managing partner of Evirosell (a behavioral market research and consulting company), Gerald Celente of the Trends Research Institute, and Faith Popcorn of BrainReserve (all founded in New York) have published books and reports outlining major lifestyle preferences that suggest areas retailers can capitalize on. Among them are:

- *Cocooning*. Because of a renewed focus on home life, Americans are reading more, chatting online, spending more time with their children, watching more

TV, and engaging in other household activities. Home improvement is a $300 billion business. Advancing Security Worldwide reports a groundbreaking study to reveal the U.S. private security industry as a $202 billion market. One in five people work from home in America. Meal-preparation services are among the fastest-growing segments.

- *Self-gratification.* People hunger for small indulgences like imported chocolate, special-blend coffees, champagne, caviar, and vehicles for recreation instead of merely transportation. On a typical day, the restaurant industry averages more than $2 billion in sales. Personal chefs, beauty spas, specialty foods, and premium-priced sunglasses offer small indulgences for stressed-out consumers who reward themselves with affordable luxuries. Theme parks are booming, with annual revenues of $12 billion.

- *Agelessness.* Baby boomers are enjoying more vitality relative to their age than previous generations have. They don't intend to stop or concede to aging. They find comfort in familiar pursuits and are nostalgic for their carefree childhoods. This creates a booming retail landscape for products from their youth—collectibles, re-creations ('80s-style clothing and retro furniture styles), trinkets in Disney stores, and grown-up toys like four-wheel-drive cars, motorcycles, and cruiser bicycles.

- *Personalization.* Consumers crave recognition of their individuality. This includes custom-made clothes and monogramming, personal distinctions (body piercing, tattoos, and hair color), imprinted stationery, and made-to-order bicycles and cars.

- *Female business trends.* The way women think and behave is impacting business, making relationships more important than ever. Pay attention. A woman opens a new business every 60 seconds. Women control over 70 percent of household income and over $20 trillion of consumer spending.

- *Traditionalism.* Religion is back. Proms, bar mitzvahs, quinceañeras, and weddings are once again spectacular social events. People want the values their parents possessed, such as having a happy family life. Christian bookstores reap $4 billion in annual sales, and the wedding industry is booming, generating more than $80 billion in retail sales a year.

▲

- *Quality reigns.* Consumers want the best value for their dollar. They know what quality is and want guarantees and products that last. This also means quality of life, as in saving time.

- *Social conscience.* Concerned about the fate of the planet, consumers respond to retailers who exhibit a social conscience attuned to personal and corporate ethics, the environment, and education. Some retailers give employees paid time off for community service.

- *Concern for wellness.* Because people want to lead longer lives, there's a great deal of fear about aging and concern about health. Polluted air, contaminated water, and tainted food stir up a storm of consumer uncertainty.

How Will You Compete?

Now that you have assessed yourself, popular culture, and your competition—and gotten a good view of the retailing climate—how do you intend to compete? There

---

Are Antiques Your Bag?

Selling antiques is a popular business. An efficient way to get started is to rent a small space in an antiques mall. Most cities have buildings that rent spaces to a number of independent dealers. Visit several on different days of the week and at different times to make an appraisal of the vitality of the location and caliber of clientele. Talk with the dealers. Are they happy? Do their wares complement what you plan to sell?

For rent, you usually pay a flat fee plus a percentage of sales. You can expect the mall owner to provide cashier services, insurance, utilities, and advertising. About $15,000 to $50,000 in inventory should get you up and running, dealers say. Buying your inventory at trade shows, garage sales, flea markets, estate sales, auctions, and from established dealers, you'll learn a lot about the antique market. You'll need display cases and shelves, business cards, and a place to sit and do your paperwork and clean and price items. You'll probably want to have the most current edition of *Schroeder's Antiques Price Guide* (Collector Books) and *Sotheby's International Price Guide: Antiques and Collectibles* (Rizzoli International Publications Inc.). Some trade magazines that will help you stay informed include *Antique Review, Antique Week, Antiques and Collectibles News* magazine, *Antiques* magazine, and *Collectors News.*

---

are five areas of specialization that can make a retailer a contender. You must focus on being better than any other retailer in one key area. Which one do you want to be known for?

1. *Service.* Nordstrom is the retailer most customers think defines the standard for great customer service.
2. *Experience.* The Disney Store is a destination stop for shoppers who enjoy more than just a transaction.
3. *Price/value.* Walmart is synonymous with offering superior value for the money every day on every item.
4. *Product.* Zippo lighters haven't changed much since 1933 and offer a lifetime warranty.
5. *Access.* CVS is relied on for convenient store hours seven days a week.

What's Your Plan?

Writing a business plan requires a lot of effort, but it all pays off in reducing anxiety, focusing your efforts, and recruiting the right talent at the right time.

In *The Complete Idiot's Guide to Business Plans* (Alpha), authors Gwen Moran and Sue Johnson say you need to answer these questions when writing a business plan:

- *What does your business do?* Explain the purpose of your business in as clear and specific terms as possible.
- *What makes your product, service, or business different—and a better choice for customers?* Whether you're the low-price option, the provider with the best service, or the high-end specialty vendor, you need to spell out clearly what your unique selling proposition is.
- *Who's doing the work?* Businesses are only as good as their people. Who are the partners, employees, consultants, vendors, and others who will be working on or in your business?
- *Who are your customers?* Create specific profiles of the people who are going to be shelling out the money to purchase your products and services.
- *How are you going to reach them?* You can have the best product in the world, but if you don't have a game plan for letting prospects know about it or ensuring that the people who want to buy your product or service can do so easily, then you won't be successful. Create a solid plan for promoting and distributing what you sell.
- *Where's the money?* You need to figure out the finances for both starting and growing your business. Take an honest look at what your expenses will be, how

much revenue you can reasonably expect, and how long it will take for your business to turn a profit. Be careful of underestimating expenses or overestimating revenue—investors will see through fuzzy math, and that will send up red flags.

- *What does the future hold?* Your plan needs to address future opportunities, potential obstacles, and a projection for future growth.

Once you've answered these questions and pursued the leads presented above, you're ready to sit down and put all your ideas down on paper. By now, the plan for your business is really taking shape, and you're ready to move on to the next step of being an official retailer.

warning

As you formulate your business plan, you may be looking for any support you can get. Be selective about whom you give your business plan, and check out people who claim they can connect you with financing for a slight fee or "miscellaneous" expenses.

Decisions, Decisions

The long-term goals you set in your business plan will affect the decisions you make during your first year of business, and your first year in business will affect your long-term goals. You may find that there are aspects of your business you like more than you thought you would and others that are disappointing. There are some things about running a retail operation that you cannot anticipate until your business is open. A formal business plan is a tool that forces you to think beyond having "a good idea" to the many factors that go into actually doing what needs to be done to build a business that supports itself. A plan doesn't guarantee that every decision you make will be a good one, but you are better prepared for the future if you carefully think through various "what if" situations now.

All businesses require dedication, determination, enthusiasm, flexibility, and perseverance. Though retail forecasts for 2015 look healthy, you should be prepared for a sharp or prolonged decline on Wall Street, a rise in interest rates, or signs of a slowing economy, which could cause Americans to curb their buying. There are all sorts of things that can turn people away from shopping, so plan for rocky times as well as good ones.

Will you launch your own business or buy an existing one? Perhaps you're thinking about buying a franchise or a business opportunity. Whichever way you decide to go, keep the following in mind.

Buying a Business

The kinds of businesses you can purchase include franchises, business opportunities, direct sales, and existing independent businesses. Here are some facts and figures you can factor into your decision-making process.

Franchises

Franchising is becoming the dominant form of retailing in America. According to the Franchise Business Outlook: 2014 reported by the International Franchise Association, in 2013 there were 757,503 franchises in the United States, generating $803 billion. Buying a franchise is a very specialized undertaking. There are numerous books and magazines devoted to the subject, and you should read as many of these as you can. There are also lawyers, accountants, and consultants who specialize in franchises and can give you the necessary insight and facts to make a wise decision. For more information, see the Appendix and check out The FranchiseZone on Entrepreneur.com.

According to Franchising.com, franchise investments can vary greatly depending on the type of franchise, location, staffing, equipment, and the like. However, the cost of a typical single-location franchise is between $30,000 and $500,000. In the United States, there are more than 50,000 different franchise opportunities in 42 categories available. McDonald's and Burger King are the most well-known, but franchises can be found in nearly every industry, in various sizes, and requiring a wide range of financial investments. For example, you can buy a cart or kiosk franchise for $25,000 to $125,000. View franchising. com/find_a_franchise to see a list of current opportunities. Never buy a franchise without retaining an attorney and accountant who specialize in franchise operations. Make sure they perform audits and assist with your due diligence and negotiations.

aha!

For current information about franchises, check out the International Franchise Association (franchise. org) and the American Association of Franchisees and Dealers (aafd.org). *Entrepreneur* magazine's Annual Franchise 500 ranking reveals the impact of the newest trends and the industries poised for growth here: entrepreneur.com/ franchise500.

Business Opportunities

A business opportunity, in the simplest terms, is a packaged business investment that allows the buyer to begin a business. (Technically, all franchises are business opportunities, but not all business opportunities are franchises.)

Unlike a franchise, however, the business opportunity seller typically exercises no control over the buyer's business operations. In fact, in most business opportunity programs, there is no continuing relationship between the seller and the buyer after the sale is made.

Although business opportunities offer less support than franchises, this could be an advantage for you if you thrive on freedom. Typically, you will not be obligated to follow the strict specifications and detailed program that franchisees must follow. With most business opportunities, you could purchase a program for less than $500, then simply buy a set of equipment or materials, and operate the business any way and under any name you want.

However, this same lack of long-term commitment is also a business opportunity's chief disadvantage. Because there is no continuing relationship, the world of business opportunities does have its share of con artists who promise buyers instant success, then take their money and run. While increased regulation of business opportunities has dramatically lessened the likelihood of rip-offs, it is still important to investigate an opportunity thoroughly before you invest any money.

Direct Sales

The third form of business you can buy into is direct sales. These are direct-selling companies, such as Tupperware and Amway, in which you sell specific products provided by the company based on your personal contacts rather than on the reputation of the brand. With direct sales, you get a percentage of the sales of all the new salespeople you bring into the distribution system. The buy-in is usually just a stock of inventory, and there generally is no equipment. But you probably won't receive support in the way of protected territory, product promotion, or operations training. Some direct-selling companies offer sales and motivational seminars and will sell you DVDs, CDs, and marketing materials. You can get more information by visiting the Direct Selling Association's website at dsa.org.

Existing Independent Businesses

Acquiring an established business requires a greater financial outlay than starting one from scratch, but buying a business allows you to realize profits faster and receive a quicker return on your initial investment. A major advantage to this approach is that the business you're considering spending a chunk of money on has a track record to review. Obtaining outside financing may be easier, and projections should be more accurate because of known historical trends. The business already has its financial and marketing plans in action. You are paying for an established location, inventory, customer base, and trained staff.

warning

You do not eliminate all the risk of being in business when you buy an existing store. It is just as easy to inherit a bad reputation as a good one from a previous owner. The location may be bad, too expensive, or inadequate for expansion. The facility or equipment may be in disrepair or obsolete. The staff may be incompetent or disgruntled.

Entrepreneurs wanting to buy an existing business will have to do as much—or more—research and careful analysis as is required when starting from scratch. Carefully evaluate the opportunity cost of entering various industries through acquisition. Do your due diligence and make sure there aren't any hidden reasons for the sale of the business—for example, the opening of a major competitor within your market area, a scheduled road widening that would take part of your parking lot, or increasing crime in the area.

Many retailers have bought out failures or near-failures that could not be revived—even under the most skillful management. Complete and careful analysis is essential if a good buy is to be made. Verify the claims made by the seller, and look into the reputation and image of the store.

Experience on your part is essential because you will have to step right in and take over the day-to-day management. There is no time to learn on the job. Without expertise in the field, you are more apt to miss major problems and stall or set back the company's growth. Employees, vendors, and customers all need to feel confident in you from Day One, or they'll go elsewhere. Buying an existing retail operation without attention to all these details can lead to buyer's remorse.

Identifying Opportunities

The best place to begin looking for a business to buy is through your own contacts. Ask friends, relatives, and professional advisors if they are aware of any businesses for sale. Do some research on the internet. Ask your accountant and attorney if they know of potential opportunities.

Many businesses for sale are represented by brokers. The business may be advertised in the newspaper or a trade magazine, or listed with a brokerage firm. Caution should be used in following brokers' leads because high-pressure sales tactics are frequently employed.

warning

There is no substitute for your own due diligence to determine what is a true opportunity and what is not. Remember that the web is a marketing tool—just like corporate brochures and promotional seminars—and the claims and content have not generally been investigated or guaranteed to be accurate.

Some entrepreneurs simply go into a store they are interested in and talk to the owner to see if he or she would be interested in selling. Others go on the internet to see what businesses are being advertised for sale. BizBuySell.com is one such site.

Evaluating the Business for Sale

To determine the value of the business, you will need the past five years' audited financial statements and tax returns. In addition, review the most recent financial statement for consistency. Use these financial statements, tax returns, support documents, personnel records, customer lists, vendor contracts, inventory reports, and accounts receivable and accounts payable schedules to help you ascertain the true value of the business.

Some sellers may not want to reveal much information until they are convinced you are a serious buyer. It's your job to convey that you are a trustworthy, serious buyer who must have sufficient information to make a well-informed decision. It is helpful to have your CPA or lawyer accompany you on these fact-finding missions. Generally speaking, buying any company that is less than three years old poses a substantial risk because it lacks a track record.

Objectivity is important when evaluating business purchases. Don't become emotionally attached to the point that your enthusiasm clouds your judgment, and you don't ask the tough questions. You must be able to walk away from a questionable transaction. Helpful articles can be found at Business Book Press (Businessbookpress. com), the SMB Reviews (smbreviews.com), *Inc.* magazine (Inc.com), and Small Business Advancement National Center (Sbaer.uca.edu).

▲

Launching Your Own Business

You may believe you have a distinct concept that is different or better than anything else out there, and you want to create your own business from the bottom up.

Most successful small businesses provide something attractive or advantageous by taking what's already there and developing some innovative features. Have you developed an improved technique for delivering goods to the market? Drive-thru coffee and juice bars situated near freeway onramps offer added value for commuters. Some clothing retailers send store reps to the customer's office with fashions and a laptop computer for taking orders after educating employees on options for Friday casual dress. Using technology and initiative, these retailers help customers overcome time problems and deliver exceptional service in about half the time the traditional method requires.

Perhaps you have an idea that will fill a market niche. A few entrepreneurs have started up successful ventures in ecotourism and other forms of adventure travel for those with money, social consciousness, and a desire for educational value to be added to their leisure time. What is your unique proposition?

Another reason for wanting to go your own way without the safety net of an existing business model is that you have developed new markets or promotional techniques for existing goods and services. For example, more than a decade ago, Lenox Inc. aggressively promoted its bridal registry. Today, this promotional tool is now widely imitated in stores everywhere and online for weddings, graduation, Christmas, and baby gifts.

At this point, you have struggled with the question of whether retailing is for you. You have looked at the personal qualities you'll need and considered how you'd start up. You've narrowed down the type of business you want to go into, revised your business plan draft to reflect your refined thinking, and are about to make some other key decisions you hope will help you be a success in the retail industry. Now you're going to need to enlist the help of some experts.

Professional Advisors

According to Entrepreneur's Organization, the most important resource required to foster entrepreneurial growth is the advice and expertise of other entrepreneurs. Financial support ranked fifth.

Strategic advisor, Jeff Prouty, strongly urges new proprietors to put together a personal board of advisors who are experts in business, and meet religiously once a

May I Cut In?

There are several factors you need to take into consideration to help you determine if it is wiser for you to buy an existing business or start your own. Will buying this business give you a jump start into retailing or waste precious resources trying to breathe life into someone else's failed dream? Ask yourself these questions:

○ Do I have the interests, skills, temperament, and experience to step in and run this business right away?

○ Do I have enough money to buy and operate the business and still have a reserve fund for unexpected needs?

○ What are the market trends (growth, size, and position) for this business?

○ How many years has this business been in operation, and how many owners has it had?

○ Why is this business for sale?

○ What am I actually buying—physical assets, name, location, customer list, existing business, or projected business?

○ Are the books accurate?

○ Is a profit being earned?

○ Are the operating ratios compatible with industry averages?

○ What is the worth of the business assets?

○ Are the employees highly trained and productive?

○ Are the customers loyal to the present owner or to the store? Will they leave when he or she leaves?

○ How long is the current owner willing to spend assisting in the smooth transfer of the business?

○ Does the business need an immediate cash infusion? Will that solve any problems?

○ Is the owner reluctant or cooperative in providing details and answers?

quarter to discuss obstacles, goals, and processes. "You'll get invaluable feedback that will shape your actions to success. You need three types of advisors; the first is the very committed listener who only listens without offering advice. The second is grey-haired wisdom; a senior or highly seasoned expert. The third is a catalyst for change and stimulates creative thinking and new approaches. I've been participating in strategic peer groups, whose advice I budget for, for ten years. If everyone did this there would be more successful business owners," Jeff says.

Retailers' Average Gross Profit

Recent figures from Risk Management Association or RMA (rmahq.org/RMA), an association of lending, credit, and risk management professionals that serves the financial services industry, indicate that the average gross profit before taxes for various types of retailers is:

Art dealers	6.2%
Auto parts and accessories	3.1%
Baked goods stores	6.2%
Cosmetics and beauty supplies	6.1%
Electronic stores	4.4%
Florists	3.7%
Fruit and vegetable markets	2.4%
Furniture stores	4.0%
Health supplement stores	7.8%
Hobby, toy, and game stores	3.6%
Jewelry stores	5.4%
Mail order houses	2.0%
Men's clothing stores	5.1%
Optical goods	7.4%
Pet supply stores	3.4%
Recreational vehicle dealers	2.9%
Tire dealers	2.6%
Used merchandise stores	4.2%
Vending machine operators	1.5%
Women's clothing stores	4.7%

Lawyers and Accountants

Lawyers' and accountants' general business experience enables them to review contracts, legalize your business name, outline the business structure, and counsel you on operational procedures you need to follow to avoid lawsuits. Their experience with retail clients will be invaluable in: helping you negotiate the best lease or buy terms for a business or property, establishing best practices for your store, keeping you abreast of current laws and regulations, and helping you manage risk. The more complex your startup, the more important it is for you to hire professionals who have worked with entrepreneurs in the retail industry.

Bankers

As a retailer, you will deal with banks in a number of ways. If you accept credit cards, you'll need a bank that can handle merchants' accounts. Since you might want a loan at some time, it is helpful to deal with a local bank or branch with which you can develop a personal relationship. Start by getting answers to these four questions: Where do other retailers in your area bank? Is the bank you are considering FDIC-insured? What are its hours and merchant services? Does it have online banking that would be advantageous to your type of operation? Where you locate your business may limit your choices, so think about where you would be doing your banking when you are narrowing down the choices.

One piece of advice you've probably heard before is to have a relationship with a bank before you need it so that when you do, it'll be there. Christine Ward and Rick Haase of Patina teamed up with a mentor from the SCORE program to develop a five-year business plan that shows potential lenders how dedicated they are. The SCORE mentor coached them to show important details in the plan, highlighting their attention to accountability. While the first few banks turned them down, they eventually found one who took the time to really consider their plan and believe in them. Had they not invested detailed research and planning into their prospectus, they may have missed their chance to show what potential they had. These days most of Patina's ventures are timed for funding by store profits, but Christine and Rick continue to nurture banker relationships for possible needs in the future.

For more on banking, turn to "Bank Locally" on page 75 in Chapter 5.

Consultants

Consultants can provide useful services for your business. They can assist in the startup or expansion phases of your business and suggest ways to manage and promote your enterprise. You may be approached by public relations firms, store designers, or

▲

advertising agencies once your dba (see Chapter 5) is published in the local newspaper or you file your business license with the city. Do not take anything for granted. Evaluate each person's and company's track record, background, educational degrees, client list, and fees before you enlist their advice or services. Your vendors will provide a lot of free advice, which can be quite useful. Ask your suppliers, trade associations, the Better Business Bureau, and your local chamber of commerce for referrals to retail experts in areas you need help in.

Once you have made some of the important decisions discussed in this chapter, you're ready to move on to Chapter 4, which is all about establishing a location for your business.

Location

Although a great location may not guarantee success, a bad location will almost always guarantee failure. A new retail business needs to be where the customers are. You want a location with a reasonable degree of security, access to public transportation or major thoroughfares for your customers and employees, adequate parking for commercial as well as personal vehicles, room for an office, and that all-important sales space. Where you locate will determine the hours you keep, who your clientele is, and your promotion style. Also, where you set up shop will impact how long it will take you to grow. Luckily, you have lots of options.

The Homebased Retailer

The economics of homebased businesses make them attractive. SBA 2014 statistics show that 52 percent of all small businesses are home based and about half of all new establishments survive five years or more and about one-third survive ten years or more.

Many such businesses can be started with limited financial investments. The low overhead of operating a business from your study or guest room greatly increases your likelihood for survival.

Financial risk may be reduced by having little overhead, but other risks now replace it. Running a business from home requires the same drive and skills demanded of any business, plus a talent for time management, concentration, organization, and self-motivation.

Thanks to advances in technology, it is getting easier and less expensive to equip your business. Powerful computers eliminate multiple positions that were required only a few years ago. Now you can communicate worldwide, 24 hours a day, seven days a week, via phone, efax, videocall, social media, and email, eliminating time and distance barriers. Advanced technologies and outsourcing services at your disposal can help you project the same professional image as a storefront company.

Despite all this, a retail business is one of the few businesses that is difficult to run from home. This is largely due to a conflict between needing customers to come to your place of business and the penalties of having a stream of clients visiting your home. Everyone accepts the occasional garage sale, but some communities regulate how often you can have one. Most residential zoning excludes retail, so your neighbors can report you to city or county officials if your business creates noticeable traffic, noise, or parking

warning

If you're operating your business out of a rental property, co-op, or condominium you own, be sure and check your CC&Rs. Even if the area is zoned for your business, house rules may pose a problem. Check with your landlord or co-op or condo owners' association. Consult a lawyer if you have any questions about the codes or want a special-use permit or a variance.

Home, Sweet Business?

In addition to the legal, logistical, financial, and operational questions of a homebased business, you need to consider your lifestyle and living arrangements. Operating a business from your residence will require some family concessions. Is your home loud and chaotic, or quiet and uncluttered? Does your condominium or apartment have thin walls or heavy-footed tenants upstairs? Can you devote the time and space that are needed to serve your customers? Different businesses require different amounts of privacy, focus, and schedules. Assess the physical and emotional challenges of having your business in your home before deciding it's the right base for your operation.

problems. Some communities prohibit commercial vehicles or cars and trucks with signs on them from parking on the street.

One option for retailers who want to work out of their living rooms is to sell their goods and services from booths or tables at craft fairs, in cooperative booth space at emporiums or expositions, by mail order, or at flea markets. You can also sell retail on the internet. Seminar leaders, real estate agents, custom book producers, calligraphers, carpet cleaners, interior designers, direct mailers, catalog companies, tailors, pattern makers, feng shui consultants, personal commemorative makers, and genealogists report thriving while working at home.

There are many things you can do by yourself or by hiring people part time or full time. Do you love music, parties, and people? Try starting your own disc jockey service. If you have a knack for working with computers, your business could be based on computer tutoring, installation services, troubleshooting, or buying assistance. Combine people's concern for security and time, and start a home inventory business, auditing the possessions of homeowners for insurance documentation in case of fire, storm, or robbery.

Cotati, California, tiny home designer Jay Shafer not only works from home, but cleverly designed his businesses so he holds no inventory for clients to view, nor to build with. Shafer's first company was Tumbleweed Tiny House Company, in Sebastopol, California. The new owners found a hot market for tiny homes in Colorado Springs, Colorado, and transferred the business there, keeping a second office in Sonoma, California. Shafer set Tumbleweed up so interested clients could view his tiny houses online and order them pre-built for delivery or build them on their own with purchased plans from his site. They would take virtual home tours on his website and visit the demo model in Sebastopol, if they wished. Each time a pre-built home was ordered,

▲

Jay would rent a space to build, trucks to haul materials, and hire builders to help with labor. Materials were ordered per job and delivered right to the work site. No storage or showroom required. Jay's new company, Four Lights Houses in Cotati, California, offers exquisitely styled new tiny home designs and consultation services for the do-it-yourself crowd.

In the beginning of his career, New York City-based Matt Murphy, of Matt Murphy Design, created his high-end handbags, catalog, and website from his apartment in Los Angeles. He had a showroom and office in the space, which gave him the freedom to design his "architectural bags" all night, fulfill orders, and do business overseas without having to hail a cab.

Commercial Locations

If working at home is not for you—or it simply won't work for your particular business—be advised that the best location combines visibility, affordability, and lease terms you can live with. Brick-and-mortar retailers need to be where the action is, so deciding where to put your business is every bit as important as the business you decide to go into. It's risky to move into an area where there has always been trade assuming that there always will be. Study the business and consumer pages to see where you can find business support services and a growing community of people with regular incomes and interest in the goods or services you plan to offer.

Placing an eco-wares boutique, Ethique Nouveau (ethiquenouveau.com), in an affluent area of Minneapolis was a good move for entrepreneur Charlotte Cozzetto. As a long-time resident of the area, she had a strong sense that an earth-friendly boutique with more of a mainstream style, would fill a need for the hungry, green community. Unique ideas like hers require a sense of combining social backdrops with business. Forecasting the creative ways her green audience may be served with a simple retail location, was important when Charlotte chose her 800-square-foot store front. The "boutique" style layout of the sunny, showroom floor encourages circular travel pattern and works well for store events, as well as making all of the merchandise visible at one time. The basement is used for meetings, seminars, and supply storage.

Neka Pasquale chose San Rafael, Mill Valley, and San Francisco, California to open stores in because

stat fact

According to Vator News, The Trusted Source for Emerging Tech, in 2014 ecommerce will see $1.316 trillion in sales, which is 5.9 percent of the total worldwide retail market. By 2018 sales are predicted to reach $2.5 trillion which is 8.8 percent of the total retail market. Are you prepared to serve these hungry online shoppers?

of the health conscious crowds working and living in those areas. Juicing, plant based cuisine, spas, and alternative health care businesses heavily populate the San Francisco bay area, appealing to residents with disposable income and a desire for natural beauty. All of these industries have the ability to create beauty from the inside out for their clients, and Urban Remedy is no exception.

Researching Locations

Take the time to analyze the areas that appeal to you. There are three phases of choosing a location for your retail business: selection of a city, choice of an area or type of location within a city, and identification of a specific site.

In choosing a city, investigate these main factors:

- Size of the city's trading area
- Population and population trends
- Total purchasing power and who has it
- Total retail trade potential for different lines of trade
- Number and size of competition
- Quality and aggressiveness of competition

Once you have a general idea of what city you like, choose an area or type of location within that city by evaluating these:

- Customer attraction power
- The nature of competition
- Availability of access routes to the stores
- Zoning regulations
- Geographic direction of the city's expansion
- General appearance of the area
- Sales and traffic growth prospects of the trade area
- Demographics of neighborhoods

These are factors in narrowing down your site choices:

- Traffic flow
- Complementary nature of neighboring stores

tip

Check whether there's a city master plan for your location. When Stillwell House Antiques owners Ron Knox and Paul Gallagher found the perfect historic house for their first shop in Manalapan, New Jersey they were concerned because it was on one of the town's last remaining farms. But when they learned it was part of an open-space preservation effort, they knew it was safe.

- Adequacy of parking
- Vulnerability to competition
- Cost of the site

Match the Area to Your Customers

Whether you're looking at a freestanding building or one in a strip mall, you have to do your homework. If you want to open a clothing store for young women 12 to 24 years old, for example, you would not want to locate in an area where the majority of residents are retired. Rather, you'd want to have schools, music stores, and snack shops that target this age group within walking distance of your business.

Use the Scribble Maps (scribblemaps.com) app to create your power zone. Place an "X" where your business will be. Then draw three circles that represent 5, 10, and 15 miles from you. This is where your bread-and-butter customers live and/or work. Will their demographics support 75 percent, 20 percent, or 5 percent of the sales you need? Google Trends is a great research tool to identify the location of differing appetites around the world. It tracks the frequency of search terms by rank, location, and language. For example, the San Francisco bay area comes up high on the list when searching the term "raw food" making Pasquale's raw juice and snack concept well placed for success. You also want to see if the population is growing or declining. Are there seasonal variations in population that favor your type of business, or will you suffer when students, families, or snowbirds leave town? And you will want to check out the activity during the week, weekends, daytime, and nighttime to see if it's in alignment with your business plans.

Make your own analysis of the market and fact-check the figures a rental agent or developer gives you. In this respect, money for professional help is well spent. Companies such as Nielsen Claritas have demographic site reports available for sale online (claritas.com). You can get lifestyle consumer segmentation reports by zip code, retail trade potential in various areas, a list of shopping centers, demographic trends, age by income, and other useful information.

Pinpointing the specific site is particularly important. In central and secondary business districts, small stores depend on the traffic created by large stores or a group of stores. These stores depend on attracting customers from the existing flow of traffic. However,

> **tip**
>
> Each year, *Entrepreneur* magazine ranks the top cities for small business. When you are looking for the most advantageous environment for your startup, begin with a peek at the "Ten Best Cities to Start a Business" listing on Entrepreneur.com (http://www.entrepreneur.com/slideshow/226485). Do your own analysis with its criteria for the areas you are considering.

where sales depend on nearby residents, selecting the trading area is more important than picking the specific site.

Type of Products and Location Choice

Another factor that affects site selection is the customer's view of the goods you sell or the services you offer. Customers tend to group products into three major categories: convenience, shopping, and specialty goods.

tip

A destination store is one to which customers will make a special trip to shop. Customers value the goods and services offered and tend to be more loyal and willing to travel longer distances to reach it.

Convenience Goods

Convenience goods are usually low-priced, frequently purchased items that require little selling effort, are bought by habit, and are sold in numerous outlets. Candy bars, newspapers, cigarettes, and milk are examples. Quantity of traffic is most important to stores handling convenience goods. The corner of an intersection that offers two traffic streams and a large window display area is usually a better location than the middle of a block. Such downtown convenience retailers as low-priced, ready-to-wear stores and drugstores have a limited ability to generate their own traffic. Convenience goods are often purchased on impulse in easily accessible stores.

In addition, the greater the automobile traffic, the greater the sales of convenience goods catering to drive-thru traffic. For the drive-thru store selling low-priced items, the volume of traffic passing the site is key. The consumer makes frequent purchases and wants things like gum, bottled water, soda, and chips readily available. Consumers are reminded when passing a convenience goods store that they need a particular item.

If consumers must make a special trip to purchase food and drug items, they will want the store to be close to home. Studies show that the majority of people in the central city patronizing these stores shop within one to five blocks of their homes, and in suburban locations, the majority of customers live within three to five miles of the stores. For rural locations, the average driving time is 10 minutes, with 20 minutes being the maximum time customers will travel to a convenience store.

tip

At C-store (convenience store) locations, customers are willing to pay a little extra for the one or two items they are in a hurry to pick up in exchange for not having to wait in long lines. Express counters are also strong sellers of impulse items.

Shopping Goods

Shopping goods usually have a high unit price, are purchased infrequently, and require an intensive selling effort. The customer does price and feature comparisons, and products are sold in selectively franchised outlets. Examples include men's suits, automobiles, and furniture.

For stores handling shopping goods, the quality of the traffic is important. While convenience goods are purchased by nearly everyone, certain kinds of shopping goods are purchased only by segments of shoppers. Moreover, it is sometimes the character of the retail establishment rather than its type of goods that governs the site selection. For example, a conventional men's clothing store generally does best in a downtown location close to a traffic generator like a department store. On the other hand, a discount menswear store tends to require an accessible highway location.

tip

If you plan to offer shopping goods, you should not locate too far away from your potential customers. Most of your customers will live within five to ten miles of your store. The size of the trading area for a shopping goods store can be determined by a customer survey, automobile license checks, sales slips, charge account records, store deliveries, and local newspaper circulation.

In many cases, buyers of shopping goods like to compare the items in several stores by traveling only a minimum distance. As a result, stores offering complementary items tend to locate close to one another. Another excellent site for a shopping goods store is next to a department store, or between two large department stores, where traffic flows between them. Another option is to locate between a major parking area and a department store.

A retailer dealing in shopping goods can have a much wider trading area than convenience goods stores. Without a heavily trafficked location, this more expensive type of store can generate its own traffic. In this case, a location with a low traffic count but easy accessibility from a residential area is a satisfactory site. Consumers buy these goods infrequently and make deliberate plans for these purchases.

Specialty Goods

Specialty goods usually have a high price tag, are bought infrequently, and require a special effort to make the purchase. Precious jewelry, expensive perfume, and rare antiques are in this merchandise category.

Specialty goods are often sought by customers who are already "sold" on the product, brand, or both. Stores catering to this type of consumer may use isolated locations

Park It

New restaurateurs often underestimate their parking needs when selecting a location. It is important to remember that customers want the most convenient access, especially during bad weather and at night. When scouting your location, see if there is off-street parking, parking meters, or time limits on street parking. Will you provide a paid lot, share a lot with other businesses, or rely on a commercial lot nearby? Check out any fees and business hours, as well as the possibility of valet parking or validating tickets for private lots.

because they generate their own consumer traffic. In general, specialty goods retailers should locate in neighborhoods where the adjacent stores and other establishments are compatible with their operations.

Retail Compatibility

Most merchants prefer to be with other retailers. Only the exceptional operation, such as a restaurant or a freestanding discount house, can survive in isolation. A cluster of stores creates more traffic, exposes more people to your business, and creates a buying atmosphere that a single store cannot. Customers are attracted by crowds and like their shopping trips to be social outings.

Having said this, you want to make sure that you select the right community and site for your particular type of store. Will the other businesses generate traffic for your store? Or will you be located near operations that may clash with yours? For example, a children's store in a service center of hardware stores and automotive repair businesses does not get enough exposure to its target audience to be successful.

Christine Ward and Rick Haase are the owners of seven Patina novelty gift stores in the Minneapolis-St. Paul area of Minnesota. They carefully study the demographic of their audience when deciding to open a new store, making sure it is strategically nestled on a densely trafficked area in an energetic neighborhood. The variety of busy retailers, all within 500 yards of their boutiques, ensures foot traffic for long stretches of time—both day and night. The seven neighborhoods each have major points in common—"bustle" elements such as movie theaters, funky diners, popular ethnic restaurants, and bookshops. These elements create all

the advertising Patina needs, with their exotic and ever-changing window displays. Patina has combined this stellar opportunity for viewing with an intense focus on their panoramic corner window display. It is exceptional, unusual, and ever changing, reaching out to a diverse crowd.

Merchants Associations

Most first-time business owners have no idea how effective a strong merchants association can be in promoting and maintaining the business in a given area. Always find out about the local group of retailers. The presence of an effective organization can strengthen your business and save you money through group advertising and promotion programs, group insurance plans, and collective security measures.

Merchants associations can be particularly effective in promoting stores using common themes or events and during holiday seasons. The collective action of a merchants association can accomplish what an individual storeowner can't. Some associations have induced city planners to add highway exits near their shopping centers. Others have lobbied for and received funds from cities to remodel their shopping centers, including extension of parking lots, refacing of buildings, and installation of better lighting.

Ask other store owners in the area if the retail location you're considering has the benefit of an effective merchants association, how many members the association has, who the officers are, what the dues are, and what has been accomplished during the past year.

Be aware that a shopping area with no merchants association may be an ineffective one, be on the decline, or have contentious tenants or other problems. If you see a lot of litter or debris in the area, vacant stores, a parking lot in need of repair, and similar symptoms, you'll know this is not the area for you. With a little on-site investigation at different hours of the day, you can avoid problems by getting a true picture of retail life there.

Landlords

Directly related to the appearance of a retail location is the reputation of the landlord. Unfortunately, some retail landlords actually hinder the operation of their tenants' businesses. In fact, the landlord may be largely responsible for the demise of the premises and retailers' failures. For instance, some landlords restrict the placement and size of signs, forgo or ignore needed maintenance and repairs, or rent adjacent retail spaces to incompatible or directly competing businesses.

Sometimes landlords lack the funds to maintain their properties. Rather than continuing to invest in their holdings and support their tenants, they try to squeeze out whatever they can get.

In addition to speaking with current tenants, talk to previous tenants of the location you have in mind. Find out what businesses they were in and why they left. Did they fail or just move? What support or hindrances did the landlord provide?

Zoning and Planning

Your town's zoning commission can give you the latest mapping of the retail location and surrounding areas that you are considering. Here are some questions to think about:

- Are there restrictions that will limit your operations?
- Will construction or changes in city traffic or new highways present barriers to your store?
- Will any competitive advantages you currently find at the location you're considering be diminished by zoning changes that will be advantageous for competitors or even allow new competitors to enter your trade area?

Most zoning boards and economic/regional development committees plan several years in advance. They can probably provide you with valuable insights to help you decide among retail locations.

Incentive Areas and Agencies

Hundreds of local, state, federal, and private agencies offer programs designed to entice business owners to move into economically disadvantaged areas. Contact your local SBA chapter for information on federal empowerment and revitalization zones in your area. Most operate an information center to help business owners learn more about the various programs that are available and how to apply for services and programs. Businesses located in these areas receive a wide range of technical assistance, tax credits for hiring local residents and training workers, deductions of business equipment and supplies, and opportunities to apply for tax-exempt bonds to help build new facilities.

Main Street Outreach

The internet allows small-town businesses to reach beyond superstores' geographic influence. Main Street businesses use the internet to provide better service to local customers and augment sales in brick-and-mortar stores. Moving merchants from malls to Main Street is a trend across America, according to Doug Loescher, Director for Business Development and Strategy for the District of Columbia and seven year Director of National Trust of Main Street Center. "Traditionally, Main Street is where small independent businesses were located," explains Loescher. "These areas were shunned by national retailers, but with the saturation of most retail markets, a lot of national retailers have looked beyond the shopping malls and strip centers toward other locations, Main Street being one of them. However, it is still a very small-business-friendly place for retailers to locate." National Trust Main Street Center has helped more than 2,200 cities, towns, and neighborhoods of all types rebuild the economic and social vitality of their downtowns and neighborhood commercial districts.

Positive results from the program have included small towns seeing greater increases than urban districts in upper-floor occupancies, restaurants, and professional offices. Urban districts have had increases in ground-floor occupancies, event attendance, and both retail and independently-owned businesses. Larger communities have experienced dramatic increases in property values and increased numbers of retail businesses, housing units, and franchises. Smaller communities had increases in personal services, businesses, and internet usage, underscoring the change in small towns affected by superstore retail saturation. The commercial districts participating in the Main Street program have generated more than $48.8 billion in new investment, created 391,050 new jobs, and 87,850 new businesses. Every dollar a community uses to support its local Main Street program leverages an average of $25 in new investment, making the Main Street program one of the most successful economic development strategies in America.

tip

Across America, revitalization in central business districts is taking place, and retailers are central to that effort. The main thoroughfare of any downtown is frequently named Main Street or Broadway. New shopping areas, mixed-use buildings, and pedestrian malls are cropping up in these centers, creating robust economic activity.

To find out how you can get involved in the Main Street movement with the location of your business, contact the National Trust for Historic Preservation at Preservationnation.org.

Check Out the Competition

If you're going to run a plumbing store, you have to be the dominant plumbing store against all competition, so take a look at the prospective customer base as well as direct and indirect competitors. If you want to open a flower shop, you need to assess a location's profit potential in terms of what other gift shops, supermarkets with flowers, floral vending machines (yes, these do exist), fresh and silk flower wholesalers, and mass merchandisers there are.

Selecting a Shopping Center Location

Shopping centers are distinctly different from downtown and local business strips. The shopping center building is pre-planned as a merchandising unit for interplay among tenants. Its site is deliberately selected by the developer for easy access to pull customers from a trade area. It has on-site parking as a common feature of the layout. The amount of parking space is directly related to the retail area. Customers like the shopping center's convenience. They drive in, park, and walk to their destination in relative safety and speed. Some shopping centers provide weather protection, and most provide an atmosphere created for shopping comfort. For the customer, the shopping center has great appeal.

warning

One or more large department stores or major discounters traditionally draw shoppers to malls. An enclosed mall without an anchor store may not be able to generate enough traffic to be a viable location for your business. If the leasing agent promises that a star store is slated for that role, negotiate for lower rent until the big store opens, and have your attorney put an escape clause in your lease should the anchor back out.

Can You Qualify?

Developers and owners of shopping centers look for successful retailers. If you are considering a shopping center for a first-store venture, you may have trouble. Your financial backing and merchandising experience may be unproven to the developer. Your challenge is convincing the developer that the new store has a reasonable chance of success and will help the tenant mix.

Whether a small retailer can get into a particular shopping center depends on the market and management. A small shopping center may need only one children's shoe store, for example, while a regional center may expect enough business for two or more.

To finance a center, the developer needs major leases from companies with strong credit ratings. The developer's own lenders favor tenant rosters that include the triple-A ratings of national chains. However, local merchants with good business records and proven understanding of the market have a good chance of being considered by a shopping center developer. So if you or your store manager has a good reputation and track record in retailing in the area, you may be able to make a strong case for acceptance into the center you want.

Center Costs

In examining any shopping center location, get answers to questions such as these: Are its shoppers your prospective customers? Would the center offer the best sales volume potential for your kind of merchandise or service? Can you benefit enough from the center's access to a market? If yes, can you produce the appeal that will make the center's customers come to your store? Can you deal with the competition of other stores?

How much space do you need and where do you want it? Naturally, the amount of space you want will determine your rent. Many merchants need to rethink their space requirements when locating in a shopping center. Rents are typically high, so space must be used efficiently. What amount of space will you need to handle the sales volume you expect to have? Be sure that it has adequate interior space for sufficient inventory, an area for an office, and possibly a receiving and shipping area. You should also consider the necessity for adequate space for expansion when business picks up.

Your location in a center is important. Do you need to be in the main flow of customers as they pass between the stores with the greatest customer pull? Who will your neighbors be? What will their effect on your sales be? What will rent really cost? In most non-shopping center locations, rent is a fixed amount that has no relationship to sales volume. In a shopping center, the rent is usually stated as a minimum guaranteed rent per square foot of leased area against a percentage. Typically, this is between 5 and 7 percent of gross sales, but it varies by type of business and other factors. This means that if the rent calculated by the percentage of sales is higher than the guaranteed rent, you pay the higher amount. If it is lower than the guaranteed rent, then you pay the guaranteed rent amount.

But this guarantee is not the end. In addition, you may have to pay dues to the center's merchants association. You may also have to pay for maintenance of common areas. Therefore, you must think of "total rent" when considering what you can afford to pay. Can you draw enough sales to cover the true rent of being in a center?

Don't forget that you still have to pay for light fixtures, counters, shelves, painting, floor coverings, and installing your own heating and cooling units. Some landlords provide a cost allowance toward completion of your retail space. This "tenant allowance" is for storefronts, ceiling treatment, and wall coverings. The allowance is a percentage of their cost and is spelled out in a dollar amount in the lease. Some developers will help you plan storefronts, exterior signs, and interior color schemes. They provide this service to ensure storefronts that add to the center's image rather than detract from it.

Specialty Leasing

A new trend that can help you feel out whether a location really works for your business is pop-up retail. Pop-ups, or temporary store rentals, in the past have been mostly associated with seasonal merchandise such as Christmas or Halloween, but today this variety of opportunities can help showcase any kind of product, for any length of time. At Storefront (thestorefront.com) you can rent space for a retail event, a small space within an already established store, an entire store, or fair and festival booths by the day. We found a curio cabinet space for rent for $9 per day, a lovely gallery for $199 per day, and a mobile store van for $500 per day, all in trendy neighborhoods in San Francisco. New York had partial and full galleries, beauty shops, and SOHO lofts available for daily rental between $200 and $8,000.

About 80 percent of America's 1,300 enclosed and regional shopping malls have temporary tenants, which include kiosks and carts. There are between 10 and 40 carts per mall at the Simon Property Group malls of Indianapolis, which rely on carts to add color and variety, as well as to generate income. Entrepreneurs can display their wares in a prime, high-foot-traffic location with little investment. Some cart operators move in just to capitalize on busy holiday seasons, and others remain year-round.

tip

Trade journal *Specialty Retail Report* says that carts and kiosks are good startups for young entrepreneurs due to the low investment required and their ability to thrive even during economic downturns. Use a cart to find out about price points, who your customers are, what the demand for your products is, and to start a customer database. To succeed, offer something anchor stores don't carry.

▲

Where's It Going To Be?

While answering these 16 questions certainly won't exhaust all possibilities, it may help you decide on the best retail location for your business:

1. How much retail, office, storage, or workroom space do you need?

2. Is parking space available and adequate?

3. Do you require special lighting, heating or cooling, or other installations?

4. Will your advertising expenses be much higher if you choose a relatively remote location?

5. Is the area served by public transportation?

6. Can the area serve as a source of employees?

7. Is there adequate fire and police protection?

8. Will sanitation or utility supply be a problem?

9. Is exterior lighting in the area adequate to attract evening shoppers and make them feel safe?

10. Are customer restroom facilities available?

11. Does the store have awnings to provide shelter during bad weather?

12. Will crime insurance be prohibitively expensive?

13. Is the trade area heavily dependent on seasonal business?

14. Is the location convenient to where you live?

15. Do the people you want for customers live nearby?

16. Is the population density of the area sufficient?

Rent for in-line stores is about four times the rent for carts and kiosks. You can buy an RMU cart for $4,000-plus or rent one from a mall. Carts and kiosks can be a lower-cost way to launch a retail business or to supplement an existing business. The potential for products is endless.

Urban Remedy operates a pop-up store, or RMU cart, in San Francisco, California. It functions well and requires less labor than the retail store locations, yielding smart rewards from placement in a health focused area—yoga and spin class studios abound with thirsty athletes looking to fill their temples with only the most pure, healthy snacks.

At Bloomington, Minnesota's Mall of America, about 100 temporary tenants dazzle 70 million visitors a year. Cart rental rates average $2,300 or 15 percent of total sales a month, depending on the time of year, and all temporary tenants must pay $1,500 or more in "key money," which pays for a store designer to design and build a cart with the right look.

Street vendors and swap meet and fair concessionaires need to check with the city or county in which they want to do business for the regulations and specifications for the types of products, hours, and displays that are allowed.

Everything Is Negotiable

Once you've decided what kind of space you want and where and how long you need it, it's time to consult a lawyer to discuss what specific issues you need to address to negotiate the best lease for your business. Core points to review carefully are occupancy date, chargeable floor space, which renovations or tenant improvements the landlord will do or pay for, services to be provided, liability, and renewal or termination terms. Once you're close to reaching an agreement with the real estate broker, leasing agent, or landlord, your attorney can make sure that everything is in writing to clearly define each party's obligations.

Retail space is usually rented on what's called a "net lease" basis, meaning that you arrange for most of its services. Unless your premises are tied to the building's mechanical systems, the costs for most services—such as heating and air-conditioning—are your responsibility.

The breadth of your use clause (the specific use intended for the space) will affect your ability to assign your lease or sublet the premises. The broader the definition the better. If you've leased the space to sell ski equipment, for example, and business lags because of a lack of snowfall, you want to have the option of opening a juice bar instead.

In addition, it's a good idea to get a restrictive covenant to prevent the landlord from leasing space in the same building or nearby to a business that competes with you. How far this provision extends will depend on the type of area you're located in. In a city, it might be a few blocks, whereas in the suburbs, it could be a few miles.

With shopping center leases, you are customarily charged for maintenance of common areas and for the mall's marketing efforts. Find out what the mall's plans are for any structural alterations or remodeling, resurfacing the parking lots, or replacing the roof. These can be devastating assessments for a young business. Requirements for hours and days of operation, employee parking restrictions, participation in community service events, gift certificate and loyalty programs, and storefront appearance may not fit into your business plan or capabilities. Make sure you will be capable of conforming to these requirements.

Starting from Scratch

A few of you will decide to throw caution to the wind and start your new business from scratch, including constructing a new building. You want to take advantage of current market conditions and design a building that's exclusively yours. A disadvantage to this approach is the cost of complex financing and legal clearances required in buying and building out property.

Starting a new business in the mature, densely populated retail industry does not, by itself, immediately present customers. The need to cultivate the market over time delays a return on your investment, which adds to the length of time you'll be paying interest on nonproductive money. This may require the infusion of cash over a longer period of time just to keep the doors open. Plus, your new business will have to compete with existing businesses that may already be successfully established in prime locations. A specialty restaurant may be the exception, as there is roughly a 90-day window of opportunity to get a buzz going among locals, visitors, and food critics to catapult your chef to stardom and you to profitability.

Location in a Nutshell

Selection of a retail location requires time and careful consideration. A retail firm cannot survive in a poor location because customers will avoid patronizing a place that is not easily and safely accessible. Choosing a location should never be rushed through. If you haven't found a suitable location, don't plan to open until you're sure you've got what you want. Remember: Opening a retail business in a poor location is fatal.

Legal and Finance Issues

You're about to fully commit to starting your own business. You're confident you're a retailer at heart with a good idea in mind, a location that will serve your customers, and a written plan to implement your dream. The next step is to cross your t's and dot your i's.

Today's business world is fast and often furious, and laws and regulations are changing all the time. Because of this, it's impossible for you to run a successful business and be an expert in everything.

You'll want to line up a number of professionals you can rely on to help put your deal together and keep it moving toward your goals. The professionals you'll want to hire may include an architect, a lawyer, an interior designer, an accountant, a graphic designer, a merchandiser, and a buyer.

One of the advantages to having a franchise or licensed dealership is the expertise you can draw on from the parent company. If you're starting from scratch, you can look for guidance from your suppliers. Erik Ekman considers the feedback of his key opinion leaders in creating new designs for his custom athlete vans in Portland, Oregon. In creating Outside Van, Erik connects with leading athlete contacts he made during his years as a professional snowboarder knowing that each is a trend setter and highly visible. He supplies these key opinion leaders each with high-end van that other sports nuts will see and ask about. Carefully choosing which people to pour his time and money into helps the vans sell themselves without advertising.

To ensure that you get off on the right foot, hire an attorney with startup expertise who can give you advice to grow on. You can use his or her knowledge of the pros and cons of each business structure to determine which one is best for your venture. You can get insight into your lease, buy-sell agreements, licenses, ordinances, bonding, zoning, financing, and human resource hurdles. An experienced business lawyer can minimize your exposure to IRS, occupational, employment, and safety problems. Don't wait until the last minute to line up competent legal counsel you trust. You don't want to put your fate into the hands of a total stranger.

Neka Pasquale had to learn as rapidly as her quickly expanding employee team has grown in the last few years. She was used to just working with four or five employees and when Urban Remedy's growth exploded, so did the odds of hiring people who weren't so trustworthy. "I am a really trusting person and I want to believe in the best in people. You have to prepare yourself for lying, stealing, and cheating. I hate to say it, but it happens. I hired someone to work in a high level position whose character was not in alignment with the company's." Pasquale understands now that it is "just good business" to follow legal procedures with employees, have them sign non-compete waivers, and monitor expense and monetary procedures before

tip

There is little paperwork involved in setting up a sole proprietorship. Get the necessary selling permits and other licenses, and notify the city, county, or state of your intention to do business under an assumed name (dba). You pay taxes on the business income as if it were personal salary and assume full liability for anything that goes wrong. You also pay self-employment tax for Social Security and Medicare coverage.

they get out of hand. Entering into written agreements without the advice of counsel is not wise.

You can reduce the amount of professional fees you have to pay by doing some homework—researching the answers to questions, making some decisions, and knowing how to do part of the paperwork yourself. There's a growing number of books on the subject of forming your own business available from Nolo Press in Berkeley, California, and Simon & Schuster in New York City; also check out *Entrepreneur* Magazine's state-by-state startup guide series, *How to Start a Business in. . .* , for your state. Write or call the Small Business Development Center nearest you, and visit your local library or bookstore for some of the publications listed in the Appendix.

Forming a Business Entity

Forming a business entity is a big step with long-term consequences. While it is possible to change the legal structure anytime in your company's life, it is time-consuming and costly. Converting from a partnership to a C corporation or limited liability company will pose few problems, as will switching from a sole proprietorship, or partnership to an LLC. Converting from a C corporation to a partnership, sole proprietorship or LLC, however—or getting in and out of an S corporation—is more complicated. Think carefully before you finalize your business structure. To ward off impatience and other pressures, look at the three- and five-year projections you put in your business plan to help you stay on course.

If you're like most retailers, you will open as a sole proprietorship. There are no special steps required other than obtaining a business license. You may need to file a notice of a fictitious firm name and present it to your bank to open a business account, but there's not a lot more required for you to start selling your products or services.

A partnership is formed through an oral or a written agreement, but a written agreement is advisable. To form a limited liability company, you need to file articles of organization with the state. A separate document, the operating agreement, outlines the rules for managing the firm. A lawyer will charge you about $1,200 to $3,000 for filling out the paperwork. Forming a corporation usually costs between $500 and $2,000 upfront, according to Fred S. Steingold, author of *Legal Guide for Starting and Running a Small Business* (Nolo Press). There is a substantial amount of paperwork involved, including filing articles of incorporation and paying a state filing fee, which varies from $100 to $150.

In 1989, Erik Ekman met his wife and future business partner while his van upfitting service continued to grow. Since the partnership formed organically of mutual interests, registering for wedding gifts at Home Depot was romantic, money saving, and productive. Some partnerships just keep multiplying power—Ekman and his wife bought a small house with their savings and in two years renovated it, flipped it, then bought a much grander abode with the profits, just the same way they use profits rather than credit to grow Outside Van.

Protect Your Name

Corporations must register their corporate names with the secretary of state, state Department of Corporations, or commissioner of corporations. Each state's laws on this are a little different. But in every state, you must get permission to use your trade name before incorporation. You have to select a permissible name, make sure it's distinguishable from any corporate name already registered in the state, and then send in an application (with a fee) to reserve the legal right to use that name to identify your business.

Antique shop owners Ron Knox and Paul Gallagher named their Manalapan, New Jersey, shop, Stillwell House Antiques, after the family who owned the historic farmhouse in which they are located. Urban Remedy in Richmond, California, provides large quantities of raw organic vegetables and fruits in juice form to nourish customers. "It's the remedy for the urban lifestyle. We are all rushing around like crazy and don't have time to chop up a bunch of vegetables." says Neka Pasquale. Each juice can contain up to two pounds of vegetables, making this liquid nutrition a real time saver. *National Lampoon* singled out the Electric Fetus as the worst name for a business, and Ringo Starr wore an Electric Fetus T-shirt to the 2010 Grammy Awards. Co-owner, Keith Covart recalls the first year of business and how the company was named; "1968 was an electric time and we wanted a strange and thoughtful combination that reflected that."

Any person who uses a trade name other than his or her surname, or any organization that goes by a name other than the last names of the owners, must register the name with the state or county as a fictitious business name. This usually means filing

A Name to Remember

Though Matt Murphy's business name is catchy—Matt Murphy Design—he warns that using your own name can get tricky, should you ever want to sell your brand. It's possible to lose the rights to branding with your own name, if you're not careful.

a certificate with the county clerk stating who is doing business under that trade name. This is called a dba (doing business as).

If your state has no central fictitious name registration, you may want to check more than one county's records to see if anyone else in your state is using the name you propose for your business. Otherwise, several businesses might use the same name in your state, and if you want to expand your operation, you may run into difficulties.

Your name is the cornerstone of your brand, and the identity of your company is a major component of your success. Because image is such an important part of marketing, a lot is riding on your name. Your signage, business cards, name tags, uniforms, vehicles, word-of-mouth advertising, private-label lines, and website will depend on the integrity of your name, so you'll want to guard it carefully.

Separate from the state law issue is the question of whether or not your name has any trademark value because it distinguishes your goods or services from those of other companies. If so, you can register the name for federal trademark protection, which entitles you to stop others from adopting or using it. You must complete a registration form from the U.S. Patent and Trademark Office in Washington, DC.

There are two very different contexts in which your business's name may be used. One is the formal name of your business for purposes of bank accounts, creditors, and potential lawsuits. The second is the name you use to market your goods or services (trademark or service mark). Whether someone is using the same trade name as yours is of less practical importance than if they were using the same trademark, or using the same trade name as a trademark as well. If your corporate name figures into your future marketing plans, you must search for use of the name as a trademark in addition to complying with the corporate name registration requirements. If someone else is the first to use your name as a mark, it doesn't make any difference whether you or they have previously registered it as a fictitious or assumed name. They will still have the right to exclusive use of the name in the marketplace. Unfortunately, it's fairly common for a small business to choose a name that's similar to that of another enterprise.

There are several ways you can conduct a trademark search to avoid such problems. You can visit uspto. gov and do a search; pay a search firm; use a computer database; manually consult trademark registers, directories, industry journals, and other library resources; or use the phone or mail to consult state agencies. This can cost you from nothing to a few thousand dollars. Trademark searching is a competitive business, so

tip ⓘ

Though his family business was doing well in the late '90s, Gary Vaynerchuk convinced his father to try selling wine on the website he'd purchased and developed—a new concept for that time. That foresight and adventurous spirit brought the $4 million business up to $45 million in just five years.

be prepared to negotiate. Nolo Press has a self-help guide, *Trademark: Legal Care for Your Business & Product Name*, that shows you how to protect your business and lists several books, software packages, and services that may help you.

Domain Name Registration

Once you have your business name, you'll need to decide on a domain name. Purchasing and registering it can be done through your ecommerce provider or you can handle it yourself through Register.com, Domain.com, DomainNames.com, Networksolutions.com, or GoDaddy.com. You can try out versions of the name you'd like on these sites and they will tell you if it's available or offer other solutions for you. For example, you may not be able to buy www.JudysDelicousCandy.com, but www.JudysDelicousCandy.biz or www.JudysYummyCandy.com may be available. Owning the domain can cost as little as $9.99 per year.

What Kind of Money Will It Take?

Many startups are financed with less than $100,000. Regardless of outside cash you may be able to raise, the SBA coaches new businesses to have one dollar in cash or business assets for every three dollars of sought loans.

Matt Murphy "bet the farm" with the $50,000 he'd saved up while working his way through graduate school at Universal Studios. Remarketing himself as a handbag designer, graphics and branding artist required a cohesive look to show how the various talents come from the same source of quality. This highly creative entrepreneur handled his own site and branding debut.

In 1968, Keith Covart and his three friends, Roger Emslie, Dan Foley, and Ron Korch, pooled their resources to start Electric Fetus. "We each came up with about $2,000. I had no money, but I had a friend who was an attorney at the bus company where I worked and he agreed to co-sign on a loan for me. Roger borrowed from his grandmother," Keith remembered, with a smile. "We started out small and after that, only expanded when we made the money to finance it."

If you only have $5,000 in cash, you should be looking for a business whose total startup cost is in the $15,000 to $50,000 range. The low end of that spectrum caters to those with little or no experience and the high end to an experienced business owner who can show banks a track record of repayment ability from documented cash flow management. For a list of startup costs for different types of retail businesses, check out "Retail Opportunities" starting on page 77.

> **tip**
>
> A resale number or seller's permit is required by all states that collect sales tax. The permit allows you to buy merchandise at wholesale prices without paying sales tax, but you must pay the state sales tax on taxable merchandise when sold at retail. Usually, the consumer pays the sales tax at the time of purchase.

Unsolved Mysteries

Some unforeseen expenses that can throw off your startup expenses projection are:

- ○ Increase in taxes
- ○ Difficulty attracting customers
- ○ Changes in consumer styles, preferences, and demand
- ○ New competition in your market that takes away some of your revenue
- ○ Price increases from your suppliers
- ○ Accidents involving you, your employees, or best customers
- ○ Increases in insurance, utility costs, or vital supplies like heating oil or gas
- ○ Lawsuits
- ○ Fines

So what will it take to get you in business? Set up a budget and list your operating expenses for the first three months—the time it will take to stock the store, advertise your opening, and hire help. Go down the worksheet and itemize everything you will need to open your doors and acquire that first customer. There are so many variables that you might want to talk with retailers in your market as well as a knowledgeable SCORE counselor (Score.org) whose background is in retail. The tips you gather can guide you in seeing if you have enough cash on hand to do the deal, or what you'll need to get from advances on your credit cards, loans, and vendor assistance. Talk over your projections with your accountant. For a sample list of startup expenses, turn to page 79. For a "Startup Expenses Worksheet" you can fill out for your own business, turn to page 80.

Ready, Aim

Figuring out how much money you'll need is the most difficult yet vital step in the process of opening your business. It is, after all, an exercise in goal-setting. You are asked to predict what you think will happen in the first few months of something that doesn't exist yet. It's a lot easier if you are buying an existing business or a franchise because some historical or average figures can guide you.

Prepare for the unexpected when charting your startup budget. If your retail business will be your sole source of income, you will need to bankroll money to support yourself until your new venture turns a profit. Typically, the amount of money you need will equal six months' to a year's living expenses for you and your family. Jay Shafer was working in a grocery store and as an art professor at the University of Idaho when he used $500 of saved money to build his prototype house, which he lived in for many years. When he got the first contract to build someone else a house, their deposit funded the necessary elements to sustain the project, as did further projects, until his venture began to thrive.

Homebased Businesses Aren't Free

Although a homebased business won't have all the expenses of a leased-space business, it is rare for

tip

There are five things an entrepreneur should be prepared to show a loan officer: a business plan that shows how you will use the financing to operate the business, proof that you pay your obligations when due, that you have enough equity money, that your team has enough experience to implement the plan, and that your sales prospects are strong enough to repay the loan.

any type of retailer not to have startup expenses. You will need supplies and business equipment. Laws and ordinances governing homebased businesses vary widely from community to community. Know what is required before you start your pet-walking, hair-braiding, bridal consulting, or other kind of homebased business.

A homebased business may need a license to operate, a seller's permit, and a federal ID number, depending on your industry and local requirements. You should also check fire department permits if you use flammable materials; air and water pollution control permits if you plan to burn any material or discharge any waste into the waterways; liquor, wine, and beer licenses if you sell liquor, even through the mail; and health department permits if your business involves food or food preparation.

You may be sufficiently covered under your existing homeowner's or renter's policy, or you may need additional insurance coverage. Check with your insurance agent. And to find out what tax benefits you may qualify for with your homebased business, seek the guidance of an accountant who is familiar with homebased deductions. He or she can calculate your cash needs with and without the tax deductions, in case tax laws change and you receive no benefits beyond savings on rent and utilities.

Bank Locally

Regardless of your location, as a businessperson, you'll need to set up your accounts. You want a bank that wants your business. Look for a full-service financial institution that caters to small businesses in general and retailers specifically. Your goal is to find one that has the products, services, and fees that fit your needs.

The basic items you will want to compare among financial institutions are:

- Business checking account
- Business interest checking account
- Business savings account
- Cash management services
- Merchants' deposit
- Payroll service
- Online banking services
- Lines of credit (seasonal and revolving)
- Small-business loans (short-term, long-term, collateral, equipment, accounts receivable financing, factoring accounts receivable, cosigner)
- SBA-approved status
- Wire transfers

- Deposit box rental
- Foreign currency exchange

Even if you're like tiny home designer, Jay Shafer of Four Lights Houses and New York purse designer, Matt Murphy, and you've saved up enough money to start your business without having to take out a loan or get outside investors, it's always a good idea to be on a first-name basis with your banker. Matt has a good working relationship with his bank but adds, "No one is extending credit on the premise of hope. It's both a blessing and a curse to be as diversified as I am. We live in a world were people are categorized by a single occupation and if one's profile extends beyond that, they [bankers] have trouble understanding it. Banks need concrete examples."

Put the bank manager and head of the loan committee on your mailing list; say hello or wave when you're in the bank; and make a point to share some exciting news with them about sales, new personnel, or your community involvement. By being someone they know and respect who doesn't want anything from them, when you do approach them to get some new equipment or remodel your store, or even to provide a reference, they will know who you are.

Strategic planner Jeff Prouty's advice on choosing a banker is to find someone who thinks about the big picture. One of the most important people in his inner business circle is his banker, who is astute enough to think about the kind of life Jeff is trying to build rather than just the balance sheet. "He's always thinking about me, trying to help me. I was really tired of working with private bankers who'd leave their firms every few years. I wanted a long-term relationship with a person (not just an organization) who intended to stay put. When you're deciding on a banker, ask that person where they see themselves in 10, 20, 30 years from now. Try to get the founder, CEO, or owner of a local bank as your personal banker, because then you know they're not going anywhere. If you can't get that and are dealing with a larger, national bank, then ask that banker if he or she owns shares and if they're in it for the long haul."

Retail Opportunities

Here is a sampling of brick-and-mortar and online businesses with approximate startup cost estimates gathered from researchers and retailers. Your actual investment and rewards will vary according to these key factors: location (home, cart, store), size (square footage, number of clients, breadth of inventory/services, capitalization), market, and structure (franchise, purchase, startup). *Primarily online-based businesses will contain an asterisk and the figures will reflect the spectrum of the physical manifestation of the business and the online version.

Business Type	Average Annual Revenues	Estimated Startup Costs
Alterations	$9,000–45,000	$500–8,000
Amusement arcade	$70,000–200,000	$90,000–125,000
Antique dealer	$15,000–100,000	$25,000–60,000
*Apartment finder	$35,000–90,000	$2,000–10,000
Art gallery	$30,000–1 million	$35,000–100,000
Balloon decoration	$12,000–16,000	$500–1,000
Bed-and-breakfast	$24,000–300,000	$150,000–850,000
Carpet cleaning	$10,000–30,000	$500–20,000
CD exchange	$50,000–130,000	$60,000–100,000
Child care	$25,000–60,000	$3,000–20,000
Coffee shop	$6,000–500,000	$20,000–250,000
Costume/novelty shop	$60,000–170,000	$30,000–50,000
Dance instruction	$40,000–60,000	$20,000–45,000
*Dating service	$50,000–500,000	$5,000–100,000+
Detective agency	$25,000–100,000	$10,000–12,000
*Editorial service	$25,000–100,000	$2,000–7,000
Elder care	$25,000–60,000	$5,000–11,000
Flower shop	$80,000–100,000	$30,000–90,000
*Genealogy service	$20,000–55,000	$3,000–10,000
Gift baskets	$10,000–100,000	$2,000–40,000

Retail Opportunities, continued

Business Type	Average Annual Revenues	Estimated Startup Costs
Graphic design	$30,000–140,000	$5,000–20,000
Jewelry design	$25,000–80,000	$5,000–10,000
*Mail order	$10,000–120,000	$1,500–50,000
Makeup application	$30,000–60,000	$4,000–10,000
Massage therapy	$20,000–50,000	$5,000–8,000
*Meeting/event planning	$85,000–250,000	$8,000–31,000
Mobile DJ	$25,000–130,000	$4,000–20,000
Party supply store	$22,000–110,000	$40,000–120,000
Personal fitness training	$20,000–120,000	$2,000–5,000
Personal shopping	$20,000–40,000	$1,000–4,000
Pet grooming	$25,000–45,000	$16,000–20,000
Photography	$40,000–300,000	$8,000–175,000
*PR agency	$40,000–100,000	$2,000–10,000
Restaurant	$100,000–1 million	$50,000–500,000
Sign painting	$15,000–50,000	$3,500–8,000
Tanning salon	$40,000–70,000	$40,000–50,000
Tattoo studio	$40,000–60,000	$10,000–25,000
Tax preparation	$40,000–100,000	$6,000–8,000
Toy store	$35,000–100,000+	$90,000–125,000
*Travel agency	$40,000–120,000	$4,000–6,000
Tutoring service	$30,000–90,000	$2,000–100,000
Wedding consulting	$25,000–150,000	$2,000–11,000
Women's clothing store	$50,000–75,000	$30,000–175,000

Startup Expenses

Here is a list of sample startup expenses for a hypothetical motorcycle sales and service shop:

Accountant setup fees	$500
Advertising (social media type)	$3,000
Cash register	$4,000
Computer system	$9,700
Fixtures	$8,700
Grand opening	$2,500
Insurance	$8,000
Inventory setup and pricing	$3,000
Legal fees	$4,000
Licenses and permits	$350
Miscellaneous expenses	$1,000
Office equipment	$10,000
Opening inventory	$75,000
Payroll account	$5,000
Remodeling	$12,000
Rent/security deposit	$12,000
Retail seller's permit deposit	$1,500
Shop equipment and tools	$15,000
Shop supplies	$1,000
Signs	$9,200
Supplies (office, cleaning)	$1,200
Utility deposits	$2,000
Subtotal	$188,650
Miscellaneous expenses (10% of subtotal)	$18,650
Total Startup Expenses	**$207,300**

Startup Expenses Worksheet

Accountant setup fees	$
Advertising	$
Cash register	$
Computer system	$
Fixtures	$
Grand opening	$
Insurance	$
Inventory setup and pricing	$
Legal fees	$
Licenses and permits	$
Miscellaneous expenses	$
Office equipment	$
Opening inventory	$
Payroll account	$
Remodeling	$
Rent/security deposit	$
Retail seller's permit deposit	$
Shop equipment and tools	$
Shop supplies	$
Signs	$
Supplies (office, cleaning)	$
Utility deposits	$
Subtotal	$
Miscellaneous expenses (10% of subtotal)	$
Total Startup Expenses	**$**

6

Operations

The glamorous side of retailing is where the merchandise is located and customer action is taking place. What goes on behind the scenes, however, is vitally important because the support systems you put in place are what keep your business alive and well.

▲

Store Policies

Store policies are the broad guidelines that outline the general practices to be followed by all employees to achieve your goals. Take time to think these various details through and then schedule times for each task to be done and who is to do it. Policies are more than daily procedures and work rules; they are a road map for success.

Rather than running your business in an informal, by-the-seat-of-your-pants manner, before you open your business, write down rules that outline every one of your expectations. Once you are open for business, things will happen very quickly, so you want to be able to create the work ethic and atmosphere you want in your business before you open. By focusing on the details now—under fairly unpressured circumstances—you will be able to meet decision-making demands when under stress, and your employees will do what you want them to do. On the next few pages, you'll learn what several retailers' days are really like.

Hours

The retailers we interviewed for this book told us this line of work has two kinds of hours: business hours and store hours. There are many tasks that need to be done besides selling—receiving, preparing and tagging merchandise, cleaning and facing shelves, freshening displays, counting the cash in the cash drawer, ordering new merchandise, checking on special orders, notifying customers of the status of their purchases, returning damaged goods, recording markdowns, answering the phone, and a multitude of other invisible, but necessary, tasks. These are all included in business hours because you obviously can't accomplish all these tasks during store hours.

Determine your hours of operation. If your business is in a shopping center you will most likely be required to remain open certain hours as part of your lease, especially if you rent in an indoor mall.

If you are an independent consultant, such as Erik Ekman, having a "by appointment only" policy suits your business well and is actually a time and money saver. Ekman's clients sometimes spend hours giving

tip

Be ready for business by having the right assortment of coins and bills to fill the till each morning. This money is set aside the night before when the register is balanced and the next day's deposit is readied for the bank. Always start with an even amount—$100, for example. Plan ahead for busy weekends and special events. Make sure you plan around bank holidays so you're not caught short.

him the information he needs to design their ultimate, livable van and the process can span months. Initial consultations begin on site, wherever either he or his key opinion leaders are when the questions start, "Hey, that's a cool van. Where did you get it? How much did it cost?" begins the dialogue. Promoters of Outside Van do much of the consulting for Ekman, providing detailed information about the process at sporting trade shows, outdoor competitions, and recreational hot spots. By the time would be purchasers make an appointment much of the initial information is exchanged without even having a retail location or a conversation with him. This entails quality time for phone or in-person appointments. Controlling the hours dedicated to "work talk" is important to Ekman. He and his wife have a strict policy now of never talking about the business at the dinner table. This helps prevent them from getting burned out. Creating custom designs requires a lot of creativity and the hours spent collecting information for his field representatives, or promoters, can mesh with his personal life because of having so many common interests and similar lifestyles. Learn to set limits for yourself. Write up a plan that includes which social activities are cross over into business and which don't, what your realistic hours per week should be, including networking functions and online socializing, extra time spent on the weekends spent taking up the slack from the week, casual phone conversations that turn into business, and stick with the plan. It's easy to always be working and even if you love what you do, it's not healthy to never have an off switch.

If you are like music store co-owners, Keith Covart and Stephanie Covart Meyerring, or eco-wares boutique owner Charlotte Cozzetto, and operate completely independently of other shop owners, you are free to set your own hours.

Electric Fetus is open seven days a week. Keith Covart says, "We used to be closed on Sundays but when other music stores started staying open on Sunday, we did, too. We always stayed until the last customer went home in the old days, whatever time that was." Now Electric Fetus is open 78 hours per week. Stephanie and Keith also structure scheduling to match customer flow, such as on "New Releases" day. Around 300 new releases are delivered to the store on Tuesdays, which draws customers greatly anticipating their favorite artist's latest creation.

Local bands sometimes stop in at Electric Fetus's central Minneapolis location and play a set or two. With enough notice, even a day or two, an alert is put out on Twitter about the musicians' eminent visit and the store is filled to capacity with

tip

Homebased workers need a lot of self-discipline to grow a retail business. Keeping standard 8-to-6 weekday hours keeps you in sync with most storefronts (8 to 5 for most service businesses) and gives you a set time frame in which to complete your tasks.

adoring fans. Stephanie staffs accordingly to the ebbs and flows of this sometimes dramatic business.

After 17 years running Patina with a 50- to 80-hour- per-week schedule Christine Ward and husband made a concerted effort to reduce their schedules to 30 to 40 hours so they we could spend more time with their kids. "Every day is different for me, Christine says, but an average week involves stopping in at each of my seven stores to check the ambience, music being played, tidiness, energy of the staff, and how the customer interactions are going. I'm always checking to make sure that displays utilize the proper usage of our inventory and do a general check in with the manager and visual merchandiser of each store. Of course, there's all the mundane stuff, too, like making sure the toilet is flushing properly and that the heat is working. I stop in at my office every day, too, to inspect new product shipments and check in with Human Resources. My store hours mirror the hours of the other businesses near me. We

Layaway Record

Salesperson:		Date:	
Customer:		Telephone:	
Address:			
City:		State:	Zip:

Quantity	Item/description	Price/unit	Total

Pickup date:	Total due:	
Delivery schedule:	Deposit:	
	Balance:	

always extend hours during the holidays and staff is encouraged to let customers into the store as soon as possible in the winter, even if they aren't ready for them, just to get them out of the frigid cold."

Credit Policies

Many small retailers sign up for MasterCard, American Express, or Visa and willingly pay the small percentage to let a bank operate their credit departments for them. You will need to decide which credit cards, if any, you will accept. Base this decision on what sort of merchandise you sell. Is it a high-ticket item your customers will be unable to pay cash for?

Also determine under what circumstances you'll accept personal checks. Most retail businesses that accept checks ask for a form of picture identification from the customer writing the check. Other businesses ask for more detailed information, such as a home or work telephone number. Your bank may be able to recommend policies, or even offer electronic check verification services, that will help you cut down on the cost of accepting bad checks.

You may also want to consider providing a layaway option for your customers. See below for a "Layaway Record."

Customer Service Policies

How do you want returns and exchanges handled? Will you offer gift-wrapping? What about alterations? Deliveries and special orders? Customer service can be as simple as saying hello to customers as soon as they step through your doors.

Your employees are the front line of customer service. Set your policies in writing and make sure everyone understands how you expect your business to be represented.

See the "Merchandise Return Form" on page 86 and the "Discount Worksheet" on page 94.

Housekeeping

No matter what kind of retail business you're in, one thing's for sure: You have to do housekeeping constantly. Retailers believe that a consistent standard for cleanliness and orderliness gives them several advantages over stores that don't have a cleanliness standard. Customers are safer, their confidence in you is higher, and your sales are enhanced by a well-kept enterprise. Business owners all try to set an example for employees by sweeping, restocking, filing, and dusting as needed rather than waiting for a set time.

▲

Merchandise Return Form

Date: _____

From: _____

Address: _____

_____

Telephone: ( ) _____

Quantity	Invoice/order	Item/description number	Price per item	Total
				$
				$
				$
				$
				$
				$
				$
				$
				$
				$
				$
				$
				$
				$
				$
				$
				$
				$
				$

Credit as:	Total return:
Exchange:	Quantity:
Store credit:	Amount:
Cash:	Check number:
Charge:	

Reason for return:

_____

_____

_____

_____

Depending on your lease, your landlord may take care of exterior landscaping and building maintenance. If you own the building, however, it's all up to you. Add one more list of tasks to oversee. Air conditioning, elevators, lighting, and computer terminals all require technical maintenance. Floors, restrooms, and workrooms also require care and daily attention. Retailers who neglect repainting, cleaning windows, replacing worn fixtures, and basic janitorial service often pay for it in reduced customer traffic.

Security Policies

Each year, American retailers suffer billions of dollars in crime losses. To decrease the chances of robbery, retailers say to limit the amount of cash you have on hand. Bank deposits should be made at different times of the day so that potential robbers cannot be sure when cash will be leaving your business. A safe should be located on your premises, which is not visible from outside the store. Do not keep large amounts of money in it for any length of time or for predictable time periods if at all possible.

> **aha!**
> Keep yourself organized by following the tips in *How to Get Control of Your Time and Your Life* (Mass Market) by Alan Lakein, attend a Franklin Covey seminar, or use a software program like Microsoft's Meeting Maker or a smartphone.

Although the retailers interviewed have not had many problems with crime, they say that it is something you need to be on the lookout for in your daily operations. See page 89 for a "Petty Cash Form," page 93 for a "Cashier's Till Record" and page 95 for a "Daily Cash Record."

You will find more information on security in Chapter 15. Also ask your local sheriff's department or police agency to suggest what instructions you should include in your employee manual and training. When law enforcement agencies distribute fliers notifying you of scam artists working the area or shoplifters hitting other retailers, make sure all employees get the information right away. Keep an employee bulletin board in the back of the store where you can post important notices.

All in a Day's Work

In addition to selling their existing collection, antique shop owners Ron Knox and Paul Gallagher consult with clients and help them find specific pieces through their wide network of sources. "We'll go to people's houses and help them integrate the pieces into their homes and teach them about what they're buying," says Knox. "We don't want to just sell them a painting. We want them to understand why this

Business as Usual

Here are just a few of the tasks you will need to perform to operate your business:

○ Meet with customers, suppliers, and employees

○ Fulfill orders and deliver service

○ Keep the books (general ledger, accounts payable, accounts receivable)

○ Order supplies

○ Prepare balance sheets and profit-and-loss statements monthly, quarterly, and annually

○ Maintain employee records

○ Do payroll

○ Buy, manage, and control inventory

○ Display merchandise

○ Market the business through advertising, promotions, and public relations

○ Correspond by internet or mail with suppliers and customers

○ Prepare and print daily cash reports, purchase orders, and necessary business forms

○ Create and maintain relational database for sales, service, and supplier records

○ Print mailing labels

○ Make signs

○ Print and affix price tags

○ Draft and print direct-mail offers

○ Design and print promotional pieces

○ Prepare personnel schedules

○ Prepare budgets and compare year-to-date figures against those that were budgeted

○ Track shipments in and out of store

Petty Cash Form

Keep a petty cash fund of about $25 for small store necessities. When the cash is depleted, write a check to bring the balance back up after posting disbursement to the appropriate accounts listed on the petty cash slips. Do not mix the petty cash with cash register funds or the till will not balance with the sales report at the end of the day. Petty cash receipts can be purchased through stationery or general merchandise stores, or you can print some up on your computer.

Received by: _____

Date: _____

Item: _____

Amount: _____

Account: _____

Item: _____

Amount: _____

Account: _____

Total:

Please staple sales receipt(s) to back of petty cash form.

is a good painting and have it make some connection with them." The pair also has a network of restoration professionals with whom they work to help repair and refurbish antiques to their fullest possible potential. For the antiques business, a seven-day workweek is not unusual.

An important part of most retailers' operations is keeping abreast of what is going on in their particular industries.

Knox and Gallagher go to numerous auctions, network with other dealers, pore through online auctions and offerings, read trade journals, and attend antiques shows around the country to keep on top of recent offerings and opportunities. Staying up on industry and consumer news has to be incorporated into their monthly tasks so they don't get left behind.

For some retailers, sometimes a day's work stretches well into night. For Neka Pasquale, starting Urban Remedy while pregnant and running the business as a single mother was challenging at first but soon became her new normal. Her son, Frankie can sometimes be seen running and playing at after hours work events as personal and business merge.

Freshly Squeezed Time Management

In a *Business Insider* interview with time management expert, Laura Vanderkam (lauravanderkam.com), the inside story on how high achievers squeeze the most out of their life minutes is perhaps not surprising. Her book, *What the Most Successful People Do Before Breakfast*, reveals ways to get more out of our 24 hours. Her top tips are:

- Wake up early. Ninety percent of the top executives do this, and so should you.
- Exercise before you start your day so it can't fall by the wayside. Being in shape helps performance in every way.
- Plan your day in the morning, while you are fresh.
- Check and respond quickly to emails in the morning rather than all day long so you can stay focused on bigger things.
- Work on a number-one priority project in the wee hours of the morning before distractions can occur.
- Budget an hour a day to work on a project you are passionate about. It is important to feed your soul for long-term health.
- Spend time with family or friends every day. Whether it's 45 minutes or just a phone call, close time with those we care about nurtures well being.
- Network over coffee for social engagement and solid connections.
- Carve out a 20-minute session once a day to meditate and clear your mind. It will keep you fresh and functioning.
- The daily gratitude list—write down as many things as you can think of that you would be sad to lose. It will increase your joy and improve your attitude.
- Read the news to stay stimulated and abreast of what may affect your creative ideas and business plans.

New York City designer, Matt Murphy, admits to sometimes working around the clock to meet deadlines. He's on the phone or email all day tracking shipments, negotiating prices for materials, checking on production, and planning his next collection. Essentially, his business is never closed because he has catalogs to plan, pricing to strategize, showrooms to visit, and retail buyers to sell. Once or twice a month, he does an interview with the print or broadcast media, and he also has to go to trade shows and be seen at fashion functions. On top of that, there are special orders to fill, signature fabric to design, and prototypes to create.

aha!

Part of operating a business is establishing ties with your community. Get to know the other retailers in your area and join community groups and business associations. Attend monthly meetings or send a representative to keep you visible, involved and informed.

Whether you're selling prom dresses, groceries, or stereos, you have to take time to make intelligent use of the data you collect on a daily basis. Everyone interviewed said this is one of the most difficult challenges they constantly have to deal with. Keeping track of the numbers on a daily basis, then interpreting them on a weekly, monthly, and annual basis and deciding what they mean in terms of buying, pricing, discounting, and profit-taking can be stressful.

"You really have to be adaptable in retail," comments one retailer. "Every business is different. There is no standard practice or manual you can follow. A lot of it is learn-as-you-go. I talk with other retailers to get some ideas on how to manage my people and handle customers better. There are so many variables in location, capabilities, product mix, customers, and computers that you just have to try what you think will work, do it, and see."

In retail, every day is different, which appeals to people in this industry. (See the "Raw Juice Maven's Daily Routine" on page 92 for an example.) While much is unpredictable, all the retailers we interviewed said if you don't attend to business, you won't have one. You'll learn more about retail operations in upcoming chapters as we expand your perspective from the owner's viewpoint to a close-up on employees and customers.

A Raw Juice Maven's Daily Routine

A typical day for Pasquale goes like this:

5:30 A.M.   Her three-year old son and alarm clock name Frankie wakes her up and she plays with him for at least an hour.

6:30 A.M.   Neka and Frankie make breakfast together so he is continually learning to cook.

7:45 A.M.   If Pasquale is lucky she has time for a shower before she rushes to drop Frankie off at school on her way to work.

8:30 A.M.   When Pasquale arrives at Urban Remedy's Richmond California facility, any of the following combinations below may happen on a typical day—the needs are always changing, and often at the last minute.

Create new raw juice and snack recipes, go through several versions of each until they are fine-tuned and finalize ingredients list. Give recipe to accounting department determine profitability. Submit data to food laboratory to determine exact nutritional content. Submit data to office staff to create labels for product. Communicate new recipes to kitchen staff.

Half day teaching kitchen staff new recipes.

Keep abreast of news from each of her three local stores, determine how she can help her managers surmount each issue smoothly. Some of typical issues that can arise are glitches in the POS store systems. Fine tuning of the way orders flow through the hierarchy of customer, to online software (Magento) to customer service team, to kitchen managers, to shipping department, and back to the customer upon deliver of product.

Write nutrition related articles for magazines such as Harper's Bazar and Men's Fitness.

Participate in product photo shoots.

Cashier's Till Record

Date:
Name:
Amount start of day:
Amount end of day:
Over/under:
Deposit:
Deposit date:

Item	Start of day	End of day
Pennies		
Nickels		
Dimes		
Quarters		
Half dollars		
Ones		
Fives		
Tens		
Twenties		
Fifties		
Hundreds		
Checks/other		
Total:	$	$

Cashier's signature: _____

Discount Worksheet

Prepared by:_____   Date:_____

Clearance:_____

Special promotion:_____

Advertised in:_____   Run dates:_____

Item description	Wholesale price	Retail price	Dates valid	% discount	Final unit price
	$	$			$
	$	$			$
	$	$			$
	$	$			$
	$	$			$
	$	$			$
	$	$			$
	$	$			$
	$	$			$
	$	$			$
	$	$			$
	$	$			$
	$	$			$
	$	$			$
	$	$			$
	$	$			$
	$	$			$
	$	$			$
	$	$			$
	$	$			$
	$	$			$
	$	$			$
	$	$			$
	$	$			$
	$	$			$
	$	$			$

Daily Cash Record

Date:

Page No.:

CASH PAID OUT

Name:
Amount:
1
2
3
4
5
6
7
8

Total paid out:	$
Total receipts:	$
Less paid out:	$
Balance:	**$**

CASH RECEIVED FROM

Name:
Amount:
1
2
3
4
5
6
7
8

Total paid out:	$
Total receipts:	$
Less paid out:	$
Balance:	**$**

Remarks:

_____

_____

Store and Website Design

I magine you are a customer entering your store or website for the first time. Are you drawn with a magnetic pull to a dynamic interface you can't help but interact with? Do the setting and visual cues give the impression you want them to?

Are you an upscale, trend-setting, discount or mainstream business? Are you futuristic, contemporary, or traditional?

Your branding is determined by the identity you set for yourself in your business plan. Both your website and physical store should convey that branding and support your mission. Consider whether elegant columns, chandeliers, neon or natural light cohesively communicate your store identity and then match that style on your website. Instead of just imagining the colors, textures and design of your store, create a variety of virtual models and try them on for size with SmartDraw's (smartdraw.com) free download.

The Store Planning Process

Your store plan has two key elements: store design and store layout. Design is concerned with atmosphere, image, interior design, and exterior design factors. Layout involves the internal arrangements of each department, selling and sales support allocation, and the evaluation of space productivity.

To set up your store, consider consulting with architects, interior designers, and lighting engineers. Skillfull designers know the best location for air conditioners and elevators and can build flexibility for growth into lighting, sound, and wiring systems that can save you money. They understand the hottest design trends and are connected to the sources to make them come to life.

Preparing a "design brief" that covers the objective, budget, target audience, description of style, and preference for materials will help your designer stay on track and within your budget. Here is a guide to writing that brief: justcreative. com/2008/09/26/how-to-write-an-effective-design-brief.

Whether you design your store yourself or hire a professional, you should be inspired first. Visit successful retail businesses and look at award winning store designs like those found here: A.R.E. Design Awards (aredesignawards.com). Take notes on which designs would or wouldn't fulfill your goals. Be critical and analytical. See the "Store Planning Worksheet" on the next page for more information.

Let's take a look at your store design opportunities from curbside to checkout counter.

Exterior Personality

Customers enter your business partly on their impression of its exterior. Much like the homepage of your website, it can convey stability, friendliness, style, service, value, safety, etc. Therefore, the external lighting, signage, size and shape of the windows, and style and positioning of the entryway should project the image you want them to and be distinct from a distance.

Store Planning Worksheet

In evaluating your physical facilities plan, answer the following questions:

1. Is adequate emphasis placed on space productivity?
   ❑ Yes   ❑ No

2. Are flexible fixtures used wherever possible?
   ❑ Yes   ❑ No

3. Does signage provide adequate information to shoppers?
   ❑ Yes   ❑ No

4. Does the atmosphere support the other elements of the marketing plan?
   ❑ Yes   ❑ No

5. Is merchandise arranged for easy cross-selling wherever possible?
   ❑ Yes   ❑ No

The key information you'll want to have ready for your design team includes:

❑ A profile of your target customer (age, zip codes, lifestyles, spending patterns)

❑ Requirements for the types of products to be stocked

❑ The store's positioning (fashion attitude, price levels, philosophy, etc.)

❑ Planned product mix for store (required stock density and presentation needs)

❑ Proposed departmental complements (what goes next to what)

❑ Window and internal display considerations

❑ Stockroom requirements

❑ Back-office requirements

❑ Staff room requirements

❑ Checkout requirements (wiring needs for electronic point-of-sale equipment, credit authorization telephones, and security equipment)

❑ Specific needs for fitting rooms, customer service desks, seating areas, showroom, etc.

❑ The length of time the decor is required to last before updating

❑ A target price per square foot you are prepared to pay

Though you have many options in the design process, you may have to compromise by restrictions set by your landlord and local authorities. You may have to work around preservation protected architecture, or neighborhood requirements for colors, materials, or sign design. Retailers advise that it's best to start out with a clear picture of what you want so you can negotiate toward that and keep most of your well-crafted identity.

tip

To find a firm that can handle your new construction or remodeling project, contact the Retail Design Institute (retaildesigninstitute.org), the National Retail Federation (nrf.com), or American Society of Interior Designers (asid.org).

Overhead Sign

A sign identifies a store and gives a clue about the goods inside. The tone, character, and design should be in sync with your brand. It should function as a magnet to drawing people in, so spend time and money to come up with a strong one. Signs can attract customers from far away if they are striking, well-lit, and unobstructed. Check the visibility various vantages to verify your intended effect.

Signs come in various fonts, materials, and lighting options. The elements of metal, stone, wood, stucco, neon, and light boxes covered with translucent facings are mixed to create pleasing combinations. Dynamic digital signage can be continually changed online. View clever examples at Digital Signage Today (digitalsignagetoday.com). Your sign plans can be a deal-breaker in negotiating a lease, so address them upfront with your landlord and city.

Maintenance is mandatory to keep your sign looking new in the presence of weather, chipping, and failing neon and electrical elements. If your sign looks old or damaged or your sidewalk is unkempt and icily dangerous it will cost you sales.. Keep some rock salt on hand for winter and tidy up your exterior daily.

Show Window

The large show window is "the eyes of the store," and your principle promotion tool. View Cole's Hardware (colehardware.com/cole-hardwares-award-winning-windows) and retailstorewindows.com to see different ways light and design show windows.

Discounters and food retailers tend to use a lot of the glass in show windows for promotional posters. Fashion retailers use it to promote the latest look. Luxury retailers often have understated, refined windows that imply a lifestyle, minimally displaying products.

Consider your merchandise, foot traffic demographic, and intended effect when planning your show window and its lighting style.

Christine Ward's Patina stores showcase trendy houseware, jewelry, and gifts in fantasy museum styled window displays that beckon passersby. Aptly placed, the stores often dominate their respective blocks with softly illuminated windows that give mysterious hints of a story within. Window panels are divided into themes by color and fantasy, but many products are mixed together within one "story" so that viewers will see items they may not otherwise seek out. "It's a way for us to present a lot of merchandise in a palatable way. Each window is an explosion of color—a mini story that people get lost in," says Christine. Once dreamy-eyed customers enter the store, the stories continue, each freestanding display inviting a complete walk around with merchandise on all sides. The cash register and gift-wrapping station is at the center of the store, surrounded on all sides by hundreds of pieces of jewelry under lit glass.

Closed-in window backs, used in many lingerie and fine jewelry stores, enable the window decorator to exercise a lot of creativity in the display, shutting out interference from the store interior protecting shopping customers' privacy. The display should be kept current with fresh price or other eye-catching signs that are professionally prepared. Rotate merchandise and change color schemes every two weeks or so. Keep your display clean.

Your windows are theatrical stages so the "stars" should be displayed center foreground and secondary merchandise on the sides and in back. Take advantage of themes, seasons, holidays, and trendy events to make your display interesting and appealing. Refer to *Chase's Calendar of Events* (McGraw-Hill) for a list of dates to create your themes with

Whatever type of window display you choose, make sure the windows are easily accessible for regular cleaning. The bulbs in your window-lighting systems should be safe and easy to for staff to change without disturbing displays or calling an electrician. Lighting decisions should consider window glare and "blinding" passersby.

Entrance

Ease of entry into your store is important. In this respect, stores located inside shopping centers have an advantage because often the entire storefront can be the entrance. Location of the entrance, customer transportation mode, and time of day all contribute to your entrance's impression.

warning

Fire regulations, building codes, zoning regulations, possibly Occupational Safety and Health Administration standards, and standards set by the Americans with Disabilities Act will also determine the way your store looks. Contact your local planning department to see what requirements apply to your situation.

The doorway should be inviting, wide, and easy to enter. Door design will follow the flow of the exterior look and display subtle "Push" and "Pull" signage to ease traffic flow. Entire open walls and security gates at closing time replace doors in shopping malls.

Retail expert Jon Schallert of The Schallert Group in Longmont, Colorado, says customers are attracted to stores with lots of other customers, and vivid color schemes. Motorists look for easy parking lots to navigate and clear signage when deciding where to shop.

Designing Your Store Interior

Layout is one of the most critical factors in retail stores and can maximize or impede sales. Designing the layout consists of allocating storage, workrooms, and receiving sections for specific use, strategic placement of fixtures and equipment, and considering the flow of humans and merchandise within.

Access for the physically challenged requires special attention. You'll need aisles wide enough to permit shoppers to pass each other without colliding and at least 28-inch passageways behind counters and showcases for salespeople to maneuver. A skilled designer will see things you may not notice but your customer will feel.

"When our store was renovated into the 40,000 square foot Wine Library that exists today, my parents created a very fancy store. I, personally, wanted something brick-and-mortar and more cold, while my parents went with a look that featured glass and mahogany. My parents love building homes and ended up building a home instead of a business. They wanted people to be impressed, but I was worried about people thinking our prices were too high," says Gary Vaynerchuk of his New Jersey wine shop. Moderate prices are just one of the things that keep customers coming back.

It's About the Experience

Michael Bills, Executive Director of Innovation & Entrepreneurship at Max M. Fisher College of Business

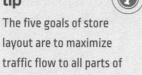

tip

The five goals of store layout are to maximize traffic flow to all parts of the store; maximize the sales space in relation to nonselling areas; maximize merchandise exposure; maximize stop and look points; and achieve maximum department identification and coordination.

believes that independent retailers need to dedicate themselves to making every part of the experience reflect the store's brand, including the products, the packaging, the events, the corporate identity, the website, and ultimately, the retail environment.

Specialty stores should deliver personal and meaningful solutions that cater to customer aspirations, solutions, and narratives. For example, Caribou Coffee, the nation's second fastest-growing coffee retailer, uses décor influences from the American outdoors, creating an image that is distinctly different from the company's key competition, Starbucks.

Mass merchant and category killer store designs leverage breadth, providing sophisticated tools that focus on quantity purchasing and help browsers find the right product. Take note of these elements next time you're in one.

Choose Your Approach

Of the four main approaches to retail store layout—grid (most popular), free-form, boutique, and maze (see "Four Approaches to Retail Store Layout" on the next page). The grid is based on rectangles and is generally found in small stores. Shoppers most often turn right when they enter a store, pass showcases or counters, make a sharp left turn and walk by displays, then come up along the other side of the store toward the register. Variety stores and supermarkets favor this format because it uses space efficiently, promotes a formal, businesslike atmosphere, simplifies shopping, ensures maximum exposure of store merchandise to the shopper, and is ideal for self-service. However, it is rarely used in specialty-goods stores because customers like to browse leisurely before purchasing.

A free-form environment permits flexibility and is characterized by graceful curves and arcs. This encourages leisurely perusing, longer visits, and impulse buys. The disadvantages are greater stock-control and shoplifting problems than with other layouts for the inefficient path design.

To create small specialty nooks in boutiques, designers combine grid and free-form layouts making it easy for special interest customers to view one small area. This supports the intimate, personal feeling of boutiques

The maze channels traffic flow with blocks that coax customers into special areas. Proponents believe it encourages a complete tour and asking for sales assistance. Opponents say it creates consumer frustration, discourages buying, and creates blind sections for shoplifters to thrive.

Other influencers of traffic flow are alternating colors of departments, leaving air-space over doors and partial walls, and limiting carpet use, which creates and breezy feeling. Consider the way you want your customers to circulate. Are they time pressured or passive?

Every Foot Counts

Every square foot of your store costs money, so apportion your space carefully. Typically the space you allot for each merchandise type should mirror its annual sales percentage, the highest profit makers taking the front of the store—the highest traffic area. Check with your trade association or the National Retail Federation for display tips pertinent to your merchandise.

Place impulse items near the cash register and sale merchandise in a wide aisle in a special display "obstacle" rack. This will train customers to look for them there.

Inventory Influences Layout

The layout of any store depends on the amount of space available and the type of products or services offered. In very small stores, layout is inflexible. A counter, at which one or more employees can work, separates customers from the entire merchandise display that is behind the counter. In larger stores there's often room for counter and rack displays for 360 degree viewing.

The layout of dressing rooms, display suites, locked cases, and open displays must be conducive to customer viewing, navigating, touching, pricing, trying on, and paying for merchandise.

Consider the best environment to help your customer understand your product, whether that involves friendly, warm conversation, trying it out or on, or quiet time to contemplate features. Understanding the emotions behind different kinds of purchases will help you do this.

If your store is an emotionally fulfilling, social destination with a homey comfort level, you are your own advertisement. Duplicate the feel of your (imagined) typical customer's home with music, plants, light, and décor. Coffee doesn't hurt, either.

Electric Fetus is a place one feels at home, with its soft lighting, creaky wood floors, and foyer display filled with vintage candy brands from the fifties. The charm of the small "rocker lifestyle" retail space that precludes the actual music shop holds a sampling of funky handmade clothing, scented oils, and mix-your-own incense options. When music lovers cross into the LP, CD, and DVD area, they are treated to over 52,000 different new and used titles to choose from and listening stations for sampling before buying. Within two years of opening his store, Keith was able

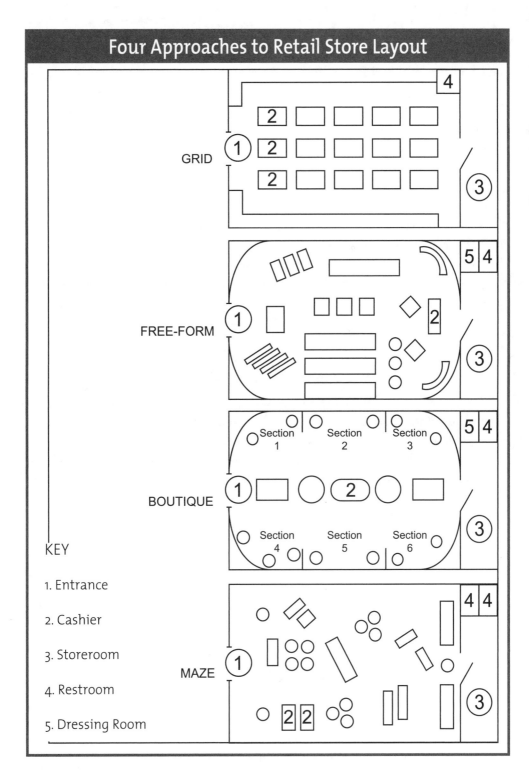

Four Approaches to Retail Store Layout

GRID

FREE-FORM

BOUTIQUE

Section 1 Section 2 Section 3

Section 4 Section 5 Section 6

MAZE

KEY

1. Entrance

2. Cashier

3. Storeroom

4. Restroom

5. Dressing Room

to afford, by benefit of a great distributor in Chicago, to order and sell thousands of each title. Electric Fetus is known for having the widest variety of both alternative and mainstream titles to choose from in the area, as well as knowledgeable clerks.

At the Springfield, New Jersey, Wine Library customers and clerks get into passionate, educated discussions about the best wines for specific occasions. They don't use kiosks and feel that knowledgeable, genuine, human help is one of their biggest assets. "The human element brings so much to the table," says Gary.

Aisles

Your main aisle should be large enough for two-way traffic and display your top selling items. Main aisle end caps (the areas at the ends of each aisle) are a good place to display specials, discounts, and new arrivals.

Browsing customers tend to move counterclockwise versus customers who know exactly what they want and move clockwise. Identifying the majority of your customers as either group will no doubt influence the wonderfully creative aisle displays you create.

Self-Service and Check Out Techniques

Is your store going to be mainly self-service or customer-assisted? Our desire for immediate information makes us a culture that would rather browse displayed information than wait for a salesperson to assist us.

Retailers are recognizing this customer preference and opting for self-service kiosks, LED monitors, open shelving, directive signage, and baskets or carts to collect and compare merchandise with. Benefits to retailers include lessened employee investment and hassle of the train-hire-fire process. View a selection of kiosks and digital signage displays here: advancedkiosks.com and mitsubishi-presentations.com/retail-monitor.

Higher priced, special order, or secured merchandise still requires great customer service and a chance to strengthen the human connection—for those purchases remember that a well-designed checkout area with color-coded to size, easy to reach bags for the cashier keeps wait times short for customers and lessens employee fatigue. Shoppers will leave if the line is too long.

Flooring

Flooring needs to be beautiful, extremely durable, and resistant to the steady tracking in of dirt and in cold climes sand, salt, and water. Polished concrete, asphalt, stone, linoleum, and vinyl wood, fit this bill and are available in gorgeous design options. Carpet requires more maintenance but offers softer acoustics and may be used in

A Place for Space

These five fundamental space allocation principles should guide you to:

1. *Show all merchandise to all customers.* The more merchandise customers see, the more they will buy. Entice customers to visit all departments with the strategic location of signs, special values, escalators, stairs, dressing rooms, and certain merchandise. (Many supermarkets place convenience items such as bread and milk at the rear of the store to drive traffic storewide.)

2. *Give choice locations to the most profitable items.* High-markup and impulse items should be very visible.

3. *Discourage shoplifting.* Keep small, expensive items under lock and key, use convex mirrors where blind spots cannot be eliminated, and install visible security cameras. By keeping everything wide open, salespeople can observe everyone in the store.

4. *Experiment to stay exciting.* Adjustable, movable fixtures accommodate changes in layout and displays, so shop accordingly for cabinets, shelving, lighting, and movable walls.

5. *Locate related lines and departments next to each other,* such cosmetics and accessories, with jewelry and cookbooks with gourmet utensils, for maximum cross-selling.

environments with less weather elements coming in the door. Keeping your floors safe, clean, and dry to avoid accidents are a must.

Ceilings, Walls, and Color

Ceilings and walls can create whatever effect you want them to. Low ceilings pared with deep, jewel toned colors create a positive, intimate environment. Opulent textures and colors such as velvet burgundy wallpaper, and dark walnut paneling give a sedate, luxuriant feel. Light and natural materials like grass cloth and cork feel down to earth and relaxed. High ceilings combined with glass, chrome, and unadorned, white walls lend a cool, sometimes impersonal feeling

aha!

Polished or stained concrete is resistant to box dragging and foot traffic and comes in a variety of faux finishes that can be customized. Get inspired by how these retailers use concrete floors here: exposedfloors.com.

with echoing acoustics often associated with high-end merchandise.

Walls and ceilings can be covered with photographic or painted murals, textured wall treatments, or mirrors which expand the perception of space. Consider what your products will look like against the walls before making any decisions. Employee dress code should compliment and blend with your décor just as accessories to an outfit.

Fixtures and Lighting

Typically, a retail business needs fixtures for several purposes: display, selling (or self-service), stock, and certain work activities. The type of lighting you choose determines how your customer will see your products and should be consistent with what they will see when they get home, or returns may be made. Interior designers and lighting consultants can advise you on this.

Look for fixtures and lighting that will stand up under heavy usage and cleaning, are easy to move around, and are flexible enough to use in different ways. But don't invest too much of your initial capital in them just yet—Craigslist.org is a good place to peruse pre-owned fixtures, lighting, and décor pieces with an open mind and a creative eye. Store liquidations and estate sales on Craigslist can yield unique pieces that can be refurbished or customized to your needs.

Nonselling Activities

Nonselling functions like accounting and phone calls should occur at the back of the store keeping the front reserved for selling only. Generally, office/storage space should take up only 10 to 25 percent of your total floor area.

Effective Presentation and Convenience

Try to create an air of spaciousness in displays, and wherever possible avoid displays that block the view of other parts of the store or the locations of cashiers. The objective of a good display is to boldy feature priority items. Signs can help, but can distract if you use too many or they are busy or unprofessional. Only use professionally made, simple, clear signs.

Whenever advertising special offers on the radio, in a newspaper, or through internet ads, be sure to highlight the location of the sale and reiterate the offer terms in your store with high contrast or vividly colored signs.

Retail expert Anne Obarski says it's essential for specialty stores to move products on a regular basis to keep the look fresh but be alert to customers who need help locating items. If you have customers that rely on your fast service and convenience, it's not advisable to move inventory frequently. Grocery, drug, and convenience store shoppers are an example of this. Convenience store shoppers especially look for a one-stop-fast-shop experience in which everything they need is right in front of them so place the highest-demand consumables in the front of the store for a quick exit strategy.

Building Your Website

Building the right website to uniquely service your business doesn't have to be hard, in fact, defining your specific needs and choosing the right providers and tools can make it simple and relatively easy.

The New Functions of Websites

The function of a website for a brick and mortar retailer has changed greatly in the last few years as mobile device use has become the prevalent way to locate merchandise. The National Retail Federation's Big Show 2015 summed up the new ways retailers are pairing their websites with physical retail locations to appeal to today's mobile minded, tech savvy customers. NRF illuminates a multi-step involvement process using an airline sale as an example of how the retailer has not just one, but seven opportunities to engage in positive customer service—customers search for what they want, make a reservations, change various options within their reservation, check in for the flight at the airport or online, get on the plane and use wifi, get off the plane and look online for where there luggage will be, check out their frequent flier status, and receive a customer satisfaction survey. Consider these contact points as you plan the elements of your website.

Assessing Your Needs

Is your physical store a place to socialize and fulfill orders made online or is it where most shopping will occur? Would you like shoppers to be able to understand exactly what they want before they even set foot in your store? Even if you don't care about that and think they can do it all when they get to your store, your customers care about it. You're better off constructing your website with features that will let your customers find out everything they want to know about your products and company replete with shipment, delivery, and pick-up options, without ever setting foot in your store. This shows your customer that you care about their comfort in the shopping process and guarantees that they will set foot in your store.

What Will Your Site Do?

The website is a place to handle everything from finding and identifying merchandise to becoming educated about products and setting up shipping or pick-up. When the order is complete customers often choose the store pick-up method instead of paying shipping charges and that gives the store a chance to give a human feel to the transaction. This is all the more reason for the website and physical location to share consistent style, customer service experience, and overall feel, since customers often will experience the physical and virtual realms of your business all in 48 hours or less.

Just as you did in the design of your physical store, now is the time to consider how people feel as they enter the main page, which functions like the entrance and front door of your store. Do they feel welcome, catered to, and respected or confused and harried? Do the colors and options make them feel organized and on task with the shopping mission or does it make them want to back out and get out?

In Store Use of Your Website

The NRF says 84 percent of people use a digital device to lookup products while in your store or before coming to it before making a purchase. What are some of the ways you'd like your website to serve customers who are already in your store? Listing your website functions will serve you and both remote and onsite customers will help you build a great website. Use the list below to inventory needs.

My website helps customers who are in my store by:

- Quickly locating merchandise they are looking for
- Finding the right color and size
- Letting them compare features on several products
- Price checking items
- Searching for specials and offers
- Reserving merchandise in a shopping cart
- Scheduling delivery of large items

My website helps me by:

- Utilizing captured data for future connections and selling opportunities
- Helping me stay organized and abreast of inventory changes
- Letting me see who has liked me or my blog on social media channels
- Helping me see which areas of navigation are and are not working through site analytics
- Create a professional presence and act as a virtual business card

Website Components

Begin brainstorming your site design with a list of areas customers will go to fulfill their desire for knowledge. Write down the main reasons a client will land on your website and what you'd like to occur after they do.

- *Welcome.* The look of this page should say everything about you and mimic your mission and branding with images, layout, and design. A current website trend is featuring a huge, striking image on the welcome page, rather than many.
- *Company philosophy and mission.* This is about who you are at your core. It is where your ethics intersect the products you sell and the way you treat the world, including customers and employees. Make sure this page conveys that.
- *About us.* This page is your opportunity to show off your talent. Feature photographs and descriptions of team members and their qualifications and achievements. Cross-link to community involvement, business-to-business relationships, and philanthropic endeavors.
- *Product pages or "shop."* Divide these pages up the way you organized your store, according to merchandise type, color, or theme, and you will be on the road to establishing brand consistency.
- *Landing pages.* Landing pages are where you are routed to when you click on a product for details and options. They are for all education about products for your customers.
- *Checkout and shipping.* Look at mass marketplaces like Amazon and Zappos to see how ease of shipping is handled. If you are going to be shipping purchases internationally you need to choose an ecommerce builder with the ability to convert currency. Go through a demo of checking out with each of your ecommerce options to experience how happy or frustrated your customers might get.
- *Help and support.* There should be a section that addresses FAQs to all things related to your site and a phone number people can call to get fast answers. 24/7 access is best and instant messaging chat is helpful.

Imitate What Works

Take cues from wildly successful marketplaces such as Zappos and Amazon when designing your website for ease of shopping.

- Display your logo and contact information at the bottom of each page, and icons that allow viewers to get back to their shipping cart and the home page at any point in the ordering or perusing process.
- Enable automatic features that show coordinating products underneath the main featured product. These might be things required to use the main product, such as cables or rechargeable batteries for an electronic, or matching earrings for a necklace.
- Show related popular, best selling, or similar products in a line underneath the product. This might be shirts with other collar options than what is being viewed or additional flavors in a snack product.
- Offer several delivery options, including pick-up in the store, and gift-wrapping with a personalized card.
- Set up confirmation of order status with order number to land in the customer's email at several points in the purchasing process. This gives confidence the transaction is underway. Offer a 1-800 customer service line for any questions.

Choose a Website Builder or Hire a Pro

You can design your own website with access to good photo editing software like Photoshop and a low cost website building service such as Wix.com, GoDaddy.com, BuildYourSite.com, Fatcow.com, and Web.com. They offer step-by-step guides to coach you through the process. You can also hand over all of the responsibility to a professional website developer or choose a lower cost option, such as a design student or new business looking for pieces to add to their portfolio. You may also have to hire a writer if your chosen design professional doesn't excel in that area. Make sure to read reviews, and check references for anyone you are considering hiring, rather than just looking at the fancy work they've designed. Customer service is key and will mean a lot in the future when you need quick changes made to your online presence. Look on Yelp.com for businesses offering discounts, search Craiglist.org for contractors, and ask friends and relatives for connections to low cost website designers.

Exposure

Walker Sand's 2015 Future of Retail Study finds that same day delivery, drones, the decline of cash use, and mobile pay options like Apple Pay are where retailers need to focus their efforts to take advantage of these brisk changes. Amazon is still the go-to website for most retail categories because of the aggressive price competition, ability to look at similar products with the auto generated feature below the product, and the ability to see what other people like you looked at and purchased. The fact that quick check-out and speedy shipping are just standard on Amazon is a major reason buyers keep coming back. eBay offers similar features. Etsy is another marketplace to connect your website to if you fall into the category of crafty, boutique style, handmade, or vintage merchandise. Listing your merchandise on these sites can offer great exposure for your business and website.

Why not set up your own Amazon, Etsy, or eBay shop in addition to selling products on your website? You might have a few products that could stand to compete against the major discounters on these sites and prove to be good exposure for the rest of what you do. All of the photos and product descriptions you've already put hard work into creating will serve you well in setting up a good looking shop on these sites. Here's a link to investigate the pros and cons of selling on Amazon and eBay: Shopify. com/blog/6399562-the-pros-and-cons-of-selling-on-amazon-and-ebay. Here's how to set up your own Etsy shop: www.etsy.com/sell.

One-Stop-Shop Solutions

Many of your needs can be covered by choosing service providers that perform several functions, such as:

- *Yahoo! Merchant Solutions* (smallbusiness.Yahoo.com/ecommerce)—a hosting site that helps you design an online store and set up a merchant account to accept and process credit card orders.
- *Volusion* (volusion.com), Affinity Internet (affinity.com), and 1&1 (1and1. com)—hosting companies with shopping cart, merchandising, and shipping technologies, and marketing assistance.
- *osCommerce* (osCommerce.com)—allows store owners to set-up and run their online stores for free, with ecommerce solutions, of course.

We're Hiring

Create an optional section on your website that coordinates your mission statement with your desire to find employees cohesive with it. Don't just list job openings and define roles—help readers understand the main goals of your company and how they'd support them. Yanay Zaguri's free eBook, *5 Steps to a Successful Onboarding Process* (kryonsystems.com), will help the way you write and display employment on your website.

Big Data

Capitalizing on big data is key to understanding patterns in what your customers look for on your website, what they buy, what they click on but don't buy, and where they come from. When you attach data services to your website you access information that is like a glimpse inside the collective customer mind and then you can customize a better business for that mind and capture more sales. Sales processing services such as ShopKeep (ShopKeep.com) and LightSpeed (LightSpeedPos.com) also offer data collection to businesses but it's up to you to review and use the data to your advantage and change your behavior accordingly.

Offer Video

In a Business News Daily (businessnewsdaily.com) interview Tom Malesic, president and CEO of EZSolution, a web design firm, said using videos can be like getting free commercial time and, "Consumers are more likely to purchase after seeing a video than if there was no video at all." Linking your website to your own You Tube channel is a great way to extend the product education dialogue your website begins with customers. Each thumbnail of a product can show a larger image when clicked on and as utilized on Zappos.com, a short video could be accessed to showcase the product in context. You can also embed videos on your site, but using You Tube is often easier when it comes time to make changes and update videos and key word tags that search engines use to find them.

Website Surpasses Physical Store

Some retailers have built such great websites they wind up shutting down their brick and mortar locations. By using your physical store for those things that are best done in person, such as events and social interactions, and coordinating them with website functions, you can make sure this doesn't happen - but if you want to give up your brick and mortar location for a more virtual way of life, be sure and pickup a copy of Entrepreneur Magazine's Start Your Own eBusiness. The idea of building a website so good that it could replace the income your store generates isn't the goal of most retailers, but is a good thing to have achieved if you come up against barriers to your location thriving.

Inventory

I n a retail business, the potential for product comes with wise inventory purchases. The most astute pricing strategies won't help if your inventory is wrong.

There are no lack of innovative buying opportunities. Matching the needs and wants of your specific customer to the right goods and price is your challenge. Creatively shop, but don't be distracted by all of the wonderful merchandise

▲

out there that doesn't fill your customer's cup, or your investment will most likely be unrecovered.

You Are What You Sell

Product selection is all about filling a gap in the market and positioning yourself as the authority, above other stores, to do it. Only choose products that enhance your reputation and set you apart.

All one has to do to see what makes Wine Library customers happy is read a few of their raves on Yelp.com, a consumer driven, service review website. Cheese samples, a wide variety of bottles in the $10 to $15 price range and a reserve of top-shelf varieties, coupled with moderate pricing and friendly staff are what reviewers are talking about. "Our only true method when pricing merchandise is to ensure that we are not undersold. There's no reason for us to be more expen-

---

Inventory Checklist

Don't forget the accouterments! Here are some of the things you'll need besides merchandise:

❑ Bags (merchandise, garment, and shopping)

❑ Boxes (takeout, gift, and shipping)

❑ Feedback/suggestion cards

❑ Gift cards

❑ Gift certificates

❑ Gift-wrap

❑ Guest book for mailings

❑ Layaway/installment contracts

❑ Promotional items (magnets, pens, key chains, pins, mouse pads, visors, baseball caps, T-shirts, etc.)

❑ Promotional literature (catalogs, fliers, brochures, posters, etc.)

❑ Web page ordering and store location information

sive. People have gotten very comfortable with the fact that we don't over price," says Gary Vaynerchuk.

Antique shops like Red Bank, New Jersey's Stillwell House, owned by partners Ronald Knox and Paul Gallagher, have more of a challenge when it comes to inventory management. Since they can't just order another Louis Philippe buffet made in the 1800s, inventory sourcing and management becomes a full-time job. "It's constant," says Gallagher. "We're online or we're calling our sources or we're going to auctions. You don't know when you're going to find the next great piece." But inventory depletion is death in the antique business because customers want to see an impressive collection when they enter a shop like Stillwell House, says Gallagher, so he and Knox know that if they sell one of their better pieces, they'd better be able to replace it with something of similar quality.

Quality Merchandise

What will the quality of your merchandise be? Buying products made in the United States and environmentally safe products has become a hot subject in recent years. But is the quality there? You owe it to your customers to make sure it is. Don't just accept label claims at face value. As much as the customer may be looking for those tags, if the merchandise falls apart in two weeks, they really won't care where or how it was made. They bought the merchandise from you, so they will hold you responsible.

What customers see should be what they get, and what you promise must be what you deliver. To some customers, quality will extend from the point of origin of the materials used in the item through the production process to the distribution chain and onto your shelves. Check your sources, and stay abreast of consumer action groups. Low-wage or sweatshop labor sources and animal testing are a few of the hot buttons that could alienate you from compassionate, aware, would be customers.

Selecting Your Portfolio

Buying inventory is easy; selecting the right things to fill your store's shelves poses more of a challenge. You know what kind of retail operation you have and who your customers will be. Now how do you put together your merchandise portfolio?

Keith Covart's slogan is "Find it at the Fetus" for good reason. Holding 52,000 titles makes sense when combined with its wide aisles, groovy atmosphere, and relaxed listening stations. Headphone-donning customers sometimes spend hours exploring the vast array of titles, which results in new music choices and ultimately, more sales. Combine that with the new Mix and Burn, custom music compilation making software now featured at kiosks throughout the store, and it makes sense for Keith to invest in such a large inventory.

Erik Ekman's Outside Vans are each unique to the potential sport pro he designs them for. Ekman knows just how many clothing hooks an extreme mountain biker may need on a trip to Whistler, Canada, or where the bike should be strapped in and what kind of bed would be appreciated after a day on the trails. Vans for surfers include a place to remove the wetsuit and a canopy for expanding living space. Helmet shelves, surfboard racks, and a diesel hydronic system that ensures toasty heat and a hot shower no matter the destination are just some of the special features that make each van seem like home on the road. Ekman's inventory is always changing as he creates new vans. A recent look at his inventory showed even more specialty builds. There were gear haulers, people haulers, camping vans, and company demo vans boasting custom solar racks, motorized awnings, a wheelchair lift, moto bike carriers, fancy LED lighting, and roof-mounted battery power. Each design is sleek and thoughtful, carefully utilizing each inch of space for maximum practicality and aesthetic value while catering to the different needs of four distinct audiences.

>
> **tip**
>
> Customers will pay more if they know they are getting a better quality of merchandise for their dollar. Now more than ever, value (the relationship between quality and price) is the most important area of merchandise management.

Choose products that enhance your reputation. Your prices should reflect your image and your target market. This means that you should establish your price lines and price points before you buy. You must get the highest possible markup consistent with competition and customer price satisfaction. The better the buy, the higher the markup you can make.

Charlotte Cozzetto's method of merchandising at Ethique Nouveau enhances the sense that her pieces are limited run and special. She orders small batches of unique, handmade jewelry and hard to find purses and ties, most often pricing them at the standard 50 percent mark-up rate. As a shrewd shopper, she looks for reasonable wholesale rates to afford this presentation of specialty merchandise priced to move. Shoppers get "the wow effect" and then the items are bought up. This piques curiosity and frequent store visits to see what fresh surprises will show up on her shelves next. For more on pricing, see Chapter 10.

Establishing Your Inventory

Here is a simple procedure to follow to help you decide which merchandise you should offer and which you should not. If you are dealing with electronics or clothing, you may wish to do your breakdown on the basis of brand names. If you are organizing a food business, simply list the food supplies you would have on hand the day you open.

We asked a motorcycle dealer to explain how he would use this model.

- Divide your inventory into broad classifications, such as $30,000 for motorcycle hard parts.

- Divide each broad classification into subclassifications—for example, engine parts, wheel parts, frame parts, transmission parts, dress-up parts, drive-line parts, and tuneup parts.

- Allocate a certain percentage of your capital to each sub-classification—for example, 20 percent engine parts, 5 percent wheel parts, 5 percent frame parts, 5 percent transmission parts, 30 percent dress-up parts, 10 percent drive-line parts, and 25 percent tuneup parts.

- Locate resources that will sell you the products you want to stock. Read *Hot Bike* magazine (hotbikeweb.com), the *Cycle World Buyer's Guide* (cycleworld. com/buyers_guide), and *Thunder Press* newspaper (thunderpress.net). Get catalogs from Custom Chrome (customchrome.com), Motorcycle Superstore (motorcycle-superstore.com), and Drag Specialties (dragspecialties.com).

- Make sure each item purchased gives you the best possible markup and that the retail prices will fit the price lines you have set for your operation. The store's target markup is 50 percent on services, 40 percent on accessories and clothing, and 35 percent on hard parts.

You only have so much money allocated for merchandise. The challenge you face is to achieve maximum sales from what you buy. By first determining how much of what you are going to buy, you discipline yourself to be discriminating and to keep your buys in balance with your overall inventory needs. Faced with an enthusiastic salesperson, an attractive deal, and a hunger to buy, you need all the will you can muster to remember your priorities. Overstocking in one area at the expense of other areas is a dangerous proposition. Take your buying plan with you and stick to it.

Finding Products

Thoroughly investigate the types of products you want to sell. This means being aware of nationally advertised products, what competitors are selling, and the offers of major suppliers. Your trade association and business publications report trends and identify resources you can use. Keep on top of your reading to stay informed about sources of product.

Using Buying Offices

A resident buying office is composed of buyers in national or international market centers who shop the market daily to offer their member stores information and to choose and purchase items for them. Resident buying offices primarily provide advice and counsel. Their staffs also do actual buying for their members on a contract basis.

A buying office can be your eyes and ears and can help you evaluate resources, identify price fluctuations, and keep up with trends. A buying office has its own staff of domestic and foreign buyers and can invite your buyer to information clinics.

Most professional buyers are located in or around merchandise markets. Visiting one or more of the regional markets listed in "To Market, To Market" on page 121 is an efficient way to begin building your network of buying information and sources. For example, you'll find most professional clothing buyers near the New York market. Search online using business industry terms to see what merchandising services are available in your area for your type of business.

Local art and craft fairs and farmer's markets can be a source of interesting, hand-crafted merchandise. Charlotte Cozzetto of Ethique Nouveau in Minneapolis adds them to her shopping list to find uncommon, earth-friendly, locally made goods for her shop. She spends 10 to 15 hours a week shopping online for new products and buying sources. Among her favorites are Etsy.com, an online artist vendor site. In combination with quarterly tradeshow visits, this makes for fresh merchandise, not likely seen in other stores. It's helpful to have a list of markets as resources for variety and category needs.

Independent resident buyers usually deal with small retailers, providing few services other than the procurement of merchandise. The buyer can represent many manufacturers and gives the retailer the advantage of choosing from a large assortment of items without paying a fee. The commissioned buyers are considered merchandise brokers.

Whether you're selling gloves, candy, carpets, or lawn mowers, knowledge is king. As a startup business, you will most likely be doing the buying and will rely on your vendor to get you started with the right inventory. If you engage the services of a buyer, select one who knows your customer, market, and geographic area.

Finding the Right Suppliers

Many manufacturers sell their goods directly to retailers. When there is no middleman or supplier involved, you can negotiate terms more easily. Most retailers buy from wholesalers. Some advantages of dealing with a warehouse include access to a

---

To Market, To Market

These markets are found in major cities where a large number of suppliers are located. Many may be in a single building, such as a merchandise mart, and can be important sources for you. Regional markets include:

○ *Atlanta*: Atlanta Apparel Mart (accessatlanta.com) for men's, women's, and children's apparel and accessories

○ *Chicago*: Chicago Mart (mmart.com)

○ *Dallas*: Dallas Market Center (dallasmarketcenter.com) complex includes the Apparel Mart, Home Furnishings Mart, and World Trade Center

○ *Denver*: Denver Merchandise Mart (denvermart.com)

○ *High Point, North Carolina*: National Furniture Mart (highpointmarket.org)

○ *Kansas City, Missouri*: Kansas World Trade Center (wtc-kc.com)

○ *Los Angeles*: California Market Center (californiamarketcenter.com)

○ *Miami*: Miami International Merchandise Mart (miamimerchandise mart.com)

○ *Minneapolis*: Minneapolis Gift Mart (mplsmart.com)

○ *New York*: Garment District NYC (garmentdistrictnyc.com)

○ *San Francisco*: Fashion Market Northern California (fashionmarketnor cal.com)

○ *Boston, Massachusetts*: Boston Gift Show (bostongiftshow.com)

▲

wide assortment of items close to your business, reducing the number of sources you have to deal with, and the ability to purchase in smaller quantities rather than going directly to the manufacturer. Some importers are excellent resources and connect you with manufacturers in foreign countries. However, buying inventory from suppliers is the cornerstone of many a successful retail business, so you need to know how to establish good supplier relationships.

As soon as you file your business name or take out a business license, suppliers will start approaching you for business. Ask for catalogs, brochures, business addresses, and who they bank with to avoid scams. Established suppliers cannot only be a great source of necessities but can also offer you insight into the market. Your suppliers should partner with you to succeed. They should help you interpret consumer demand, guide you in the operation of your business, and assist in solving problems.

Dealing with vendors involves active and continuous negotiation. While a good sales rep may tip you off to specials or price reductions, many discounts are available for the asking. Quantity discounts, invoice dating, shipping terms, return privileges, trade discounts, seasonal and cash discounts, as well as free merchandise all translate into dollars on your bottom line. Ask so you can receive.

Supply and Demand

Jon Schallert of retail consultancy The Schallert Group has five suggestions for finding and maintaining the best suppliers:

1. Shop for suppliers outside your typical geographic area—try different shows in other parts of the country or search online.

2. Cultivate a few suppliers who value your account rather than trying to do business with many suppliers who simply see your business as another number.

3. Once you establish this relationship, listen to their advice. The best suppliers want you to be successful and will help steer your business in the right direction.

4. Look for "limited distribution manufacturers" to avoid suppliers selling the same product to large chains in your area who can offer better pricing.

5. Look for suppliers who aren't going to compete with you via an ecommerce presence.

Several years ago while traveling with friends to Brittany, France, Matt Murphy discovered a local gourmet treasure simply called "magic salt." He fell in love with the earthy flavor-infused salt and began importing and marketing it as Sel Magique, creating an artisan, old-fashioned brand. The French cottage industry producer that creates the salt crystals from salt pans drained from the Atlantic ocean, is an up close and personal vendor for Matt, creating a one-of-a-kind, exceptional quality product that he can count on. The brand has grown to include additional salt blends, cocktail salts, chocolate, and a range of other categories.

Sel Magique is now available at over 30 retailers in the U.S. and U.K., including Barneys New York, Harrods in London, Dean and Deluca, and a range of other gift and gourmet shops.

Vendors can pop up in the most unlikely places at unexpected times. Always be on the lookout for quality product to add to your retail profile and hidden vendor opportunities.

Once you have chosen your suppliers, you want to maintain good relations so that you both profit. You have to work at understanding each other's position and be willing to deal openly and fairly with problems that arise. Both retailers and suppliers rate each other on a scale of A, B, and C. Class A is highly profitable because the partner is dependable and very cooperative. Class B is usually dependable and cooperative, and the line contributes significantly to profitability. Class C relationships have to be watched carefully and need to be abandoned before they become unprofitable. To help you rate your suppliers, we've provided a "Supplier Evaluation" checklist starting on page 124.

The more money a supplier makes from you, the better you will be treated, and the more money you make from a supplier, the better the treatment this supplier deserves from you. A business relationship will survive only if there is give and take and the bottom line is mutually rewarding. Don't make unreasonable demands on sales reps, or you will lose a valuable ally and damage your reputation in the industry.

Controlling Inventory

A computer is essential for controlling your inventory. You can program it to tell you when stock reaches a maximum level or minimum level. Automation saves you time, personnel costs, and lost opportunities by helping you act quickly to respond to the ups and downs of consumer preferences.

Electronic data interchange, barcoding, and computer operating systems: All these can be invaluable

tip

The more descriptive you are in tracking what is selling and what isn't, the better you will be at servicing your customers. Retailing is rich in nuances and subtleties. You won't want to miss a beat in knowing what's going on.

Supplier Evaluation

Here are some areas in which you can rate your suppliers' services as excellent, good, average, or poor. Likeableness and price alone won't satisfy your needs. Suppliers are your life support; choose them wisely.

	Excellent	Good	Average	Poor
Company Profile				
Size and/or capacity	❑	❑	❑	❑
Financial strength	❑	❑	❑	❑
Operational profit	❑	❑	❑	❑
Manufacturing range	❑	❑	❑	❑
Research facilities	❑	❑	❑	❑
Technical service	❑	❑	❑	❑
Geographical locations	❑	❑	❑	❑
Management				
Labor relations	❑	❑	❑	❑
Trade relations	❑	❑	❑	❑
Products				
Quality	❑	❑	❑	❑
Price	❑	❑	❑	❑
Packaging	❑	❑	❑	❑
Uniformity	❑	❑	❑	❑
Warranty	❑	❑	❑	❑
Services				
Timely deliveries	❑	❑	❑	❑
Condition on arrival	❑	❑	❑	❑
Follow instructions	❑	❑	❑	❑
Number of rejections	❑	❑	❑	❑

Supplier Evaluation, continued

	Excellent	Good	Average	Poor
Handling of complaints	❑	❑	❑	❑
Technical assistance	❑	❑	❑	❑
Emergency aid	❑	❑	❑	❑
Supply up-to-date catalogs, sales sheets	❑	❑	❑	❑
Supply price changes promptly	❑	❑	❑	❑

Sales Personnel

	Excellent	Good	Average	Poor
Knowledge	❑	❑	❑	❑
The company	❑	❑	❑	❑
Products	❑	❑	❑	❑
Your industry	❑	❑	❑	❑
Your business	❑	❑	❑	❑

Sales Calls

	Excellent	Good	Average	Poor
Properly spaced	❑	❑	❑	❑
By appointment	❑	❑	❑	❑
Planned and prepared	❑	❑	❑	❑
Mutually productive	❑	❑	❑	❑

Service

	Excellent	Good	Average	Poor
Obtain information	❑	❑	❑	❑
Furnish quotes promptly	❑	❑	❑	❑
Follow orders	❑	❑	❑	❑
Expedite delivery	❑	❑	❑	❑
Handle complaints	❑	❑	❑	❑

for managing inventory, but they are no substitute for a culture and procedures that make inventory management a top priority. Efficient inventory management can have a much greater impact on your store's bottom line than a sudden spike in sales. In fact, retailers who espouse accurate and timely record-keeping, an organized storeroom, and very little dead or slow-moving stock can handle just about anything that comes their way.

Always use written purchase orders, itemizing what you ordered and how much you are being charged. Without documentation, you may be billed additional charges or sent the wrong merchandise.

From Shipper to Shopper

Almost half your time will be spent getting merchandise from receiving to the selling floor, properly displayed and merchandised. Inspection is the first thing that must be done to make sure the merchandise is in good condition. Once accepted, process items, give them an inventory control number, and get the items onto the selling floor. You don't make any money when they're sitting where no one can find them.

Cover the basics of unpacking and handling with your employees. Don't assume that they know how to properly take care of all the different types of merchandise that come into the store.

Selling Seasons

Most buying is done on a seasonal basis. There are certain items that sell throughout the year, and there are those that drive consumers into your store during a specific

What Is It?

Classification is the assortment of items by classes. Fundamental merchandising units change little from year to year even though the actual merchandise within each classification will change. Subclassification breaks goods down into smaller identifiable units. Depth is about variety—an array of styles, colors, and prices. Width is about different product categories that can accompany the sale of your primary item.

period of time. Winter means long sleeves, boots, coats, snow shovels, cold remedies, hot food, heaters, and cross-country skis. Summer sells bathing suits, air conditioners, sunscreen, cold drinks, barbecues, and pool supplies. April is tax season, which raises the demand for photocopying services, tax preparers, and software programs. During August and September, sales spike in school supplies and clothing for students and educators.

Factor these realities into your analysis of your store's sales activity. How hot is a "hot" item? Is the interest a passing fad or a sustainable trend? Make sure you can obtain new items and promote them in time to profit, or the risk may be too great for being left with excessive stock you'll have to mark down.

Winter holiday orders at Ethique Nouveau shift from the more casual, year-round feel to total luxury. Gift-giving holidays call for extra pampering, so products that give the impression of opulence are seasonal best sellers. Whimsical, velvet handbags, extra fancy soaps, and fair-trade chocolates nestled in gold gilt wrapping, along with locally-made jewelry, "flies off the shelves," says Charlotte Cozzetto. She also stocks up on larger than usual quantities of consistent perennial favorites, like ethical children's books, for the flurry of gift shoppers in November and December.

What's Enough?

A common ratio during normal demand periods is 3 to 1. That is, to reach a certain sales figure, a retailer must have three times that amount in inventory. For example, if you have an action sports retail business, it might take a $90,000 inventory in snowboards to generate $30,000 in sales in that category during a given month. Other merchandise classifications have different ratios. In a furniture store, it might take $500,000 in inventory to generate $100,000 in sales—a 5:1 ratio. In fine jewelry, it could take $300,000 to generate $50,000—a 6:1 ratio.

A major retailing goal is to develop as much as possible in sales from the smallest possible inventory, but it is dangerous to run out of merchandise customers want. Thus, keeping tabs on sales-to-stock ratios helps you know how much merchandise you should have on hand. Trade associations usually maintain the most up-to-date ratios to assist retailers with buying. It is common to use such ratios on a month-to-month basis. Sometimes, more frequent use may be called for to measure what is needed for unusually strong demand periods, say during special weather conditions, the holidays, or tourist season. In perishable-goods retailing, stock-to-sales ratios on a weekly basis are needed in most merchandise classifications for food and plant matter.

▲

The Real Deal?

The Commercial Crimes Division of the International Chamber of Commerce (iccwbo.org) says that counterfeiting is one of the fastest growing economic crimes of modern times. International AntiCounterfeiting Coalition (iacc.org) names handbags and wallets, watches and jewelry, electronics, apparel, and pharmaceutical and personal care items as the top counterfeited merchandise. Knockoffs are inferior in content and performance and can be dangerous. Fake pharmaceutical products, for example, not only fail to cure but have also caused deaths. Aircraft and vehicular accidents have been caused by the use of counterfeit parts. Buy only from legitimate manufacturers, dealers and verifiable sources. Don't put your business and customers at risk. If an item's price seems too good to be true, it's probably a fake!

Consignment Items

Building your stock by taking goods on consignment is a smart business practice for retailers who market new goods as well as antique, art, and secondhand dealers. Because you don't have to pay for merchandise outright, you'll be able to build a sizable inventory without a cash outlay. Consigned goods can be displayed for a set period of time and should be kept in a separate category from ordered goods.

You need to establish a policy on how you want to handle consignment items. For example, will you give a store credit to the seller (usually about half what you would sell the item for), or will you pay the seller a certain percentage of cash (50 to 75 percent) when the item sells? Will you require that the seller (frequently an artisan) sign a contract that is renewable every two months, or that they automatically pick up items that don't sell after 60 days? Who will be responsible for the display of the merchandise? Can you put it on sale or donate it to charity without the seller's permission if the items are left after a prescribed period of time?

aha!

Use a different color tag for new inventory monthly or quarterly, and you'll have a visual dating system for your stock. As you walk through the store, you can see the older merchandise and be aware of the general rate of stock turnover.

Keeping Up with Change

Focus on the specific merchandise categories your business carries and stay abreast of the trends and market fluctuations influencing the merchandise you sell.

Get out there and look at what's going on. You can spot trends by visiting airports and attending cultural and social events. Visit school campuses and spend time at local resorts. Shop your competitors and go to trade shows. And monitor what people are watching on TV and at the movies.

Wine reviews from industry experts on large screen monitors help shoppers at Wine Library make selections. This depth and knowledge translates to a complete experience for those who stop in for expert advice pre-purchase The onscreen advice is minor compared with the human help shoppers have come to rely on from educated clerks. Walking in with desires for wine can lead to walking out as more educated consumers, with a wheel of perfectly paired cheese or truffles from the attached gourmet shop. It's a complimentary combination.

All the information in this chapter will help you develop a combination of courage and insight to make some profitable inventory choices. You'll find some of the forms that will aid you in keeping track of inventory on the next few pages. See the "Back-Order Record" on page 130, the "Items Needed" form on page 131, and the "Receiving Slip" on page 132. Sense what is happening so you'll have the right merchandise for your customers before your competitor does. Retail buying is a fast-track operation.

Back-Order Record

Date from: _____ Date to: _____

Item/ description	Number ordered	Number back-ordered	Date ordered from supplier	Date due/ received

Items Needed

			Date submitted:	
Submitted by:			Department:	
			Attention:	

Item/description	Quantity	Date needed	Price	Date ordered
			$	
			$	
			$	
			$	
			$	
			$	
			$	
			$	
			$	
			$	
		Total cost	$	

Specifications/suppliers to contact:

▲

Receiving Slip

Shipped by: _____

Date: _____

Order/invoice no.: _____

Shipping/package no.: _____

Received from: _____

_____

_____

_____

_____

Quantity	Item/description	Accept	Return

Received by: _____

Equipment

N ow that you own a business, occupy your space, and have ordered your inventory, what's next? You need equipment—equipment to support the various functions of a retail business. You must have the right equipment to help you order, store, display, and sell merchandise or services; manage information; and keep track of everything else.

The equipment you choose should be consistent with the volume and type of operation you run. For example, a service firm will generally not have the same storage or display requirements as a business that sells products. If you don't have a lot of customer traffic, your furnishing and amenity needs will be minimal. A single store selling nonperishable items has different needs than a three-store supermarket chain. Likewise, a furniture retailer generally requires fewer display fixtures than a women's clothing store. (To see what a restaurant would need, take a look at "Equipping Your Eatery" starting on page 146.)

You will buy, lease, or rent every piece of equipment you use. Many retailers recommend that you purchase equipment if you have the capital, since they believe it is the most economical choice in the long run and you can depreciate the equipment on your income tax. Lease equipment if you do not have enough capital to buy it, or if you want to establish a credit rating. If you lease, you may have the option to trade the equipment in on upgraded models down the line, or perhaps buy it at the end of the lease term for a preset price. Rent equipment if you want to try out a particular kind, test a retail concept, or have a seasonal rather than year-round need for it. Use the "Equipment Checklist" starting on page 148 to make sure you haven't forgotten any vital office equipment.

Equipment Sources

There are plenty of places to get good equipment. Check with other retailers to get leads on equipment sources. Then consider the following sources.

Auctions, Garage Sales, Swap Meets, and Thrift Shops

Auctions are an excellent way to get equipment and supplies at good prices. Watch the business and classified sections of newspapers as sites such as Craigslist.org or Freecycle.org for listings. At most auctions, there will be a preview where you can view the equipment before the bidding begins. You will pay a fee for a bidder registration number, and you will probably be required to pay by cash or a personal check for the full purchase amount on the day of the auction. You can also find incredible bargains at garage sales, swap meets, and thrift shops. Some retailers decide to shop this time-intensive way to save money to put into new computer systems and merchandise. It goes without saying that shopping through catalogs and showrooms is easier, but alternative sources can often supply unique equipment.

Online Equipment Sources

Searching for equipment online is easy. Simply go to your favorite search engine and type in "retail equipment," and you'll find scads of resources, the best known of which is Retail Equipment Liquidators (retailequipmentliquidators.com) and eBay, which sell used equipment and fixtures for pennies on the dollar. For electronic needs such as computer equipment and surveillance cameras, online stores like BH Photography (bhphotography.com) will spend quality time educating you on what will work best for your goals. You can buy digital signage and POS kiosks, LED and LCD display monitors, and data backup and storage systems at Newegg.com.

If you're going to be capturing part of the $638 billion spent on ecommerce (as of 2015 and rising steadily), then you'll need to register with one of the mobile app companies and follow their specific instructions for getting started.

Existing Businesses

If you are buying a business, you may be able to negotiate to buy some of the existing equipment. Pay scrupulous attention to what is and is not part of the purchase price. Ask for copies of all purchase documents, warranties, and service records. You want all the equipment you purchase in good working order, so check it out yourself or hire someone to inspect it for you. Do not take the seller or broker's word for it. When the refrigerator, safe, or cash register doesn't function properly, you'll lose more than sales. You'll lose face and credibility with your customers and employees.

Office Equipment

There are so many different kinds of office equipment that you will need for your operation, we could not possibly cover them all here. But we will cover computer hardware and software, cash registers, credit card verification systems, bar-code readers, and a few other types of technology that will help you stay on the cutting edge of the retail world.

Computer Hardware

In today's world, no retail operation can be effectively managed without some type of computer system. You need information so you can solve problems and make decisions as effectively as possible. A major function of any system is to predict today what is going to happen tomorrow. It also has to reduce the time required to make decisions. One of the major functions of a retail computer system is to process useless data into useful problem-solving and decision-making information.

Computerization of critical management tasks can make small retailers competitive in this fast-paced business. The hours you save will keep your lights on and cash register ringing up sales. The retailers we interviewed gave us this checklist to help you decide what you want your computer system to do:

- Automatic billing
- Balance the books
- Calculate and file taxes electronically
- Electronic cash register
- Financial analysis and projections
- Generate sales and trends reports
- Handle payroll
- Maintain customer and supplier files
- Maintain employee records
- Manage shelf space effectively
- Manage accounts payable and accounts receivable
- Prepare balance sheets and profit-and-loss statements
- Prepare budgets and compare actual figures against plan
- Prepare cash reports, purchase orders
- Print and store correspondence and mailing labels
- Process online and in store payments
- Produce business forms
- Produce promotional materials
- Profile customers by zip code, interests, buying habits, preferences
- Replenish stock quickly
- Set up and maintain customer files
- Set up and maintain supplier files
- Track activity by time periods
- Track advertising and promotion response
- Track orders
- Track responses to advertising and promotion

tip

Forrester Research expects mobile payments to reach $90 billion by 2017. This incorporates Google Glass and Apple Watch as well smartphones and tablets. Make sure you and your sales team are familiar with how each device operates with your chosen swipe technology.

- Track sales trends by product/service and category
- Update inventory

Retailers tell us that your hardware requirements will be determined by the software you use. For example, office suites from Intuit, Corel, and Microsoft with combinations of word processing, spreadsheet, email, information management, mobile platform management, desktop publishing, business and customer management, and database management programs list their requirements on the packaging. But as a general guideline, the basic requirements for a business computer are as follows:

- Intel Core i3, i5, or i7 processor with a current graphics card
- Windows 8.1 Pro, (soon to be Windows 10)
- 4 to 8 GB RAM (memory)
- Hard drive with a minimum of 250 GB RAM, preferably with solid state drive (SSD) memory technology for automatic, instant data backup
- External or internal DVD drive for backup
- Either a Gigabit Ethernet port or an internal AC 802.11ac WiFi card for internet surfing and file transfers

In addition, you'll probably want to upgrade to the highest-speed internet connection you can afford. Reliable public wifi is essential if you are going to offer in-store mobile payment service to your customers. You'll want to choose an internet service provider that will provide you with a combined router-modem system to function both for your main computer data needs as public wifi for your customers. Comcast offers business wifi for up to ten users at a time starting at $249 per month. You'll need to purchase a router such as the Apple Airport Extreme ($179). For DSL you'll need a cable modem, which will cost you about $350 for the setup, modem, and initial month's service; DSL lines, which run about $300 to $600 for setup, modem, and initial month's service, and ISDN, which runs about $500 for the same. Monthly service will cost you about $25 to $75per month for unlimited service.

tip

It's not the computer's fault if you lose your data. Back up data in three ways to cover all bases:

1. Cloud storage solutions such as Google Drive (Google.com/Drive), Dropbox (dropbox.com), and Apple iCloud (Apple.com/icloud)

2. External hard drives such as the Western Digital Raid 1 8TB My Book Thunderbolt.and AirPort Time Capsule.

3. Offsite paper storage. Keep paper copies of all data and store it in a warehouse or building off-site.

Whatever storage medium you use to safeguard your records, it is only as efficient as your habit of backing up your work.

▲

Rather than running the most prevalent operating system, Windows 8.1, soon to be Windows 10, now is the perfect time to start your business off with the upgrade and recommended equivalent, Windows 8.1. Retail technology consultant Joe Bushey advises retailers to keep in mind that the point-of-sale (POS) system may have different requirements. Make sure your software package will work with this configuration. Bushey says that most should.

Surge suppressors prevent damage to electronic equipment when there is a fluctuation in voltage. Some power strips look like surge suppressors, but they simply increase the number of outlets you have. Make sure you know what you're buying. Also, a $50 surge protector suppressor will not protect unsaved data in the event of a power failure. For that, you need an uninterruptible power supply, which will cost about $120. Most experts advise upgrading your system at least every three years.

Think ahead. Compare the features you need now with those you will need when you expand your inventory and number of employees. Be sure the system can grow with your business and that there is tech support. It's very expensive in terms of time and money to have to convert to a different system later. Get the best system you can afford.

Computer Software

Sales representatives and other retailers can help you zero in on the right software and hardware products for your type of business. Retailers told us that there is simply no best application for all retailers' needs. Retail is too diverse an industry to have a standardized software package.

Gary Vaynerchuk mixes business and pleasure, using Tweetdeck on his Macbook Pro. He connects to thousands of users this way on Twitter, but points out that the hardware and software he uses are not as important as engaging with people, chatting about wine, sports, and life. Gary's professional identity is storyteller as much as it is sommelier. Finding the right software and online venue to illuminate your individual style needn't be costly, just in exploration time.

You should purchase either a subscription or license for Microsoft Office Professional bundle for word processing and creating spreadsheets and the Adobe Photoshop bundle for editing and organizing your photos and creating design work around your promotions and communications efforts with PowerPoint and Publisher. You'll have to renew the license every year if you only purchase a year at a time. If you purchase the products outright you'll be prompted to upgrade them when a new version is available.

The right combination of hardware and software has the capability of delivering reports once considered too labor-intensive for the time-harried storeowner to accomplish. For example, customer buying habits can be detailed to profile personal preferences and frequency of visits, as well as what referrals they have sent to your business.

A few of the software packages you might want to take a look at for your book-keeping needs are QuickBooks Pro, Sage 50 Accounting, and Acclivity (formerly, M.Y.O.B., Mind Your Own Business) Accounting. Programs like this will enable you to enter your store's daily transactions, track invoices, pay bills, report sales, and schedule employees. Explore your options with your accountant and tax advisor. Check with your trade association for the names of programs widely used in your field, such as Wordstock for bookstores (available through a monthly subscription fee of approximately $250 per month for a small, single-user retail license to $1,200 per month for a large system with 20 users).

Look in the smaller ads and classifieds in the backs of trade magazines for the names of some software programs written specifically for small retailers in various markets. You can probably find one for every conceivable type of retail business.

The kitchen team at Urban Remedy uses Labelcalc software to calculate nutritional information and produce the legal label for juice and food products. Filemaker Pro 13 is another helpful recipe database organization system. It has preformatted recipe cards and categorical search functions that are very conve-nient. Most of the retailers we spoke with use Quickbooks for keeping finances straight. Pull up a listing for retail/inventory systems from google.com and begin your search. Ask other retailers' advice by visiting the Retail Owners Institute (retailowner.com).

Cash Register

The definition of cash register is changing. At the Nation Retail Federation's 2015 Big Show Ratnakar Lavu, EVP of Digital Innovation at Kohl's said, "We are a decade away from the end of the traditional POS. The entire process will need to change, not just the register. It is more of a business problem than a tech problem." Customers are now often met by roving salespersons with the ability to take a credit card payment anywhere in the store using apps like Google Wallet and Square or near field commu-nication (NFC) as part of radio frequency identification (RFID). Buyers either swipe their cards on the store's mobile device, wave their phone in front of a reader, or tap their phone against a reader to pay for purchases. These systems can cost retailers less than traditional POS combinations such as computerized cash registers with built-in inventory control or a register that just keeps track of income for use with a separate inventory system. Whether you choose a register system or use swipe-to-pay technol-ogy, tracking customer receipts and a detailed record of each purchase is important. Type of sale, department, salesperson, sales details, and stock keeping units (SKU) should be part of your data collection in either case. You'll also need sales broken down as taxable and nontaxable for sales tax reporting. and which sales were made by cash, check, and credit card so you can balance each account at the end of the day with Quickbooks or the internal program provided by your mobile payment system.

The register should feature four or more departments or category breakdowns, enabling you to classify merchandise purchased by type as each sale is rung up. You'll use the special department category to monitor promotions, a new line, or special items. You'll use the data you collect to analyze and evaluate trends and peg exactly how your business is doing. The more expensive POS systems will generate detailed reports for you.

Many low-volume retailers use PC-based solutions for back-end operations and an electronic cash register at the sales counter. While not as efficient or rich in information as a point-of-sale system, this will work. However, to be competitive, a business needs to grow, and volume means more sophisticated tools are needed. A Point of Sale (POS) system is a computerized cash register system, usually used to read the Universal Price Code (UPC) on each product and match it to the price. The system feeds information about each sale directly into your computer's database. A POS system can be used with a bar-code scanner or by entering numeric codes from price tags into the system manually. Many stores have eliminated cash registers in favor or paperless POS systems.

POS systems help control sales operations at both the shelf and sales-counter level. They also help identify individual customers. POS systems enable targeted marketing and sales promotion through the continuous analysis of transactions. But a small, single-location store may be hard pressed justifying buying such a sophisticated system. When making a decision, compare the price and features of any technology against the cost of doing a lot of things manually in terms of competitive pressures, time, and accuracy.

POS systems vary dramatically in cost depending on the features and functions, as well as the number of stations in your store's network. Although every business is different, to operate the applications you'll need in your retail business, technology consultant Joe Bushey provides some purchasing considerations for common equipment, as well as some sample prices for hardware and software to give you a ballpark to play in:

- *Dot matrix or impact receipt printers.* These printers have a low initial price and print on two-ply carbonless paper, but they're noisy and print more slowly than other printers. They also require ribbon changes and have a shorter product life overall. Starting price: around $250

- *Thermal receipt printers.* This type of printer is generally quiet and fast, with dark printing that doesn't fade like dot matrix printers. The downside of this printer is that two-ply printing is not an option, although the printer can usually be programmed to print two receipts. Graphic quality, if you want to put your logo or other image on receipts, is good. Starting price: $200

- *Barcode label printers.* Direct thermal and thermal transfer are the common types of barcode printers. Direct thermal uses thermal labels without ribbons. The labels are more likely to be damaged from the elements, and there are limits in the types of labels that can be used. Generally speaking, thermal transfer printers are a better bet. Thermal transfer printers use a wax and/or resin ribbon that allows the print to be transferred to a wider variety of label types, such as vinyl. These can be much more durable, even in harsh environments. Starting price: $200

- *Cash drawers.* These usually connect to the receipt printer being used to free up available ports on the computer for other devices. Always confirm compatibility, as some software requires the use of cash drawers connected directly to your computer. Starting price: $150

- *Barcode scanners.* Barcode scanners are available in a few different types and can significantly impact checkout times. For low volume, any entry-level scanner should work fine. Higher-end linear image scanners are typically much better at reading damaged barcodes or barcodes on unusually shaped items. At the highest end, omni-directional scanners or area imagers allow you to read barcodes without respect to orientation of the code. That can make scanning of items much less labor intensive. Most applications recommend "keyboard wedge" scanners, which require a PS/2-style keyboard to function. However, USB scanners set to "emulate" keyboards work in most cases. This is important since many computer manufacturers have eliminated PS/2 and serial connections. Starting price: $175

- *Credit card readers (aka magnetic stripe reader, MSR).* Credit card readers come in various configurations that include the ability to read specific tracks of data stored on credit cards or other plastic cards containing a magnetic stripe. The most common type sold today read all three tracks by default. Tracks 1 and 2 are used on credit cards. Track 3 is often used with gift, loyalty, or other specialty cards, and on some driver's licenses. Modern readers allow you to disable tracks you don't want to use and make other configuration changes as needed with little effort. As stated previously, most software specifies the use of "keyboard wedge" readers that share a PS/2 keyboard port with the card reader. Most PCs and laptops are equipped USB ports now so using readers such as Square, which simply plug into most any phone or laptop are a convenient way to go. Starting price: $10

- *LCD flat-panel touch-screen monitor.* Touch screens are becoming increasingly popular in retail environments, partly as a result of the substantial price drops on them in recent years. Again, Bushey recommends using a USB interface for the touch controller, since serial ports are becoming increasingly scarce on PCs. LCD screens take up considerably less space than their CRT equivalent (see below), a valuable consideration if you have limited counter space. Starting price for a 22" version on newegg.com: $494

- *LED lit touch-screen monitor.* These monitors allow the retailer to access functions by simply touching a screen. Starting price for a 22" version on newegg. com: $279

- *Customer pole displays.* Customer pole displays are used to communicate price information and other details while a customer transaction is entered into the POS system. These systems aren't just a convenience to customers; they often help to discourage employee theft as well. Some POS systems don't support these devices or are very limited in those they do support. Starting price: $129

> **tip**
>
> Barcode labeling feeds information about each sale directly into the computer's data bank by scanning the numeric codes assigned to an item. It can help you track stock, generate restocking orders, monitor purchase orders, and track sales/margins, stocks, and payables.

- *POS/programmable keyboards with built-in credit card reader.* These keyboards are very popular with most retailers, who like being able to label keys on the keyboard to mean something, such as changing a key from "F2" to Cash, etc. They also provide a convenient location for reading credit cards if using a nontouch monitor without a credit card reader. Starting price: $170

- *Credit card systems for processing credit card transactions.* Popular mobile versions such PayAnywhere (PayAnywhere.com), which charges 1.69 to 2.69 per swipe, and GoPayment (Intuit-GoPayment.com) which charges 1.75 percent of each swipe and includes a free card reader.

- *Credit card terminals.* Many startup retailers are choosing to go with a standalone credit card terminal. These are usually available for lease or purchase through your local bank. Starting price: around $2,150

- *POS software.* Intuit's QuickBooks POS offers direct integration with Quick Books and is easy to set up and use. This product is a good option for new retailers; you can explore other products as your business grows. Bushey says that Microsoft POS and RMS (Retail Management System) are also good products for new retailers to consider. Prices start at: $1,200

- *Cash registers.* Cash registers are becoming less common as more credit card payments are made with mobile devices and POS products come down in price, but some swipe-to-pay-systems don't process cash so the register still has a place in your store. These may work well for a very small retailer, even though they have limited reporting capabilities. Starting price: $125

Credit Card Verification System

There are several advantages of using a swipe-the-card electronic credit card verification system over a manual system: It reduces errors, charges are credited immediately to your account, paperwork is reduced, and it's fast. Debit card and check verification are available with some of the newer credit card verification systems.

Barcode Reader

The use of barcode labeling is increasingly widespread, but not all items come with bar-code labels yet. If you want to, you can print your own barcode labels using your PC and special barcode software and a label printer. Some POS systems come with this software and equipment as part of the program.

Barcodes typically enable better register management. With a barcode reader, the clerk simply scans the machine-readable numerical codes (vertical bars of varying widths) printed on consumer items, and the item is identified with the price, a print-out is generated, and payment is made quickly.

tip

Digital signs can deliver customized, real-time point-of-purchase messages. Using these signs is a way to make the in-store experience more entertaining and appealing.

Other Equipment You May Want

Other technologies transforming the retail industry are electronic funds transfer (EFT), electronic data interchange (EDI), and data warehousing. EFT allows buying and selling electronically. EDI enables you to access the databases of your suppliers and position your inventory accordingly. Data warehousing helps you convert data into useful information. IBM and National Cash Register (NCR) are leading solution suppliers for the retail sector.

Kiosks: The Missing Link

Malls are finding ways to link in-store kiosks to websites and corporate headquarters to provide ecommerce options for shoppers. Large retailers are exploring the possibilities, but it takes a long time for the behemoths to implement new systems. Small retailers are more flexible, so by knowing what your competition is up to, you can provide the benefits the technology is trying to deliver right away. In this case, kiosks are simplifying the shopping experience, reducing time spent in checkout lines, and increasing consumer convenience.

Interactive Shopping Equipment

Experts say retailers need to consider investing in in-store technologies to attract wired shoppers and to tie together their physical and online capabilities. Bushey says that small retailers should be paying attention to the interactive technology that is in larger retail stores today. "Many technologies considered cutting edge a decade ago are commonly used by small retailers today," he explains. "With the reduced costs of LCD touch-screen monitors, digital signage and kiosk applications are definitely becoming more common."

Stores of all sizes can use multimedia capabilities to capture customer awareness. Valentine's Day is very busy at Electric Fetus and revolves around the Mix and Burn kiosks. Dreamy-eyed lovers mix custom CDs for their sweeties, all day long. Stephanie Covart Meyerring staffs extra help on this special holiday to help users with their first time using the software. Not only can customers scan a bar code on most any album, with the Mix and Burn software in order to hear 30-second samples of songs, but they can also record them and add songs from separate albums to make their own "greatest hits" compilation and name it whatever they want. Users can also mix and order from the comfort of home, then pick up their custom CD's at the store. Keith Covart was the one of the first retailers in Minnesota to use this clever feature in his store. Not many other music stores have it.

Traditional brick-and-mortar outlets must embrace ecommerce as part of their business models and face great opportunities if they do it in a balanced way. Too many retailers apply the latest high tech, interactive kiosks to their show rooms and fail to balance the act with supportive, human-to-human customer service. A self service interaction with an interactive display can tell the customer about products and create an easy shopping experience but if it all happens without a real interaction the social bonding that is largely responsible for customer loyalty, is lost. "The more technology, the more you must compensate for it with a human touch," says Patricia Aburdene, author of *Megatrends 2010: The Rise of Conscious Capitalism* (Hampton Roads Publishing, 2010). "Technology for its own sake [can be] technology overkill. High tech/high touch is an exquisite balance of technology in service to the human experience of sensuality."

With small touch screen monitor systems, shoppers can view listings of a music store's most popular artists and sample music before buying,, or find more titles by the artist or more collections in a particular genre. The book-size device is integrated right in with the products on the shelves and operates with headphones or speakers, allowing more than one person to listen to the music at the same time. Any kind of retailer can use

> **tip** ⓘ
>
> Design a sample offerings package for online blogging reviewers in your industry who speak to your audience. Which products best represent you? Selection and presentation are key.

Suiting Up for Selling

Some of the kinds of store fixtures you may need are:

- Back counters
- Baskets
- Build-ups
- Carts
- Counters
- Display cases
- Display shelves
- Display tables
- Dumbbells
- Easels
- Floor stands
- Island displays
- Pegboards
- Racks
- Register stands
- Sales counters
- Self-service stands
- Shelving
- Showcases
- Stock bins
- Storage cabinets
- Tiered tables
- Work tables
- Wrapping desks

it and can customize the content on their system to include daily or weekly advertising specials, electronic coupons and discounts, as well as full integration of point-of-sale cash registers. Retailers can cross-promote products in the store or on their websites, and cross-reference titles more simply by scanning or pushing the ATM-like button.

Sales Floor Equipment

There are many kinds of sales floor equipment (see "Equipment Checklist" starting on page 148). Here, we provide an indepth discussion of display equipment.

Display Equipment

Whether you choose to display products on high-tech shelving or in antique armoires, you must plan to spend money in this vital area. The decorating scheme of

Equipping Your Eatery

Fast-food and casual dining outlets, specialty restaurants, and other types of food-service locations call for a kitchen full of commercial food-service equipment. The equipment you'll need depends on your menu, so the first step would be to plan what kind of food you want to serve, and in what volumes. According to Janice Cha, senior editor of Foodservice Equipment Reports, *there are some necessities you should budget for.*

Cooking equipment
❑ Broilers

❑ Fryers

❑ Convection oven

❑ Ventilation hoods

❑ Steamers

❑ Pasta cookers

❑ Griddles

❑ Microwave oven

❑ Pizza ovens

❑ Toasters

❑ Steam kettles (these are usually used at huge-volume operations)

Food-holding equipment
❑ Hot holding cabinet

❑ Warming stations

❑ Drawer warmers

Prep, storage, and cleaning equipment
❑ Freezers

❑ Refrigerators

❑ Cold prep tables

❑ Vegetable slicer

❑ Steam tables

❑ Garnish rail

Kitchenware
❑ Walk-in coolers and freezers

❑ Ice cream cabinet

❑ Dishwasher and booster heater

❑ Three-compartment sinks

❑ Dry storage and shelving

❑ Woks

❑ Hand sinks

your store is an important promotional device. In addition to the aesthetic appeal of your fixtures, consider safety and convenience. Which fixtures will show off the benefits of the products you sell and make it convenient for customers to examine and buy

Equipping Your Eatery, continued

Restaurantowner.com surveyed 700 restaurant owners from different regions, from casual dining to high-end, formal service establishments and found the median prices to be as follows:

Total startup cost (no land purchase)	$275,000
Total startup cost (with land purchase)	$475,000
Startup cost per foot (no land purchase)	$95
Startup cost per foot (with land purchase)	$131
Startup cost per seat (no land purchase)	$3,046
Startup cost per seat (with land purchase)	$3,734
Cost overrun compared to budget	15%
Construction cost	$140,000
Construction cost percentage of overall startup	47%
Construction cost per square foot	$50
Kitchen and bar equipment cost	$75,000
Kitchen and bar equipment cost per square foot	$88
Land and building cost	$125,000

For more information on starting a restaurant, check out *Entrepreneur's Start Your Own Restaurant and More: Pizzeria, Coffeehouse, Deli, Bakery, Catering Business..*

while minimizing damage and theft? Chapter 7, "Store Design" and Chapter 15, "Risk Management" explore logistical elements of this issue.

Use display fixtures and equipment that complement the décor of your interior. If you have a limited budget for fixtures, you may be wise to purchase or rent less-expensive fixtures rather than cut back on the amount of inventory on display. Selling inventory provides you with profit and cash flow, after all.

Look for fixtures that will stand up under heavy usage, are easy to move around, and are flexible enough to use in different ways. But don't invest too much capital in fancy fixtures or equipment. Look into pre-owned items that can

▲

Equipment Checklist

Office Furniture

❑ Office chairs

❑ Conference table

❑ Desk(s)

❑ _____

❑ File cabinets

❑ Credenza

❑ Computer table

Office Equipment

❑ Calculator(s)

❑ Copy machine

❑ Scanner

❑ Phone system

❑ Sign maker

❑ Alarm

❑ Cash register

❑ Safe

❑ Modem

❑ _____

❑ Efax service or app

❑ Computer(s)

❑ Printer

❑ Credit card or swipe-to-pay equipment/software

❑ Specialty equipment

❑ Barcode reader

❑ Point-of-sale computer equipment

❑ Computer system for web

❑ Pricing machine

Office Supplies

❑ Bulletin board

❑ Pencils and pens

❑ Sales receipts

❑ Computer paper

❑ General office supplies

❑ _____

❑ Employee rights board

❑ Stationery

❑ Copy paper

❑ Note pads

Equipment Checklist, continued

Sales Supplies

- ❑ Paper bags
- ❑ Shipping supplies
- ❑ Hanging bags
- ❑ _____

- ❑ Gift-wrapping supplies
- ❑ Note cards
- ❑ Hangers

Sales Floor Equipment

- ❑ Gondolas
- ❑ Wall racks
- ❑ Mirrors
- ❑ Display cabinets
- ❑ Specialty lighting
- ❑ Snack machines
- ❑ Fire extinguishers
- ❑ Restroom signs
- ❑ _____

- ❑ Sales showcases
- ❑ Hangers
- ❑ Display tables
- ❑ Customer seating area
- ❑ Dressing rooms
- ❑ Drink machines
- ❑ Exit signs
- ❑ Hours sign

Back-Room Equipment and Supplies

- ❑ Broom
- ❑ Trash cans
- ❑ Vacuum cleaner
- ❑ Toilet paper
- ❑ Soap
- ❑ _____

- ❑ Dust pan
- ❑ Mop
- ❑ Paper towels
- ❑ Cleaning supplies
- ❑ Window cleaning supplies

be purchased for a fraction of the cost of new ones and can be refurbished to meet your standards.

Contact your merchants association, trade association, and business-to-business telephone directory for referrals to manufacturers, information technology specialists, service providers, and other suppliers. Visit their websites or call them for catalogs or a meeting with a sales rep. Talk with other retailers to find out which brand of equipment they use and why they prefer it over other choices on the market. Independent dealers who carry a broad line of equipment for retailers can give you insights on maintenance, longevity, service contracts, and prices. They will also be able to tell you when to expect a drop in price for the item you are interested in.

The closer suppliers are to your business, the better for reducing delivery times, shipping costs, and service. You need reliable equipment that is backed up by warranty. Whatever your decision on brand, make sure you are protected by doing business with companies that stand behind what they sell. You've got to be selling every day, so there's no room for equipment downtime.

Whew! Equipping your business is a lot more complicated than going shopping, isn't it? Balancing your bank account with the record-keeping and merchandising needs of a retail business is a challenging task. But one thing's for sure: Consulting with those who've been there and done that will help you run a successful venture.

Pricing

n retailing, the price of an article is the amount of money the retailer asks for the item. So how do you set prices? How do you arrive at the "right" prices for your goods? For some retailers, pricing is easy: Take the cost of the item from the manufacturer and double it. For the most successful merchants, pricing is a strategic act.

▲

Your pricing strategy is important for two main reasons. For one thing, the difference between what you pay for products or services and what you charge customers determines the margin, which has an immediate effect on your business's profitability. Also, price directly affects the demand for what you have to offer.

If they are right, prices have the power to attract customers. The majority of items advertised in sale ads are priced to pull customers into the store. But you must put high enough retail prices on the merchandise you sell, or you will not be able to pay your overhead expenses and make a profit. If your prices are too low, you will lose money and go out of business.

Your Pricing Philosophy

Decide on your basic pricing philosophy: Will your prices be above the market, competitive, or below the market? You may have already answered this question when

Name Your Price

Price is the centerpiece of your relations with your customers, the weapon competitors use to steal market share, and the reason for many sleepless nights. Learn from the experience of others by considering the top ten pricing factors in your decision making:

1. Availability (number of suppliers, quantity produced, and delivery)
2. Perceived image
3. Growth stage of market
4. Price sensitivity of the market
5. Legislative and financial climate
6. Prestige of the product
7. Differences in available products or services
8. Quality
9. Competition
10. Your financial goals

you decided what kind of business and image you wanted and formulated your business plan. (See Chapters 2 and 3.)

Pricing for profit is vital to your business. But pricing should not be driven by profit motives at the expense of fair, ethical tactics and competition. Profits should be the result of smart business, not a means to an end. With good business relationships and products priced correctly, you will generate sufficient sales to provide the capital you need to stay in business and enjoy some profits.

In making your pricing decisions, you need to answer these questions:

- What prices are shoppers willing to pay for the merchandise?
- Where do you want to be in comparison with your competitors' pricing: equal, above, or below?
- What is the suggested retail price proposed by the supplier?
- What are the qualities or characteristics of the merchandise that influence a shopper's perception of quality and value—style, perishability, scarcity, richness, commodity, or other?

Narrowing the decision-making process even further, give careful consideration to your specific pricing objectives:

tip

Consumers tend to equate higher prices with higher quality. Fine restaurants, designer shops, and consultants practice prestige pricing to convey an image and capture elite customers.

- *Return on investment.* Establish retail prices that will yield a specific return-of-profit percentage on your investment.
- *Maximum profit.* Set prices designed to produce the highest possible profit percentage you can expect to earn on the goods you sell.
- *Sales increase.* Prices should produce a specified percentage increase in overall store sales. Usually this involves reducing prices to sell more merchandise.
- *Improved cash flow.* Establish short-term prices to bring more sales dollars into your business.

Sometimes feelings of guilt are involved in pricing. Some price specialists claim that most consumers with limited discretionary income often have guilt feelings about buying certain items, especially non-necessities. However, if the retailer can appease these guilt feelings, the customer is more apt to buy. Therefore, consider giving incentives to buy expensive items or give a shirt or tie away with a three-piece suit.

Pricing Impression Psychology

Attracting customers is so important to some retailers that they will take a loss on an item to drive traffic to their businesses. Supermarkets often keep prices low on a few basic items that customers can easily compare prices on to give the impression that all merchandise in the store is priced lower than the competitors. Tour operators retailing holiday packages use lower prices to stimulate demand in off-seasons. Home improvement stores might discount home-insulation materials during the summer months to get an off-season head start on competitors.

tip

In the secondhand business, there is no such thing as a manufacturer's suggested retail price. Every item is unique in terms of age, condition, rarity, and desirability. The longer you're in the business, the more knowledgeable you'll be about pricing unusual objects. Read catalogs and books, speak with contacts at auctions and estate sales, and use your common sense.

Jay Shafer coaches potential clients on the Tiny House Blog (tinyhouseblog.com/tag/jay-shafer) who debate the merits and higher cost per square foot of building tiny homes. But one might argue that to design such a small home that functions well is much more of a challenge than a traditional larger one. His designs take hundreds of hours to create and every fixture, appliance, and detail is of high quality and purposeful. Customers who purchase his plans realize this once they do some research.

If the image you want for your store is one of high-quality luxury goods, then the prices charged would need to be higher than average, or you will lose credibility with your target customers. If your stock is lower-priced merchandise, your customers might doubt the exclusivity of your store. Be consistent and know who you want to serve.

You do not always have to sell for the lowest price. For example, most consumers will pay a little over normal supermarket prices for goods at the local convenience store. They are willing to pay for the ability to buy certain products late at night and on Sundays and holidays. These are perceived as extra customer benefits. Remember, the majority of people weigh retail prices against their perception of value for money.

Price and the Product Range

The more variety you have in your product range, the easier it is to combat lower price activity by the competition or to test a new line. If you have other product types you can rely on to sell at full margin, you can afford to be more flexible in your pricing activities than if you rely on a narrow portfolio.

20 Questions

New business owners are often tempted to give the business away to get sales, but this is not an advisable practice. Realistic pricing indicates your confidence in what you are selling, and if you value your service, so will customers. Keep these questions handy and use them over and over again to keep you true to your brand identity:

1. What role do you want price to play in your overall retailing strategy?
2. Will you price below, at, or above the market?
3. Will you set specific markups for each product?
4. Will you set markups for product categories?
5. Will you use a one-price policy rather than bargain with customers?
6. Will you offer discounts for quantity purchases or to special groups?
7. Will you set prices to cover full costs on every sale?
8. Will the prices you have established earn the gross margin you planned?
9. Do you understand the market forces affecting your pricing methods?
10. Do your prices reflect which products are slow-movers and which are fast-movers?
11. Will you experiment with odd or even price endings to increase your sales?
12. Do you know which products are price-sensitive to your customers? At what point will a slight increase in price lead to a noticeable drop-off in demand?
13. Which products will draw people when put on sale?
14. Do you know the maximum price customers will pay for certain items?
15. Do you know what the lowest price point is on some products before customers hesitate to buy because of the perception that something must have less value, functionality, or quality?
16. Is there a specific time of year when your competitors have sales?
17. Do your customers expect sales at certain times of the year?
18. How will you react to competitors' price changes?
19. Have you developed a markdown policy?
20. Will you take markdowns on a regular basis or as needed?

If you stock mostly branded goods, then your pricing will be largely determined by the competition, either locally or nationally, because there are not usually large variations in the prices charged by the major brands to small retailers. After all, a pair of Levi's 501 jeans is the same product wherever it is purchased, and it is readily identifiable, so the only comparison a customer needs to make is on the price.

Private Label

On the other hand, if you have products made especially for you, or if your products are mostly unbranded, then careful price planning can provide profit opportunities. Private-label products can usually be bought at lower prices than branded goods since they don't carry marketing costs. Since your private-label goods are unique to you, they give your business the chance to price them according to what you think the market will bear.

Social Price

The social price is the nonmonetary cost of buying a certain item. One social price is time. Time spent doing one thing means the buyer has to give up time available for another activity. This is the "time is money" concept. Another social price is effort. When you have to bring your old refrigerator to get a discount, this takes effort and causes fatigue. Lifestyle is another social price. The last social price is psyche, meaning self-esteem, privacy, or peace of mind. You can not only use this awareness in your pricing structure, but also in your selling activities, advertising, and promotion.

Think about ways you can make your customer comfortable doing business with you. For Neka Pasquale, sending out samples to "promoters" across the county is time and money well spent. These promoters are usually young, hip women who either blog or video blog about products they believe in, and their friends and followers listen. Enhanced your word of mouth effect by giving a few people who like to broadcast their likes your products in a generous way. Find popular bloggers on YouTube who seem to have followers that would like what you produce, and send out a sample basket with a nice note attached to that blogger and watch what happens.

Pricing Restrictions

There are several restrictions on the prices you can charge your customers. For example, art dealerships, consignment shops, and auction houses set minimum prices and bids that items can be sold for, or the items are taken off the market. Cards, magazines, and books have prices printed on them, so the maximum markup is predetermined. Be sure to learn all the regulations affecting your business. Check with your lawyer, small-business counselor, CPA, or government consumer protection agency about price-setting practices in your state.

Pricing Strategies

The most commonly used pricing strategy retailers can employ is cost pricing. Simply stated, you calculate all your expenses—direct and indirect—and then add a profit. The second strategy is competitive pricing. This involves meeting the going price for similar products in your local market. The cost you paid is not taken into account here. Finally, market-value pricing looks at what the market will bear. Market-value pricing is generally used for unique products or services that have few or no competing products on the market. You can take higher markups here.

Adopt a pricing policy that fits your needs. When you decide on a price, make sure you can still be profitable. Determining your company's total costs to operate can be a tedious and slow process, but it is imperative to assess costs when you are establishing pricing.

Unfortunately, you cannot control all items that go into the calculation of costs. For example, prices of raw materials may fluctuate, or your utility company may approve a rate increase for your service. How quickly you are able to respond to those items may impact the viability of your business. The soundness of your assumptions should be carefully tested before you risk all you have invested.

Whatever your pricing philosophy and objective, remember that you must always be ready to react quickly to changes in market conditions. A successful pricing policy is sound, logical, and flexible at all times. Pricing merchandise and price adjustments require time and thought. Whether or not you achieve a net profit will probably depend largely on your skill in this area.

If all of this seems too overwhelming, you can hire a retail pricing service or marketing specialist to develop a pricing plan for you.

Price Lines

Few stores can be everything to everybody. Most retailers must be satisfied to target only part of a given market. You identified your target customer in your business plan. Once a market segment has been determined, then you should purchase the merchandise and price it to reach those within the segment. Price lines should reflect a store's overall image. If you want to reach the middle- and lower-income levels, you'll search for lower prices in the marketplace. If, on the other hand, you want to draw from upper-income populations, you will search for higher-quality and higher-priced items.

A price line is the top, middle, and bottom prices at which a retailer offers a certain classification of merchandise to customers. For example, writing instruments can be purchased from a large number of resources and offered at 30 or more retail prices. However, dozens of prices complicate the inventory and confuse customers and salespeople. So to simplify the operation and demonstrate good merchandising, a retailer might restrict the price line to four categories: under $5, $10, $20, and more than $35. This price line would indicate that the retailer is after the middle to low end of the market. If you have a selection of 20 different price points instead of four, your salespeople will have five times as many prices to keep track of, your customer will have a wider selection to choose from, and there will be more difficulties with inventory control. Price simplification is an important merchandising tool.

Pricing Principles

Price points are the specific prices you choose within your price line. They are important because research indicates that more people will buy an item at one price than at another—even if the difference between the two is only a few cents. Suppliers can often help you select the best price points. For example, should you sell an item for $12.95 or $13.50? Stay with the lower price as long as a sufficient gross profit and store image can be maintained.

Your pricing strategy is a key element of your marketing plan. As you've probably concluded by now, there is no easy, precise formula for pricing goods and services, but it should not be a random or impulsive process. Price-setting is a pragmatic search for what works best to achieve your overall market objectives and maximize profits. Applying these principles can help you achieve your goals:

warning

Undercharging and giving away too much service and advice are among the biggest causes of financial ruin for service businesses, warns Jan Norman, author and business columnist for *The Orange County Register* newspaper.

- *Divide your price lines into three zones: prestige, popular, and competitive.* The prestige price zone is the one at the top of the line that will improve the image of your store and enhance the rest of the line, but not chase customers away. The popular zone is in the middle, where most purchases are made. The competitive zone is at the bottom, where you might price an item simply to compete with another store located nearby. All prices in a line can fall into any of these zones.

- *Try to find merchandise that will fit into your predetermined price lines and points.* Savvy buyers are specific with their vendors. ("Do you have a silk sweater set that I can retail at $39.95 and get my regular markup?") Such a buyer knows what will attract customers under current market conditions in her market area. Price predetermination is a self-disciplinary skill you'll want to acquire. Setting specific price points before going to vendors can keep a new entrepreneur from starting out with the wrong inventory.

- *Be careful not to lock yourself into fixed lines and price points.* There are many reasons price lines must be adjusted upward and downward and price points changed. Stay abreast of economic conditions, consumer buying habits, and your competition in all channels.

Pricing Your Services

Service industries should also follow these guidelines while recognizing that the process of pricing becomes more abstract than tangible product pricing because real costs are often not directly associated with the service. Service providers often say that they enjoy what they're doing and feel guilty about getting paid for painting a picture, working in the garden, or sharing what they have learned with other people.

Competing on price until your new service business is established is a very common strategy. But if yours is a repeat business, like car maintenance, making your fees the lowest in town may not be wise because it will be difficult to raise your prices for the same service once you're established. What you charge should depend on your expenses and time, the quality of your service, your market, competitors' prices, your experience, and what your customers are willing to pay.

With some service businesses, price-charging guidelines may be available from your licensing agency or professional association. Do some research to determine the going rate. Check with your local chamber of commerce or *The Encyclopedia of Associations* in your library. Read career, industry, and business articles in your local newspaper, trade newsletters, magazines, and online. Check with expositions, the Economic Development Department in your area, and employment agencies. Ask consumers in your market what they pay and what they expect to get in return.

fun fact

Findings from Swapalease show that three out of four moms are the decision makers regarding choosing a vehicle for their families. Women are more comfortable than men haggling during the buying process, but men tend to ask for more money off of the MSRP. Read more about this study at swapalease.com.

Patina stores offer not just a price for every customer, but also a feeling. The key to Patina's success has been offering a wide variety of inexpensive, funny, novelty gifts alongside unique, high-end housewares with a one-of-a-kind feel—this, and a consistently warm reception for customers and their dogs. Dogs are offered a biscuit, teenagers with small budgets are treated as nicely as their wealthy parents, and sales clerks offer endless patience to those who'd like to try on jewelry from the rows and rows of local artisan contributions. The small gifts sell like hotcakes during the holidays and free giftwrapping draws the crowds as well, who may think of Patina as a place to get inexpensive gifts, but often walk out with much more than they planned on.

Once you know the minimum you should charge to avoid losses, add the following elements to determine a profitable rate for your services:

Material/supply costs (cost of goods) +
your time (competitive rate for your labor) +
overhead (health insurance, Social Security, taxes, loan payments, etc.) +
percentage of profit you want to make
(research will give you a reasonable range) =
your price

It may take some time for you to determine what price will satisfy both your needs and your customers'. With a service business, prices can fluctuate based on a particular job or extenuating circumstances. Consult with your bookkeeper or accountant for help in determining what you need to charge to build your business.

Concepts of Retail Price

tip

All merchandise does not deserve the same markup. Markups vary depending on the price elasticity of the product, price concessions of vendors, whether the product is used as a price leader, and other variables.

The difference between the invoice cost and the original retail price is the initial markup. Maintained markup is the difference between the invoice cost and retail sale. Maintained markup differs from initial markup by the amount of any reductions.

Retail specialists suggest that you work only with the retail markup percentage. Retail markup percentages can be calculated on either a cost basis or a selling price basis. Here's how to work with the retail markup percentage:

(Retail markup in dollars ÷ retail selling price) x 100
= retail markup percentage

Manufacturers and wholesalers generally compute their markups based on their costs:

(Retail markup in dollars ÷ cost in dollars) x 100
= manufacturer markup percentage

Most astute retailers rely on the retail markup approach because it is a quick and useful way to see if an item is profitable for you to carry. However, retail enterprises that sell custom-made items or have direct labor may be better off calculating their markups on the cost basis. If an item costs $9.75 wholesale, and you keystone it (double the cost of goods), you will sell it for $19.50. Your markup percentage, based on cost, is 100 percent ($9.75 divided by $9.75 times 100). Your markup percentage, based on retail selling price, is 50 percent ($9.75 divided by $19.50 times 100). Bakeries, computer consultants, appliance repair shops, embroidery businesses, and the like usually use the cost approach.

There are many practices retailers follow when it comes to markup. The approaches introduced here will provide some insight into the problems and possibilities you will encounter.

We just used the term keystone, which means "double the cost." If you buy something for $5 and sell it for $10, you have taken a keystone markup. Small, less sophisticated merchants use this simple method. However, this approach does not allow for individual markup selection and often ignores what competitors are doing with identical merchandise. This method also does not account for the realities of retailing that reduce your margins, such as selling articles marked down to lower-than-retail prices, damaged merchandise, employee discounts, and shoplifting.

Particular markup percentages are usual and customary in a number of trade areas. For example, the traditional markup for hardware is 40 percent of the retail price. If a retailer pays $6 for a hammer, he or she would sell it for $10. For jewelry, the markup range may be 400 to 800 percent. Those who follow the principle of trade acceptance want to be competitive with others in the trade and do not analyze individual items in determining markup.

tip

Stay informed on the top retailing failures and study patterns. Which types of businesses does the current market crave, and which do they disregard? Office Depot, Family Dollar, Coldwater Creek, Dots, Blockbuster, Sears, and Staples once shined in the retail industry and in 2014 they are all closing their doors. Ask yourself what is outdated about their offerings.

Still other retailers believe that you should always go for the highest price for any item as long as you don't drive the customer away. Advocates of this theory usually specialize in items that are unfamiliar to customers and not handled by competitors. They are guided by the law of supply and demand, keeping prices high as long as demand is high. Many of these retailers would rather sell less at higher prices than more at lower prices. Does your business concept fit into this model, or would another markup approach be better?

The good-buy theory is a popular one because it rewards good buying and can enhance the store's reputation if used well. You can increase the markup on an unusually good buy and still offer your customers a great deal when you have scooped the competition.

Still another approach is the high-start/quick-drop-back position. Retailers using this approach are looking for an immediate reaction from the market and are willing to drop back to a lower price to get mass distribution. They can legally advertise that an item that was offered at a higher price is now offered at a much lower price. First-of-a-kind or first-in-the-market opportunities can be leveraged to skim buyers off the top and quickly capture the secondary market by capitalizing quickly on consumer reaction.

warning

As much as 50 percent of all markdowns occur because one or more of the six laws of marketing are broken. Pay attention to price, promotion, place, product, perceived value, and positioning.

Some retailers set pricing on the basis of achieving volume sales at different price levels. The market penetration pricing technique enables retailers who interpret and calculate correctly to gain greater volume with little loss in gross profit. Those retailers who make mistakes lose gross profit without a corresponding increase in sales. For example, a retailer aims to get 10 percent of the market on car batteries at one price—say $69—and anticipates capturing 15 percent at $49. The lower the price, the greater the market penetration. The thinking is that many people will not buy until the price drops to a certain level below the present price.

Calculate for Competitive Advantage

How much should you mark up a product? This decision involves many factors, including the amount required to pay overhead and show a reasonable profit, and the price at which competitors are selling an identical or similar item. A third factor is the kind of purchase made. Sometimes an exceptionally good buy will allow a higher-than-normal markup that will still meet competition and satisfy the customer. If the item will be used as a leader to attract customers into your store, perhaps a smaller markup is in order.

With these and other variables to consider, there is no one absolute formula to follow. Normally, the actual markup amount is based on your best judgment. Ideally, the best markup is one that will give you the greatest gross profit and still bring the customer back to the store. The danger in determining retail prices is setting them so high that customers are lost to competitors.

The sum total of all your markups on all items during a given period of time—less markdowns—is your gross profit. Gross profit is what you use to pay your overhead expenses and is one of the most important concepts in retailing. If the total income of your store for the first 12 months is $100,000, and you take a 50 percent markup on all items sold and there were no markdowns, then your gross profit would be $50,000, or half the total income. From this $50,000, you must pay all your expenses—labor, rent, advertising, etc. What's left is net profit.

The Benefits of Discounts

There are a variety of ways discounts can promote your business. The most obvious examples are post-holiday and summer clearance sales. The objective is to stimulate sales turnover during a normally quiet period and to clear remaining stock of seasonal merchandise and make room for incoming stock. Pricing can be used as a tactical tool to deal with problem products in midseason.

Loss Leaders

You can dramatically reduce the price of a single product or small group of products to bring customers to the store in hopes that they'll buy other products at full

▲

Extra! Extra!

When it's time to clear out merchandise to make room for new and hotter-selling items, you want to move reduced-priced items quickly. It's difficult to close out products that are seasonal, fashion-oriented, artsy, or edible, but here are five things you can do:

1. *Use price points instead of percentages.* Customers relate to dollar signs faster and more easily than percentage points.

2. *Set up small displays in your clearance area.* The same principles used in selling your full-price merchandise apply to markdowns, too. You want it to sell, so make it attractive.

3. *Do not let your clearance items look like junk.* As much as possible, keep this merchandise looking fresh.

4. *Keep the markdown area well-lit.* Customers don't like shopping in dark corners, and the light will make items more appealing.

5. *Use tables for large quantities of clearance merchandise.* Put the tables in the traffic pattern of the customer, encouraging impulse buying.

price. As a new retailer, you can use a "get acquainted" offer to drive business, placing the special merchandise at the back of the store so people will see the rest of your goods as they walk through the aisles to pick up the special offer.

Quantity Discounts

There are a few ways you can use quantity discounts. One is to stimulate volume sales and increase the size of individual transactions. For example, wine merchants might offer reductions on a case of 12 bottles. What you are essentially doing is passing back to your customers some of the savings in handling and administration costs you get from selling in bulk while increasing your net margin.

This tool can also be used to reduce the price on problem stock without putting it on sale. For instance, "buy two, get one free" on frequently purchased items such as T-shirts, underwear, file folders, and toothpaste can boost sales.

Trade and Organization Discounts

As part of your community service—or just good business—you may want to offer discounts to local clubs and associations. Sports and clothing retailers can often generate substantial incremental turnover by offering a discount to youth groups, sports clubs, and so on. Another possibility is offering discounts to electricians, firefighters, schools, or nonprofit organizations. You can establish yourself as a great source for uniforms and supplies and generate long-term loyalty and profitability.

Pre-Season Discounts

Whether you own a fashion retail outlet, holiday decoration cart, or gardening shop, you can introduce new products and build awareness of your business by offering early-season discounts. By offering sharp discounts before the start of bulb planting, the Fourth of July, or a sporting season, you can identify the winning lines to invest in for the main selling months.

Voucher Discounts

Another way of quietly reducing prices and managing the timing of customers' spending is to use discount vouchers. This involves giving the customer X number of vouchers for every Y amount spent; the vouchers are redeemable against future purchases within a fixed time frame. This technique stimulates the current sales period and provides an incentive for the customer to return to the store during a specified future period to make further purchases with the vouchers. You delay having to pay for the discount, which will benefit your cash flow. Furthermore, customers usually spend more than the amount on the voucher when they come in to redeem it, and a number of customers will lose the vouchers or forget to redeem them by the expiration date, in which case your cost for the promotion goes down.

save

Your suppliers can be your partners in profit by working with you to promote your business. The more you sell, the more they sell to you. Ask your vendors to work with you by sharing the cost of discounts on redeemed vouchers or reducing the costs for merchandise bought for special promotions.

General Markdowns

Although every retailer's goal is to always sell at full retail price, everyone makes overly optimistic or bad buys. You may be forced to lower the price to attract customer attention and encourage buyers. After the holidays and between seasons, retailers must deal with markdowns and clearance items. Sometimes, especially in fashion merchandise, markdowns for the year can be more than 15 percent of original prices.

Many markdowns are due to lackluster displays, insufficient product information, improper placement, or poor customer knowledge. If you misinterpret consumer demand, buy too much merchandise, or select the wrong colors, sizes, or styles, review what went wrong with your staff and buyers. The more information you have about your market, the better you will get at having inventory that sells at full price.

Another common cause of markdowns is coming up with the wrong price to begin with. Weather, economic recessions, and other unusual external events can also force you to cut prices to move merchandise.

tip

Blogging is important to your business. Google favors you based on how many relevant blog posts you create with quality content for users looking for your kind of topics. Do you want to be found and promoted to higher page rankings? A blog as part of your website will take the whole site to stardom if you're a good enough writer and give your market what it craves reading about.

It's easy for merchandise to become damaged or soiled while in the store. When this happens, take immediate markdowns to move the items so that returns to the manufacturer are not required. The ideal markdown is one that will move the items quickly without cutting into profits more than necessary. If an item was offered to customers at $9.95 and didn't move, try it at $6.95 before lowering the price to $5.95.

Don't follow one mistake with another. Sometimes it is better to admit a mistake, take a deep markdown, and go on to some successful purchases with the money received and free up your buying dollars and valuable space for full-price items.

Often, entrepreneurs in the fashion business drop prices of slow-moving merchandise to 10 percent above cost. This enables them to pay their overhead and still break even on the merchandise. You can use this principle when reducing prices for an annual clearance sale.

Warehouse stores use the 10/30 principle, reducing the price on slow-moving merchandise 10 percent every 30 days until it sells. Still another markdown theory is early price reduction in the season while customers are still in a buying mood. This technique can be used for newer and better styles that may be turned over many times and can generally bring in more money. When you cut prices slowly over time, you rarely stimulate any real buying, and this can damage the image of your store because you have merchandise around too long.

Here's to You!

Focus on your own success, not on creating failure for your competitors, suggests author, marketing consultant, and professor emeritus of marketing at the Harvard Business School Benson P. Shapiro. He offers a seven-step guide to resisting the pressure to slash prices to compete:

1. Create customer value by providing a reason for the customer to do business with you.

2. Focus on the customers who want what you have. You can't be all things to all people.

3. Be different!

4. Don't compete with yourself. Simple product lines and service offerings are the easiest to manage and the most profitable.

5. Set your prices to reflect the value customers place on the quality or the quantity of your products or services.

6. Deliver on your promises. If you don't, your customer will have a good reason to negotiate and focus on price.

7. Be courageous. If you set a price and say it's not negotiable, don't negotiate or you lose your credibility.

At the end of a season, some retailers give distressed merchandise to charity. Others prefer to recover what they can in cash quickly and sell the odds and ends to retail specialists who often bid less than 10 cents on the dollar of the retail value.

True Costs

There needs to be a healthy balance between the accountancy view of your business and the marketing view. Retailing is more than numbers—it's relationships as well as salesmanship. You have to sell the intangible (goodwill and dreams) as well as the tangible (goods and services). Successful retailers pay attention to the soft side as well as the calculated part of doing business. Are your instincts and feelings about things paying off? Will they enable you to extend your retailing experience another year or cause your store's demise? You must understand the financial consequences of your decisions and the constraints of money on your choices.

Patina owner, Christine Ward laments, "One time we ordered direct from a vendor in Italy especially for the holiday season. I should have done more research for an international order. It was large order that didn't go well and we ended up not receiving the merchandise until December 15th. Now I order domestically."

The lesson? You need to stay alert to the true costs of stocking various products. Prime retail space is expensive. High interest rates punch up inventory costs. Therefore, it is vital to ensure that every foot of floor space is earning an appropriate return.

True costs include all the factors that contribute to the retailer's ability to provide a consumer with goods or services, and the way you price your inventory should cover these costs. For instance, in a menswear store, a suit will take up twice as much space as a pair of trousers but may only sell at half the rate. Therefore the "rent" cost of a suit should be four times that of trousers and the interest charge for the square footage of space it takes up should be double. Since suits require a higher level of personal selling, they should carry a higher proportion of the selling staff costs. There will be similar differences between the true costs incurred by a furniture store and those in a self-selection lamp store. From day one, you need to have a clear picture of the direct product profitability of all the merchandise ranges you stock.

Pricing menu items is difficult for the new restaurateur. Pricing can depend on volume, portion size, and seating. It may be necessary to price items according to what you feel the customer will pay. Even if you decide you have to maintain a food cost of 35 percent to make a profit, you may have to weigh various factors. For example, certain items on your menu may be priced too high to be accepted by the public, and some items will necessarily have to be priced below your targeted range in order to attract the lunch crowd to your dinner house. This policy may mean pricing one item at a 25 percent food cost and another at a 45 percent food cost. You have to determine the selling mix of these items, as well as the portions, to stay in business.

Knowing the real costs of providing goods—wholesale cost, shipping, preparation, merchandising, selling, etc.—will help you select and price the inventory that will keep your business viable.

On the internet, just as on the boardwalk, consumers are looking for the best deal. Armed with wholesale and competitive information, consumers might try to haggle with you to lower the price you will sell a particular item for. They may also ask you for quantity, senior citizen, student, teacher, or organization discounts. These days, it's a fact of life that retailers will lose some sales to sites like eBay and Priceline.com. Because of this price pressure, one of the biggest challenges a new retailer faces is building a brand that customers will value and support with their wallets.

The Unbeatable Pricing Strategy

A new business has the ability to customize products for small market segments, to respond quickly to changes in the market, and to cultivate personal relationships with customers to satisfy their needs. Small businesses cannot compete on price with big-box retailers, but they have an equal or better chance of competing on value. As a small retailer, your best pricing strategy is to provide both tangible and intangible benefits, rational and emotional ones, to your customers.

:: Human Resources

U ntil now, you've mainly been concerned about what it will take to get your store open—the location of your business, layout and image, proper pricing procedures, lining up vendors, etc. Making sure you don't burn through your money before the doors are open is no doubt at the top of your priority list. Good—you're planning to succeed.

Having said that, what if you get what you want? What if you are flooded with customers on opening day? How will you greet, direct, answer questions, ring up sales, and wrap and deliver the goods all by yourself? Even after the shoppers go home, your work won't be over. You'll have the store to clean, merchandise to re-shelve and display, register to balance, deposits and orders to make, and other paperwork to complete before opening the next day. Still want to do everything yourself? Can't afford to hire any help? Think again.

As the quantity of work to be performed expands, you must hire employees who can play these roles: display coordinator, buyer, controller, receiving clerk, stock person, delivery person, manager, bookkeeper, operations manager, and cashier. One person may hold the skills of several positions—that's called a great hire.

When you start out, you will handle the lion's share, if not all, of the business functions. Small retailers usually divide the work in half: You, as the owner, manage the operations, and you're assisted by someone who manages the merchandise. At the Minneapolis, Minnesota, gift shop Patina, Christine Ward and her husband Rick Haase, oversee the buying, business and sales management, and merchandising departments. They used to do all of those jobs themselves until a year after opening Patina the business could justify adding team members. They still accompany their buyers on national buying trips and trade show excursions. Their buyers are very helpful to them, especially since each was originally an in-store employee before becoming a buyer. This ensures they are well-seasoned with home trend knowledge and understand the end result of each purchase. As your business grows, you will probably need a general manager, operations manager, merchandise manager, marketing manager, and financial manager.

Each manager has prescribed areas of responsibility with measurable goals and written procedures for each. Operations managers are in charge of building mainte-nance, delivery, purchasing, and personnel. Merchandise managers are responsible for the purchase, flow, and movement of merchandise to the customer. Marketing managers are in charge of all advertising, promotions, visual presentations, and pub-lic relations. And financial managers are responsible for all computer data, financial controls, and reports.

You don't want to wait too long before hiring the right manager to relieve you of some responsibilities and ensure all duties are being completed, including fol-

aha!

Establish a mission-driven team with total customer satisfaction and company profitability as the pri-mary goals. You and your employees are interdepen-dent. Together, you can achieve your goals if you measure your decisions and actions against this simple, two-part guideline retailers gave us: "Do what is right for the customer and what is right for the team."

low-ups on merchandise requests. If you are not able to get answers back to your salespeople for customers in a timely manner, it frustrates customers and costs sales.

Assessing Your Needs

Consumers often form their impressions of a store by evaluating its sales force. So look for initiative and problem-solving skills in multi-skilled employees who can ring up repeat sales for your business and keep customers satisfied.

Regardless of merchandise type, retail salespeople assist customers in finding what they are looking for and try to interest them in buying. They describe a product's features, demonstrate it, and show various models and colors. Therefore, you need to hire people with experience in your trade area—or at least people with a willingness to learn.

While these are the basic requirements for selling items, not all sales approaches are the same, and not all salespeople will fit your line of goods or store. For example, some sales personnel, particularly those selling expensive and complex items, need special knowledge or skills. Selling automobiles requires explaining the features of various models, the meaning of manufacturers' specifications, and the types of options and financing available to prospective buyers. Selling fine jewelry involves a certain level of expertise beyond that required for a costume jewelry clerk.

Stephanie Covart's buyers have been with Electric Fetus for decades. They can wisely buy and educate customers on a wide range of music because each of them has a love of music spanning the '40s, '50s, and '60s in addition to current trends. Each has been studying music for years, as well as the floor staff, who have to prove their education of music before getting hired with a test.

In addition to selling, all employees need to know how to make out sales checks; receive cash, check, and charge payments; bag or package purchases; and give change and receipts. Depending on the hours they work, they may have to open and close cash registers. This may involve counting the money; separating charge slips, coupons, and exchange vouchers; and making deposits at the bank. Attention to detail and basic math skills are important.

Depending on the type of store and your policies, your workers may also handle returns and exchanges, wrap gifts, stock shelves or racks, arrange for mailing or delivery of purchases, mark price tags, take inventory, and prepare displays. Neatness and artistic talent are very useful. Salespeople must be aware of special sales and promotions, recognize possible security risks and thefts, and know how to handle or prevent such situations.

How Many People Is Enough?

The quick answer is as many as it takes to ensure complete customer satisfaction. In reality, simple economics preclude this. There are as many answers to personnel needs as there are types of retail businesses. Nonetheless, here are a few points to consider in deciding how many staff members your business requires:

- *Size.* A single-floor firm will need fewer staff than a multifloor store of the same size.
- *Type of product.* The higher the price and complexity of the product, the more personal selling is required. More personal selling means more people.
- *Operating hours.* The number of workdays and the hours of business may require shifts and flexible work times. Changes in holiday business will also affect staffing.
- *Patterns of trade.* The concentration of sales at certain times of the day or on certain days of the week will affect staffing needs.
- *Sales density.* The higher the sales per square foot, the more staff you'll need.
- *Business location.* A homebased business increases its chances of experiencing zoning problems with every employee it adds.

tip

Hiring tip from strategic advisor, Jeff Prouty: "When choosing a potential employee examine how that person brings energy to the room, the process, and the people around them. People who are genuinely happy in life bring that to the job, but just asking questions in an interview doesn't reveal that accurately. Think Winnie the Pooh and ask, 'Are they a Tigger or an Eeyore?'"

Hiring

The first phase of hiring is the more impersonal aspect of personnel administration: creating plans, formulating policies, and setting up procedures. This involves recruitment, selection, hiring, compensation, employee health and welfare, maintaining personnel records, and the like. Then come the more human aspects of managing human resources—the personal, in-the-flesh people business.

A natural tendency of many new retailers is to hire family members and/or friends as soon as help is needed. Avoid doing this. Your relationship with these individuals may interfere seriously with your in-store supervision of them and your focus on what you need done. Of course, there are exceptions. Some partnerships are smashing successes: Keith Covart eventually bought out all three of his business partners and in 2007 began sharing ownership of "the Fetus" with daughter, Stephanie Covart

Meyerring, and loves it. Stephanie's husband, Aaron, also came onboard a few years ago, so it is truly a family run business. Christine Ward and Rick Haase make a dynamic family duo with their combined talents and after eight years of really hard work are finally cutting their hours back a little to enjoy the benefits. The point is not to hire one of your family members and friends without seriously thinking through the possible impact on your business's bottom line. "If you load your business with friends, you have a group of people who think like you. It doesn't necessarily allow for a healthy, well-rounded perspective. There is the possibility of it actually hurting your business," cautions Keith.

Labor Practices

A person who operates a business with employees outside the immediate family must comply with a host of statutes regarding fair employment practices. These statutes relate to things like terms of employment, safety on the job, provisions for retirement, and workers' compensation and unemployment insurance. The fairness principle requires that decisions related to employees aren't made arbitrarily and that policies are applied equally to all employees. The law gives employees certain rights, and as an employer, you are responsible for knowing the law and abiding by it.

Some retail employees working in large companies belong to unions that represent their common interests. The United Food and Commercial Workers International Union has 1.3 million workers at the checkout stands, in the food aisles, and behind the deli and meat counters of neighborhood supermarkets. The Service Employees International Union accounts for two million employees. The Retail, Wholesale, and Department Store Union has over 60,000 members. Consult your lawyer and SBA counselor regarding labor laws in your state.

Hiring Procedures

There are several methods for attracting and evaluating potential employees. Educate yourself on proper hiring procedures. Information on this subject is available at local libraries, community colleges, Small Business Development Centers, employment services offices, career development centers, and seminars.

Make sure your job announcement is attractive, accurate, meets government equal opportunity criteria, and is listed in the right places. Each job posting should be well-thought-out to emphasize the positive aspects of the job, including benefits and potential for advancement (see sample ads on page 176). The medium used to advertise should match the type of person you hope to hire. For example, if you are looking for an experienced store manager, advertise on LinkedIn.com. If you're looking for an entry-level candidate, you will probably target young people, so post

Job Advertisements

Ad for a Salesperson

We want your energy and ability to contribute to our success. You must be highly motivated, enthusiastic, friendly, and energetic. You must have sales experience, a strong customer service attitude, and the ability to consult with customers on purchases. Neat appearance and the ability to work in a fast-paced environment are essential. Employee benefits and room for advancement are available to the right candidate.

Ad for a Store Manager

We're looking for candidates who are merchandise-oriented and want to be involved in all aspects of running a retail store. Candidates should have three or more years of retail store management experience, strong people and communication skills, strong sales and motivational abilities, some computer skills, visual merchandising, inventory control experience, excellent customer service skills, and a sense of style. Excellent salary, benefits, and an opportunity to grow with the company with exponential rate increases can make an appealing package for the candidate who shows promise.

ads on college job boards or church and community newsletters. Signs in the store entryway or on community bulletin boards may be helpful, too. You can also pass the word along to current employees to suggest friends or acquaintances, work with employment agencies, or list the opening with the state Department of Employment Services or on the web.

When the time arrives to hire higher-level employees such as assistant managers, buyers, and bookkeepers, you need to be more imaginative and aggressive in your pursuit of qualified personnel. LinkedIn, trade journals, professional association newsletters, and relevant industry websites, are good places to find seasoned, skilled, relevant prospects, often with referral status. Discussing your needs with suppliers and other retailers is another way to find employees who can often "hit the ground running."

Some firms pay a bonus to any employee who brings in a new hire. Others spend thousands of dollars on classifieds, only to report that word-of-mouth referrals still seem to bring in the best candidates. Outstanding salespeople must be recruited, developed, and then shown they're appreciated.

It is often easier to train inexperienced people to sell your line of goods than it is to retrain salespeople who have developed undesirable attitudes and habits. Productivity can be developed in candidates who have a few desirable traits: friendliness, attention to detail, persistence, patience, and creativity. For example, one La-Z-Boy franchise has had success recruiting waitresses and hairdressers, as well as people who have worked in clothing stores, to sell their furniture. These people are used to working with the public and handling difficult situations. If they're good, they have the patience and know-how to listen and work with people.

Auditioning talent can be more revealing than a series of interviews. Trying potential job candidates out on the floor for customer feedback and putting them through slightly stressful busy periods can be an opportunity to see how well they'll perform in the future.

Background Checks

There is no crystal ball to ensure that the employees you hire will be loyal, honest, and hard-working. Verify an applicant's background yourself or hire someone to do it for you—everyone from the store manager to the shipping clerk represents your business and references cannot always be trusted.

Howtoinvestigate.com is an online organization that outlines information sources and procedures for you to accomplish a background check. Local investigation firms can also be found in your town with a simple Google search, as well as through your police department and lawyers association. They will do background criminal checks on prospective employees for about $50 to $250, depending on the agency's fee schedule and how many jurisdictions the agency checks.

Retail jobs are an easy starting point for immigrants to get into the workplace when first coming to the United States. Employers must have proof that the employee has the right to work in the country, as required on U.S. Citizenship and Immigration Service (USCIS) Form I–9. To find out which requirements your business must meet, visit the U.S. Citizenship and Immigration Services website at uscis.gov, and click on "Employer Information."

New employees must provide you with either one document from List A (Identity and Employment Authorization) or one document each from Lists B (Identity only) and C (Employment Authorization only):

List A
- U.S. Passport or U.S. Passport Card
- Permanent Residence Card or Alien Registration Receipt Card

- Foreign Passport with I-551 stamp or temporary I-551 printed notation on machine-readable immigrant visa (MRIV)
- Employment Authorization Document card with photograph (Form I-766)
- Foreign Passport with Form I-94 or Form I-94A with Arrival/Departure Report bearing same name on passport with endorsement of non-immigrant status and specific work endorsement
- Passport from the Federated States of Micronesia (FSM) or the Republic of the Marshall Island (RMI) with From I-94 or Form I-94A showing nonimmigrant admission under the Compact of Free Association Between the U.S. and the FSM or RMI
- Foreign passport with special documents issued by the Commonwealth of Northern Mariana Island (CNMI)
- Foreign passport that contains a temporary I-551 stamp or temporary I-551 printed notation on a machine readable immigrant visa (MRIV)

Top Ten Things Employees Want

In business today, a lot of focus is placed on customer satisfaction, but without employee satisfaction, very little can be accomplished. As you hire people, establish your policies and procedures, and run your business, keep these ten motivators in mind to develop a top-quality team that is loyal and productive:

1. *Achievement:* to be challenged by worthy goals
2. *Balance:* flexibility in scheduling to have a life while earning a living
3. *Respect:* to be considered professional and left alone to do their jobs
4. *Community:* support and validation from co-workers and customers
5. *Opportunity:* the chance to learn new things and advance their positions
6. *Stability:* leadership, fairness, organization, and job security
7. *Communication:* access to information and openness about what's going on
8. *Reward:* appreciation of their work through fair compensation and recognition of a job well done
9. *Environment:* a healthy, positive, pleasant atmosphere with comfortable working conditions
10. *Pride:* personal satisfaction in their day's work

List B

- Driver's license or ID card issued by a state or outlying possession of the United States with a photograph, date of birth, physical description, and address
- School identification card with photograph
- Voter's registration card
- U.S. military card or draft record
- Military dependent's ID card
- U.S. Coast Guard Merchant Mariners Document (MMD)
- Native American tribal document
- Driver's license issued by Canadian authority
- Acceptable List B documents for those under 18
- School record or report card
- Clinical, doctor, or hospital record
- Day-care or nursery school record

    *See uscis.gov for special notations that can be used in place of these for the disabled or minors who are unable to produce these documents.

List C

- U.S. Social Security account number card that is unrestricted
- Certification of Birth Abroad issued by the U.S. Department of State (Form FS-545)
- Certification of Report of Birth issued by the U.S. Department of State (Form DS-1350)
- Original or certified copy of birth certificate issued by a state, county, municipal authority or outlying possession of the United States bearing an official seal
- Native American Tribal document
- U.S. Citizen ID card (Form I-197)
- Identification Card for Use of Resident Citizen in the United States (Form I-179)
- Employment authorization document issued by the Department of Homeland Security (see uscis.gov for details).

Compensation

According to the U.S. Department of Labor, retailers hired 4,261,630 salespeople in 2014 to work in stores ranging from small specialty shops employing a few workers to giant department stores with hundreds of salespeople, and self-employed representatives of direct sales companies and mail-order houses. This occupation offers many opportunities for part-time work and is especially appealing to students, retirees, and others looking to supplement their incomes. The average hourly earnings of all workers in retail trade were $17.28 in March 2015, compared to the average hourly earnings of $24.86 for all workers in the United States, according to the Bureau of Labor Statistics.

You can pay sales employees hourly or on commission but you must pay all employees at least minimum wage regardless of the commissions or bonuses they earn. The commission method is generally practical only for stores providing one-on-one customer service to sell high-priced items such as expensive clothing, jewelry, electronics, furniture, and computers. The advantage of this form of pay is that it ties employees' income directly to their job performance. Add to these three approaches the opportunity for employees to win special rewards or bonuses for meeting or exceeding goals for sales and service.

warning

Employees who feel they are appreciated, compensated fairly, and treated respectfully have the incentive to be more productive and positive than those who feel overworked and underpaid. If the poor performers receive the same compensation as the go-getters, it won't be long before you have a mediocre staff and lose all your best workers.

Most managers and full-time employees expect health coverage, paid time off for illness or vacation, and some perks like paid educational opportunities, trade show attendance, and merchandise discounts. Without offering some benefits in your compensation package, you will find it difficult to compete for quality employees. When considering what to offer your workers, compare the perks with the costs of high turnover—decreased morale, time interviewing new employees, training new people, interruption of customer service, public perception of instability, loss of person's know-how, etc.

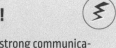

aha!

Build strong communications with your employees through weekly store meetings, a periodic newsletter, an annual company meeting, sponsorship of academic or athletic teams, a suggestion box, or scheduled social get-togethers with families.

After They're Hired

Once you have invested the time and effort in recruiting and hiring skilled new employees, don't rest on your laurels. There are several things you can do to make sure your diligent hiring efforts don't go to waste.

Allowing poor communication between management and employees is one of retailers' biggest mistakes. Regular store meetings are a good way to

The Employee Bible

Here are some of the topics you should cover in your employee manual:

- ❍ Company philosophy
- ❍ Company benefits, including medical care, time off, discounts, and allowances
- ❍ Hours of operation and reporting hours
- ❍ Procedures for reporting an illness, absence, or family emergency
- ❍ Dress code, including uniforms, safety gear, or badges to be worn
- ❍ Standards of behavior regarding smoking, alcohol, drugs, gum-chewing, language, personal telephone calls, and visitors
- ❍ Customer communication etiquette
- ❍ Procedures for dealing with unhappy customers
- ❍ Procedures for dealing with suspected shoplifters or other illegal activities
- ❍ Procedures for making suggestions for company improvement
- ❍ How to use all equipment
- ❍ Procedures for serving customers
- ❍ Where to get product or service information
- ❍ Emergency procedures

educate employees on new products or services and let them practice demonstrating their benefits. Have employees report customer feedback and requests for out of stock merchandise. Employees should be told when new products will be arriving and when replacement items will be in stock. Employees want to be asked for their opinions and see some of their ideas implemented.

Provide Incentives to Employees

Employees should constantly be encouraged to perform in a quality manner. When you or a customer is pleased with an employee's performance, let everyone know about it. Personal and public recognition has a multi-tiered affect. It communicates what you value to your workers and customers, which can generate more achievements and satisfaction. Rewards can be treating a star employee to a lunch, bonus, afternoon off, or reserved parking. You will be hiring from the same labor pool as other local businesses. How can you get your employees to perform better for you? Your acknowledgment, rewards, and overall management will make all the difference.

Employee and Operations Manual

Operating a retail business can be fun and rewarding, but without effective management procedures, it can also be a lot of headaches. If you put the proper systems in place so that your store is more or less on autopilot, you'll be successful. The reason franchises generally work well is that they use proven systems; all the new retailer has to do is follow the tried-and-true policies.

An employee and operations manual provides the information your people need to do their jobs and play by the rules. It gets employees off on the right foot and instills in them habits you want to see rather than those you want to break.

Many retailers are extremely dependent on their key staff members. If a management person leaves, sales suffer because of the knowledge that walks out the door with a valuable employee. Turnover is expensive, and training new staff is a tedious, time-consuming process. Written operating procedures that explain how to perform the day-to-day, week-to-week, month-to-month, and year-to-year jobs involved in running your store will help smooth employee transitions.

By having a guide for employees, you eliminate uncertainty about what your store's policies, procedures, and guidelines are. This can be of particular importance when you need to put an employee on probation or fire someone. Having clearly stated policies can protect you from the litigation that is all too common in today's world.

Your dress code should be plainly understood by everyone who works in the store. Employees should know that they will be sent home to change if they are not dressed appropriately. Clothing, makeup, and jewelry regulations should be appropriate for your clientele because poor dressing and hygiene will drive customers away.

Managing the customer's mood is not a small task. Management of the customer's experience starts when they walk in and ends when they walk out. A warm greeting from an alert, knowledgeable, and attentive (but not pushy) salesperson will make customers want

aha!

Establish employee policies that don't attract people who are looking for an employee discount rather than a job. A lot of kids want to work in music and electronics stores, owners say, so those entrepreneurs have to screen candidates carefully to avoid low productivity and high turnover.

to do business with you time and again. For more on store policies, read Chapter 6.

Probation

It is customary to hire new people on a probationary basis. For retail employees, this period should be relatively short—for example, 10 to 90 days. This time allows you to evaluate the new employee to measure their progress and to determine if they will fit into your organization. A probationary period also provides incentive for new employees to prove themselves and to learn their jobs quickly and well.

Training

When new employees are hired, they should be trained in a well-thought-out and thorough manner. To begin orienting them to your way of doing business, give them a complete tour of the facilities, explaining what their role is in each area, what procedures to follow, and things to watch out for. Take new employees around your store or office from the front door to the back. It is important that everyone understand how their job fits into the overall scheme of things and what each person's duties and responsibilities are so people will work well together.

Continue training on a regular basis. Training is an investment in the future— your future. With rapid changes in technology and fashion, products change frequently and the challenge to employees to keep up with them is great. Encourage employees to stay informed about the latest trends in your industry by reading trade journals, local newspapers, and consumer magazines. Send employees to trade and consumer shows to pick up new ideas, interact with other businesspeople, and promote your business.

> **tip**
>
> According to the Economic Policy Institute, two thirds of the 1.5 million workers who make minimum wage will see that number go up as a result of President Obama's call to raise it. Why not offer a higher rate now to attract the best and brightest? This will set you apart as an employer who cares about quality of life and hopefully have your employees feeling grateful.

Scheduling Personnel

Scheduling employee hours is complex and can be daunting at first since you have no history to go on. In setting up the store and merchandise, employees may work longer hours during the first few weeks when the public hasn't found you yet. With time, customer patterns will emerge that make it easier to know how many staff members will be needed on certain days of the week and at what times of day.

Full-time employees work 30 to 40 hours a week and are usually paid at a somewhat higher hourly rate than part-time employees (or they are paid salary). Full-timers provide continuity for your store and develop your customer base for you. They generally have broad-based skills in the areas of sales, cashiering, special ordering, and display work. These employees make a commitment to your business and have regularly scheduled hours and days of the week.

The Electric Fetus staffs 45 employees, one-third working full time. Store events call for extra staffing, such as when a popular band plays at the store and it's packed to the hilt with adoring fans. Ethique Nouveau is open Wednesday through Saturday, and hosted mostly by a store manager, with Charlotte filling in on Saturdays. For the many special events held in the store she adds staff as needed. Volunteers with similar values, wanting to lend support, frequently help out at events.

Part-time employees may work year-round or seasonally when you need additional help in sales, gift-wrapping, inventory, and service. They can be scheduled for your heavy-traffic hours and days or on an as-needed basis. These workers are frequently students, retired people, or parents of school-age children, and their schedules can be set to accommodate school and/or seasonal schedules. Establishing four-hour shifts allows you the flexibility of having people work partial days as well as adjusting staffing needs. Some of your part-time workers will stay with you for years and provide exceptional service.

Invite employees to submit schedule requests and make every effort to accommodate them. However, don't be casual on the accountability side. Let employees know you are counting on them and expect them to arrive on time and ready to work. Overstaffing, understaffing, and no-shows disrupt other workers and can jeopardize your business. By maintaining detailed sales, traffic, and staffing records, you can analyze what's working and what isn't. From year to year, you'll amass figures that will help you maximize your resources and opportunities. For a "Weekly Time Sheet" and a "Staffing Calendar," turn to pages 185 and 186.

aha!

Learn from the experience of letting an employee go. Ask yourself what went wrong and whether improved interviewing/screening practices might have prevented the problem in the first place. Ask yourself if there's anything you can do to improve your management to create an atmosphere where both your business and employees will thrive.

Employee Performance Appraisals

Annual employee evaluations help you zero in on the strengths and weaknesses of your business. At the same time each year, set up appointments with your

Weekly Time Sheet

Employee name: _____
Number: _____
Department: _____
Date from: _____
Date to: _____

	Morning		Afternoon		For office use only	
	In	Out	In	Out	Regular hours	Overtime
Monday						
Tuesday						
Wednesday						
Thursday						
Friday						
Saturday						
Sunday						
				Total hours		

Employee signature:_____

Approved by: _____

employees to review their performance. Give each employee a self-evaluation form to complete and return to you prior to your scheduled meeting. Then, review each employee's answers and prepare your points for discussion. These will include expectations for the job, personal achievements, areas where effectiveness could improve, how you can help the employee do a better job, and the employee's new performance objectives.

From the information exchanged during the performance appraisal process, you will get a clearer view of how well your hiring, training, and management practices are working and how to better motivate employees. This is often a time when new ideas for the business surface and aspirations for promotion are revealed.

Staffing Calendar

Date from: _____   Date to: _____

Employee	Mon.	Tues.	Wed.	Thurs.	Fri.	Sat.	Sun.

Performance appraisals also provide the opportunity for clearing the air about misunderstandings or mistakes and for starting fresh.

Firing

Rigorous hiring standards can help reduce the number of firing headaches you may have. Stephanie Meyerring Covart of Electric Fetus in Minneapolis, puts potential employees through a comprehensive music knowledge test, a sampling of questions customers would ask in a typical week. Surprisingly, Stephanie doesn't hire based on test results alone. She says that even she can't score 100 percent on the test, which is always changing, so she looks for candidates that have great knowledge of many genres of music, but are balanced people with social skills.

aha!

Unless an employee steals, destroys property, or causes safety problems, immediate dismissal for poor performance isn't a good idea—legally or managerially. Instead, meet privately with the employee and explain the problem. To prevent misunderstandings, you might want to have your store manager present.

The laws protecting workers' rights are complex and can easily be used against you. Check with your lawyer, local Small Business Development Center, and other advisors to make sure you understand what you can and cannot do in terms of firing an employee.

If you feel you need to discipline an employee, the first thing to do is meet with them and give a verbal warning. The next time the employee exhibits behavior that goes against your policies, provide him or her with a written summary of mandatory behavior expected within a certain timeframe. This chance to improve behavior is known as a written warning. Keep a copy of the warning that clearly states that if the behavior is not corrected, the employee may be terminated. Ask the employee to acknowledge with signature the understanding of your expectations. If, after these measures, the employee's performance has not improved in the ways you outlined in the verbal and written warnings, a termination may be in order.

Be humane if you have to let someone go. Meet in private with the employee and tell the person the exact reasons for termination. Create an atmosphere of fairness, if not compassion, and have the employee's final paycheck and paperwork ready to make a clean break.

Braun Consulting, human resources experts offers tips for firing an employee once the decision has been made. Remember that the eyes of other employees and senior management will be on you as you handle the situation. They will likely wonder if they will be fired in the same way. Prepare for firing people emotionally before it happens, knowing that eventually you will have to do it, by working on your "people skills." Remember that for the employee, being fired is a very memorable event in his or her life and the way you handle it will stay there for years. Have another manager at the termination to witness the proceedings and lend support. Let the employee also bring a witness or support co-worker, if possible. Use clear, documented explanations of why the termination is taking place. Keep your cool and be kind if the employee becomes emotional. Confirm all commitments and communications in written form made at the meeting, such as severance pay, available services, and when their last check will be cut.

You Must Remember This

Establishing a sense of community among your employees is one of the best ways to make your store successful. Employee loyalty leads to customer satisfaction, which profits everyone. Be fair, have fun, attend to business, and you'll all be proud of what you create.

12

Marketing

Marketing is a system of business activities designed to plan, price, promote, and distribute products and services to potential customers. How well you promote what you're doing is a major factor in determining how much business you will do.

Marketing is often the most creative and fun part of running a retail business. To let people know you can satisfy their wants and needs, you must be highly visible. You can publicize your business through paid, free, or partnering promotions. Paid promotions include advertising, direct mail, and your website. Partnering promotions include paring up with sites that feature vendor wares at a discount to create publicity. Neka Pasquale's business "exploded" after an invitation to be featured on Gilt City (giltcity.com) led to a non-stop interest in her products. "Someone from Gilt called me and wanted to feature my juices. I hadn't heard of them and thought maybe 50 people would be into the offer. My phone didn't stop ringing for two weeks. I sold out of everything. It was crazy and it changed everything." Aim for investigating social discount promotion sites like Gilt and try establishing a vendor relationship with one at a time to see which one works for your audience.

Putting Together a Promotion Plan

When devising a plan to promote your store, these are the things you need to think about:

- What do I want to say to potential customers?
- How will I reach them?
- What are my specific objectives for each promotion?
- How will I measure the success of my efforts?
- What is my budget?

Keep the big picture in mind while leveraging the benefits of the various marketing channels and vehicles to achieve your goals. A typical marketing plan may have 10 to 35 different marketing channels through which sales will come. The goal is to be as creative and playful as possible.

Neka Pasquale showcases Urban Remedy's lifestyle branding as fresh, green, simple, and raw. The food is raw and the décor in her stores follows suit. Rough-hewn wood shelving, mason jars of herbs and roots, and fresh flowers compliment her message, which is to eat as simply and naturally as possible. Fun is introduced to the marketing plan by pairing her food with hot topics through events. Neka recently held a film screening of *Fat, Sick, and Nearly Dead* at a local surf shop, followed by a question and answer session, and of course lots of delicious, raw food and juice. The audience members were already into fitness, many of them surfers, and eating healthy goes hand in hand with that, so by pairing the surf shop's community with her own, it created a highly social event, which builds community around the business. Impressed with the way the film's character lost weight through juicing, the audience members looked to Neka to guide them toward a similar experience with her holistic practitioner knowledge and like-minded products.

Designer Matt Murphy, got his best advertising through the notoriety of competitive projects and contests, which he still strives to win. Christine Ward paid big bucks for an ad in a major local magazine and ran additional ads in her local newspaper, but her best marketing is done through highly visible windows and lots of foot traffic.

Marketing Ideas Galore

Use this list to brainstorm ways to promote your business:

- Auction/raffle prizes
- Balloons
- Billboards
- Billing inserts
- Brochures
- Business to business partnerships
- Catalogs
- Celebrity guest appearance
- Classes, workshops
- Collectors club
- Contests
- Coupons
- Direct mail
- Event program ads (theater, sports, school)
- Fliers
- Frequent buyer program
- Gift certificates
- Gift with purchase
- Group discount card
- Internet email, banner ad, website, links, search engine registry
- Loyalty program
- Magazine ad, article, insert, bingo card

- Newsletters
- Open house
- Partnerships with schools
- Patron of the arts
- Photo opportunities
- Pledge on sales
- Postcards
- Posters
- Product demonstrations
- Radio ad, appearance, live remote
- Sales
- Shopping cart signage
- Signs: interior, exterior, building, vehicle
- Skywriting
- Special events
- Specialty items
- Social networking (see Chapter 13 for jumpstart assignments)
- Tastings
- Themed events
- TV ads, appearances, infomercials
- Volunteer opportunities
- Window displays

▲

Whether you prefer social media, store events, magazine ads, or contests, this chapter will help you start making a plan for what's most productive for your goals.

Your Grand Opening

If you built your store, you may have had a groundbreaking ceremony to let people know you were coming to town. For most retailers, the first opportunity to blow your horn is when you're ready to open your doors for business. Some kinds of businesses need greater opening promotion efforts than do others.

The opening of an auto repair shop might not need to be as lavish as the festivities for an interior design store. For restaurants and some other businesses, it is often wise to have a "soft" or quiet opening until all the kinks have been worked out. Still other businesses have a series of events targeting various stakeholders in their success. Suppliers, investors, family, and friends may be treated to small celebrations, with a fund-raising party for a local charity or group the night before the official opening.

How much should you spend on your grand opening promotion? Retail expert and author Carol Schroeder says a general rule of thumb is to spend 3 to 5 percent of your anticipated sales for the first year. If you expect to generate $200,000 in sales, you can probably afford to spend $6,000 to $10,000 to launch your business. That might include doing a barrage of pay-per-click social media banner ads, radio and newspaper advertising, as well as placing "grand opening" signage outside your store. You might consider holding a kick-off event with refreshments. Plan grand opening specials and collect names and addresses of customers who come in to begin building a database for more targeted direct-mail programs.

Advertising

Advertising offers a wide range of opportunities. You can pay to have your message put almost anywhere you find your customers.

Minneapolis, Minnesota, retailer Keith Covart keeps Electric Fetus in the cross-hairs of his music fanatic audience by advertising in a local daily college newspaper and two arts, music, and entertainment newspapers—City Pages and Vita.mn. Not to mention his constant visibility on Facebook and Twitter. The record label companies he carries in his store used to pay for radio spots, but those days dwindled as radio time became more expensive over the years. He's also a public radio sponsor of local jazz shows because he's committed to music. It's a nice plus when they mention his name on the air.

If you open a children's store, car repair business, or fast-food business, you might want to use radio to reach commuters while they're driving. If you have a photography studio or florist shop, you may want to print an attractive brochure that can be used in many ways. Which media will give you the largest return on your investment for the least amount of money and wasted effort? Check prices against circulation figures and audience profiles.

Media Mix

What media can put consumers under your spell? Compile a list of publications and other media outlets that reach your target audience. Consider social media websites, radio, TV, billboards, newspapers, transit, internet ads, magazines, newsletters, fairs, and event programs. Retailers suggest you ask the sales reps of the advertising outlets you're thinking about using to give you a rate card and demographic profile of their audience. This is free market research for you and can help

---

Is It Working?

To evaluate your advertising and marketing plans, ask yourself the following ten questions:

1. Are my objectives for advertising and sales promotion clearly stated? Do they support my marketing plan?

2. Is my media mix supportive of my marketing plan?

3. Are budgets adequate to accomplish my objectives? How are budgets established?

4. Are my creative strategies compatible with my marketing plan?

5. Do I have weekly, monthly, and seasonal plans for such activities in place?

6. Are customer service levels satisfactory? What weaknesses exist?

7. Are mail and telephone sales programs compatible with my overall marketing plan?

8. Are my after-sales delivery programs, if any, compatible with my marketing plan?

9. Are my credit programs cost-effective? Should credit options be added or deleted?

10. Is the breadth and intensity of market coverage satisfactory for growth?

▲

you decide if the price is right and the customer profile matches yours.

The media mix you choose depends on the size and type of your store, the part of the market to be served, media availability, advertising budget, and other factors. A jewelry store specializing in engagement and wedding rings might concentrate on ads on radio stations broadcasting music to young adults, or on direct mailings to young adults such as graduating seniors at local colleges, and to organizations composed of this group. A small gift basket business might send direct mail to businesses and college dorms. Cable TV may work well for sellers of furniture, cars, and computers.

Historically, newspapers have been the primary advertising outlets for retailers. Though newspaper ads are still used for large sales events such as Black Friday, and traditional newspaper advertisers, such as car dealerships, other media are now playing bigger roles. Finding it hard to compete with warehouse and department stores in the major dailies, small retailers take advantage of suburban and neighborhood weekly and semiweekly newspapers at more reasonable costs and effectiveness. Banner and pay-per-click ads placed on like-minded websites can offer a controlled marketing bill and reach a specific demographic. More detail on this is provided in the "Print and Online Advertising" section below.

tip

According to market research firm, Female Factor, women buy or influence 70 to 80 percent of all consumer purchases. To capture the attention of millennial women focus on two things: inspiring them with social causes related to your products, and communicating to them with images, especially photographs.

Co-Op Advertising

Get your suppliers to work with you in promoting goods. They can send consultants to talk to salespeople, provide demonstrators, and help your advertising efforts by providing camera-ready ad slicks or product illustrations for you to use.

Under certain conditions, some suppliers will pay part of your advertising bill. A cosmetic firm that supplies you with goods, for example, might wish to push a new product. As part of the purchase agreement you negotiate, the cosmetic firm might agree to pay 50 to 100 percent of the cost of a full-page newspaper ad for your store. This enables you to get good newspaper coverage at a discount (or for free); it also permits the vendor to get its product in front of the public at the lower per-column-inch cost for you. Look into negotiating this type of arrangement with your suppliers.

Direct Mail

You want to build a relational database that helps you identify various customer segments for direct mail and service opportunities. Segment customers by zip code, level of spending, buying habits, interests, family size, or other criteria that will enable you to match your offerings to their wants and needs. For example, if a customer has school-age children, you can send that person a mailer on back-to-school supplies.

Direct mail can effectively promote open houses, anniversaries, private sales, seasonal events, preview parties, factory-authorized sales, factory closeouts, or floor sample sales—and can generate significant traffic and sales.

Meticulously maintain customer lists so you can build relationships with your existing clients. When you send them a time-sensitive invitation, deliver a little something extra, like extending the terms of normal financing or offering a gift to the first 50 people who come in. You have to make a strong, sincere offer so you can get people off the internet and out of their homes to see what you have for them.

Print and Online Advertising

You can hire an advertising agency or graphic design firm, pay a publisher to compose an ad for you, hire a freelance professional or student, or create your own online and printed ads. Desktop publishing software comes with most computers, giving people the tools to produce visually attractive, legible promotions—catalogs, fliers, newsletters, ads, posters, mailers, postcards, tent cards (seen on tables in fast-food and other types of restaurants), brochures, sales sheets, gift certificates, coupons, menus, etc. Investing in an inexpensive digital camera will allow you to control the images you use. With planning, the same ad you create for the web can be used for print, and serve as a base for you business cards if you like. Make sure to create your visuals at 300 dots per inch for print and later you can reduce them to 72 dots per inch for the web, but not the other way around. Get some instruction online or through classes at a computer store, community college, or university on how to use desktop-publishing software like Illustrator, InDesign, PhotoShop, and QuarkXpress to produce high-quality pieces.

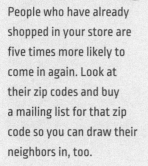

stat fact

People who have already shopped in your store are five times more likely to come in again. Look at their zip codes and buy a mailing list for that zip code so you can draw their neighbors in, too.

Take a look at what your competitors are doing. What are your prospects reading, watching, and listening to? Gather clues of style, color, language, and values from popular culture and apply them to your print materials. A lot of the research has already been done for you. Match the medium, type, content, and style of print advertising to your audience.

Be sure to tell your salespeople about the theme and placement of ads so they will be prepared when customers phone and come in. Post the print ads in the store for quick reference. Put the ad in an acrylic frame on your countertop with the headline, "As Seen On TV" (or whatever). You can also get extra mileage out of any publicity you've received by displaying it in your store, noting, "As featured in" and the name of the publication.

Website: A Must-Have in Retailing

The internet is the great equalizer, making it possible for you to reach across town, the United States, or the world, if you like. There are several ways you can go about marketing your products and services on the internet. Every retailer we interviewed for this book is marketing his or her services on the internet.

Having a website is very important. It will give your customers a place to go anytime they want to learn more about your business, or in the case of Urban Remedy and Patina, complete their own sales transactions, whether the stores are open or closed. You can create your own site with Adobe Muse (muse.adobe.com), IM Creator (imcreator.com), SquareSpace (squarespace.com) or PrestaShop (prestashop.com). To make sure you design for the most traffic flow of your target demographic, pick up a copy of *Ultimate Guide to Optimizing Your Website* by Jon Rognerud (Entrepreneur 2014). Hiring a professional designer through a word-of-mouth, an advertising agency, or design firm is a smart thing to do, too. After all, this is your company's reputation we're talking about. Your site needs to be polished, highly functioning, and well thought out with user-friendly options.

The essential elements of a great website, according to retailers and internet surfers, are:

- Store name, location, and contact information
- Product or service descriptions with prices and fees
- Pictures of products, or pictures of services being performed
- Ease of ordering online with clear instructions
- Lines carried or clients served

stat fact

Restaurant marketers who are still using old-fashioned means of advertising had better get with the program. According to the Pew Research Center, 51 percent of consumers use websites to investigate restaurants and their menus for making dining choices.

- Company background
- Store policies regarding payment, returns, repairs, and warranties
- Links to your blog and social engagement sites
- Links to related, interesting resources
- Constantly updated information that entertains or informs the visitor

So why do you need a website when you already have a storefront? Or in the case of Urban Remedy, which does most of its sales online, why does Neka Pasquale need storefronts when her website brings in 90 percent of the revenue? *Stores* Magazine's 2015 Forward Focused Report reviews the intertwining of online with face-to-face interactions, pointing out that customers get their daily dose of socializing by stopping in the store to pick items up. Discussing nutrition topics, health challenges, how the juice cleanse is going, and simply talking about the joy of food bring clients and employees together in the social scene that takes place in Uban Remedy storefronts. Many of these topics are featured on Urban Remedy's social media channels, which customers also participate in so these communication methods thrive off of each other.

As consumers incorporate online shopping into their daily lives, they will use the channel in more conventional ways, purchasing in more discretionary categories like apparel and food. This "normalization" of online shopping will drive total online revenues higher, according to Chain Store Age, but it will also reduce the amount of incremental and impulse buying. In a shopping environment with no physical barriers, online customers will continue to purchase items they could not otherwise buy—a garment not available in a local store, a hard-to-find book, etc.

Because Murphy doesn't have a standard brick-and-mortar location, his site serves as his representative. He began creating his high-end handbags from his home in Los Angeles. His business relocated to New York and has evolved and grown. The Matt Murphy Design streamlined website profiles his brand which now includes a range of professional creative services, from branding and marketing initiatives to graphic, interior, and product design. This would be difficult to showcase in an actual store. The site's slick style creates a seamless transition from one discipline to the next.

Make your site a rich experience. In addition to order information, extend your brick-and-mortar line by testing market acceptance of additional items. You can give background information on the product, its materials, manufacturer, or users. Profile employees and satisfied customers. Have a treasure hunt, quiz, game, or contest. Make it entertaining.

Springfield, New Jersey's Winelibrary.com sports a wonderland of valuable information, purchasing options, and links to other forums. The section offering 90+ point wines describes wines in an elegant language of color, flavor, "mouth feel," texture, and emotion, for the hedonistic reader to salivate over.

The way people will find you on the internet is by using search engines. Google, Yahoo!, and Bing.com are just a few of the thousands of search engines and directories web surfers can use. You need to have your site listed with as many of these search engines as you can. You can do it yourself, hire someone to do it for you, or hire a service like SubmitExpress.com for about $30 to register your site on hundreds of search engines.

You can link to other sites to increase traffic to and from these resources. Have major suppliers refer customers to you as the local provider of their brand, and in return, provide a link on your site to theirs. Linking is a great form of advertising for you because it's free and it refers people to you right away. Think about businesses with complementary products or services, organizations for your industry, directories, and general consumer sites. These partnerships might include either click-through or revenue-sharing agreements that give companies incentives to push your products. To make arrangements to link your site with someone else's, speak to the webmaster, company president, or marketing director. Another way to advertise on the internet is by buying banner advertising.

For more information on starting an ecommerce website, read *Entrepreneur's Start Your Own eBusiness*.

tip

Promotions have a dual purpose: to sell new merchandise in large volume and to sell regular or old merchandise, thus keeping inventory clean of irregular, outdated, or shopworn items.

In-Store Promotions

While advertising drives traffic to a store, the store closes the sale one-on-one with the shopper. Most successful promotions require considerable planning. A good promotion is based on good merchandise. Sometimes the merchandise is already in inventory, but many times you must make special purchases. The most common promotions include warehouse sales, parking lot sales, pre-Christmas promotions, back-to-school sales, inventory-reduction sales between seasons, anniversary promotions, moonlight sales, post-Thanksgiving sales, summer clearances, and end-of-the-month sales.

Merchandise displayed in high-traffic "power" aisles grabs shoppers' attention and usually yields higher sales than the same merchandise placed in a side aisle. Therefore, savvy merchants use these aisles to display special values, seasonal merchandise, and/or price-sensitive items.

Sales promotion is an important part of your marketing strategy. To manage the costs, you must establish an objective the same way you do for advertising, pricing, and distribution. The objectives for each promotion should be clearly stated, such as trial, repeat purchase, reducing stock levels, a shift in buying peaks, combating competition, and so on. Then select the appropriate promotional technique and dates the promotion will run, and make sure to evaluate the results once the promotion is over.

Assign dates and responsibilities for all aspects of executing the plan. In addition to briefing your staff beforehand, set target performance levels and offer incentives for exceeding goals. Don't forget to establish a procedure for collecting the required data for follow-up and evaluation. Spending must be analyzed and categorized by type of activity, such as special packaging, special point-of-sale material, special labels, extra product, loss of margin through price reductions, etc.

Special Pricing

The most obvious in-store promotion is special pricing (price reduction). Coupons, vouchers, and competitions with cash prizes are ways of attracting customers. Premium promotions (e.g., two-for-one offers), free gifts, and trade-in programs are some direct promotions of goods you can use.

Visual Merchandising

Thrill your customers with exciting merchandise vistas. The exterior of your store may help attract visitors, but it is the interior décor and atmosphere, combined with the assistance and attitude of salespeople, that convert prospects into buyers. The interior of your store, like the exterior, must be compatible with your products and services and the image you are trying to portray.

Do not overcrowd displays. Crowded displays can confuse customers and may prevent them from spotting something they would buy if it were more visible. Making a choice among three similar products is easier than among six.

Group displays into obvious categories, and if your customers are generally repeat ones, do not constantly move products to different locations since that can irritate some people. This is particularly true for grocery store, office supply store, and drugstore customers.

Arrange displays throughout the store to facilitate the shopper's journey from one area to another. Give new offerings star treatment by showcasing them either in window displays or in a prominent place near the front door. Start designing the display area by choosing a focal point for the display, such as a key piece of fishing equipment or a grouping of skin-care products. Know your merchandise so you know how to combine items into displays that make sense.

Update displays as needed to reflect items sold out or discontinued lines. Plan to change each display of large items, such as furniture or home theater suites, a minimum of four times a year with the change in season. Some markets require monthly or weekly rotations, such as music, books, food, and fashion.

You can give your store a fresh look and pump up sales just by giving items a new location. Sometimes moving a collection to a wall display or to a pedestal and spotlighting it will attract the attention it deserves. Retailers suggest accessorizing furniture and clothing to give you extra marketing mileage.

Public Relations

The effective use of public relations can increase the awareness, understanding, and acceptance of your business. Media contacts should be nurtured and utilized at every opportunity. Using public relations to your advantage is an important part of your marketing plan. Don't forget about it!

Well-prepared press releases and media kits containing photographs and background information on your company are good ways to generate media interest and articles on your new season's product line, your new employee or customer service, or a special event. When someone associated with your business is taking part in community projects or supporting a charity, let the media know. The media are often interested in human-interest stories, and the benefit to you is in keeping your company in the public eye and enhancing the relationship between your business and the community.

Getting coverage in the media is free advertising and can reach many more prospective buyers than you could hope to on your own. How do you obtain radio, TV, newspaper, and magazine coverage? Write a press release with strong descriptions and relevance to the audience. Send your press packet to the media that your prospective customers rely on for information.

aha!

Ask manufacturers and distributors to work with you in creating sizzle for your store and their merchandise. Ceiling banners and interactive media capture consumers' attention. Many manufacturers and distributors will give or sell you videos, memorabilia, and artifacts related to their brand or selling season theme to create the proper atmosphere in which to sell their merchandise.

Social
Network
Marketing

Social networking is much more than social. It can position you as an authority in your field and coax your audience to depend on your wisdom. With a little dedication, creativity, and knowledge it can be an incredible tool, not only for growing your business, but also changing the way others perceive you. Simple assignments online can multiply your relevant, real-life connections, manifesting in customers and recognition.

EMarketer's 2015 U.S. Digital Users Q1 Complete Forecast reports 259.7 million internet users primarily access social media sites with mobile devices. Over 60 percent use Facebook, 29.9 percent Instagram, and 20.4 percent Twitter.

The Perfect Site for You

The appropriate pairing of social networking style with your particular business image is important. If your laundromat is known for its family-friendly movies, which run while patrons wash their clothes, you can connect to your biggest audience (parents) by thinking about their interests. Many parents want to know about the content of movies before they let their children watch them. Creating or joining an online "G-rated movie" community on Flixter.com, a social film review site, might be a productive way to grow your laundromat's visibility with parents in your community.

Different social networking sites cater to different demographics. Online research firms help find the age, sex, hobbies, location, race, and even political interests of users, for accurate positioning of your debut. These statistics are always changing so it's a good idea to do quick searches biannually. Some networking sites, such as Facebook.com, do all the work for you within their site. Their highly specific, ad-serving

Networking Site Types

Notice the different qualities of each site and the demographics they appeal to below. Imagine the types of businesses that may benefit from networking on each them and study the qualities of their users. This list is by no means comprehensive, but includes some of the major players in social networking and will give you a good base to start with.

Stats compiled by Pew Research Center, Nielsen, and Burst Media were turned into an infographic by Alex Hillberg that you can view here: reviews.financesonline.com/most-popular-social-media-sites-review. View more stats at Digital Insights (blog.digitalinsights.in/social-media-users-2014-stats-numbers/05205287.html). Alexa (alexa.com), SEMrush (semrush.com), Compete (compete.com), and Quantcast (quantcast.com) are more great places to keep an eye on what your audience is doing. The free tool mentioned in Chapter 4, Google Trends, can help you hone your research further, with keyword geographic searches.

Networking Site Types, continued

Facebook.com, a social information and image sharing site

○ 890 million daily active users
○ 76 percent of women use it
○ 66 percent of men use it
○ 61 percent of teens are users
○ 350 million images are sent daily
○ 745 million mobile daily active users

Tumblr.com, and information sharing site

○ 54 percent of women use it
○ 46 percent of men use it

Pinterest.com, a special interest, hobbyist, image-sharing site

○ 33 percent of women use it
○ 80 percent of users are female
○ 158 is the average number of pins from female users
○ 8 percent of men use it
○ 23 percent of users tune in at least once per day

Instagram.com, an image lifestyle sharing site

○ 20 percent of women use it
○ 15 percent of men use it
○ 23 percent of teens consider it their favorite social network

LinkedIn.com, a business and professional network and referrals hub

○ 187 million monthly active users
○ 19 percent of women use it
○ 24 percent of men use it
○ 39 million students and college grads use it
○ 41 percent of visits are from mobile phones

Meetup.com, a special interest groups connector, for meeting in person

○ 20.09 million members
○ 62 percent of users are women
○ 38 percent of users are men

Networking Site Types, continued

Meetup.com, continued

○ 181,411 Meetup, special interest groups

○ 378,853 monthly Meetup events

Twitter.com, an announcement platform with limited word capacity

○ 78 percent use mobile phones to access

○ 46 percent of users Tweet at least once a day

○ 18 percent of women use it

○ 17 percent of men use it

Yelp.com, a social user business review site

○ 139 million monthly visitors

○ 64 percent of searches are from mobile devices

○ 485 million daily phone calls to businesses via Yelp's mobile apps

○ 39 percent of users are age 18–34

○ 37.3 percent have incomes over $100K

Snapchat, an image exchange site on which items vanish after ten seconds

○ 30 million monthly active users

○ 70 percent of users are female

○ 5 percent of selfies shared on social media are from Snapchat

○ 700 million photos are sent each day

Vine.com, a social video marketing site

○ Over 40 million users

○ 3 of 5 most retweeted Vines are from musicians

○ 5 Vines are turned into tweets on Twitter every second

system allows advertisers to sort and target their users by demographic, by placing your ad on the pages of like minds.

Many of these sites are community-based platforms and attract like-minded users with photos, ads, videos, special interest articles, and information. Active online socialization multiplies one's fan base, members, and friends. Creating a web presence with great online manners, receptivity, and linking oneself to specific special interest groups can expand your retail market.

Finding Your Tribe

Let's say millions of Facebook.com, Twitter.com, and LinkedIn.com users are talking about van living. If you start chatting about your van outfitting service with your exact demographic, they'll simply know you exist. Taking it to the next level is easy, but requires more thought than just hammering away on the keys with virtual friends. You'll need to invest time in cultivating relationships online, the same way you would in the actual world. If you can discipline yourself to participate online a few times a week, consistently putting forth helpful remedies, tips, and friendly chatter, you'll earn loyal followers, which sometimes turn into clients. There are no guarantees and in the beginning it may seem purely like a labor of love, but many entrepreneurs have completely changed their lives by taking social networking very seriously.

There are more than a hundred large social networking sites each with their own unique audiences. Do a little research to make sure you aren't trying to sell men's health products to the Pinterest.com crowd, whose majority of users are women. Reddit.com and Youtube.com have a higher percentage of male users and the LinkedIn.com crowd collectively has more expendable income and higher educations. Use your imagination.

In 2008 North Carolina mom Brandi Temple used Facebook to show off funky clothing she'd made for her daughters with an old sewing machine and began selling them on eBay. Starting the exposure of her creations on Facebook prompted buyers to post photos and stories of their own kids in Temple's clothes. Gradually her page achieved one million likes, she switched to selling through Facebook, and today her company, Lolly Wolly Doodle (lollywollydoodle.com), brings in over $10 million annually. Temple credits part of her success to conversing with followers and fans on Facebook. In a 2015 ABC News interview Temple advised entrepreneurs to "adapt their social media plans to what their customers are already doing, be true to their brands, and not be afraid to try new things."

Six Assignments to Get You Started

In order to get you going with your new marketing medium, try these six simple steps to getting started.

1. *List your business on Yelp.com complete with photos and a detailed description.* If you focus on stellar customer service people will naturally review you in a positive light and you'll be found more quickly in online searches.

   Do not ask people to review you. Reviewers with only one review (yours) look fake to hardcore Yelpers. Yelp.com users look for sincerity and authenticity. They get to know one another and come to rely on specific user's reviews to match their own tastes. Yelpers choose favorite reviewers and follow their advice on which restaurants, auto mechanics, or ophthalmologists to patronize, and who has the best products and why.

aha!

Do word searches for your audience and then expound on them for synonyms.

You can see how it would benefit your business to engage in discussions with users. Say a reviewer writes about the van you designed for him and has been waiting for one more part to come in to complete the project. Perhaps he is upset your employee took two days to call him back and writes something like, "The owner is unresponsive." If you write review responses, many people will see them. This is a great opportunity to offer a sincere apology, invite the customer to experience a perk on the house or simply clear up the misunderstanding. You also let the customer know that you will deal appropriately with additional employee training to ensure their next experience will be 100 percent. You've just gotten some great feedback that you may not have from someone in person.

2. *Create a business or "fan" page on Facebook.com complete with detailed information and photos.* Start conversations with like-minded users online. Use your growing visibility to announce events, specials, hot news in your industry, and ways your business helps the community. There are many user-friendly features on Facebook, which will aid you with its many uses.

3. *Give a professional, informational tutorial in your area of expertise once a week and post it on YouTube.com linking it to keywords so other users can find you.* If you make your videos funny, charming, or unusual and begin to use that as your brand, users will start to follow and engage with you online, which translates to the spotlight shining on your business.

tip

Choose established Meetups with lots of members and advertise early with reminders often for your event. If you start your own Meetup.com group for a small fee, or choose those with fewer members to be involved with, be prepared to wait longer for people to catch on to your events.

You'll also need an inexpensive video camera and some moxie to start your YouTube celebrity. Know your material before posting.

4. *Join Meetup.com.* Meetups are a great way to meet very specific hobbyists, collectors, professionals, and students of many topics. Most of their events are free or low cost. Your raw vegan food company is begging to be known by all the hungry folks in the sub groups: Veggie Cyclists, Vegetarians for Animals, Macrobiotics, and Raw Vegan Foodies.

5. *Start Instagram and Pinterest boards with inspirational images for your followers with linked resources*. Hold a contest for the most breathtaking, or funny images in your field.

6. *Create baby-boomer-specific ads for blogs expressly for seniors, such as suddenlysenior.com*. Don't forget this collectively wealthy group, who are looking to try new products and services as discussed in Chapter 2. Offer to host a senior photo portrait event with funky backdrops, costumes, a raffle, and a singles match-up dance contest or speed dating theme with another like-minded business.

Tips for Looking Good Online

- *Stay positive*. Don't respond to anyone who uses inappropriate language or verbal abuse on your pages. Eliminate correspondence with unreasonably negative users quickly and discreetly and move on.

- *Respond to critiques of your business by thanking the reviewer and telling her or him what how you plan to improve*. Then openly invite the reviewer back for another chance to prove yourself. Second, positive reviews by the same person make you look good.

- *Don't get sloppy*. Use correct grammar and punctuation and keep your presence as polished online as you would in your store.

- *Interact and respond daily*. If four days go by before you respond to that question on Twitter about the best rising agent for delicious popovers, users will pay their attention to another baking expert who gives them more immediate gratification. Keep responses brief and friendly to maximize your time or, as

---

Don't Fear the Virtual Whiner

Whining and venting online are easy—the same way over-inflated, emotional outbursts that you would probably never say in person are easy from the safety of your car. Some retailers are afraid to make themselves vulnerable online, but habitual reviewers know the difference between an unreasonable whiner and a thorough critic by reading that person's other reviews. Negative feedback is a chance for you to listen to the detailed wants of your customers, hone your service, and even keep an eye on your employees.

▲

your popularity grows you will quickly become overwhelmed and have to hire an assistant just to respond to queries. Twitter.com is great for quick, to-the-point communication because of the limit on number of characters.

- *Share just enough knowledge to keep them coming back, without telling all that you know.* Post freebies and give-away recipes that you won't be using in your next cookbook as well as tips on kitchen safety.

aha!

Purchasing Facebook ad space is inexpensive and makes you visible to the right people by floating your ad on the pages of users like you. You can buy ads as inexpensive as 1 cent per click.

Develop Your Online Personality

The more relevant information you share on your networking pages, the better people will get to know you and your business. Some of the ways you can do this are with photos, news, special deals, and contests.

- Post as many relevant and artful photos and videos as you can. Snap photos of your new silicon oven mitts and tell readers why you recommend them. There are many inexpensive digital cameras that work well for quick downloads and sharing. Some have bare bones video capabilities built right in, such as the Kodak EasyShare, which retails for around $99.

- Link to a photo album on Shutterfly.com of your most recent trip to a farmer's or open air produce market with its luscious rows of vivid vegetables and share little-known facts about the nutritional value of each. Give viewers a quick shopping list of the "must haves" for every great health nut.

- Share current news quips in your industry by posting links to pertinent stories and your opinions on them. This will open conversations between viewers and pull their connections into the mix, thus multiplying your audience.

- Pair specials on products in your store with online contests, such as: Help me come up with a name for my delicious new juice! First prize wins a dozen a free four day cleanse and discount on a weekend retreat!

- Create new surveys and post their results for your viewers with Surveymonkey. com. They can be educational, unusual, or just plain amusing. For example: "Plant eaters have younger vital organs in medical studies," or "85 percent of men report feelings of love after kale." Remember your target audience and demographic for each social networking site you choose.

Frugal Advertising, Big Rewards

Charlotte Cozzetto, manager of Ethique Nouveau, in Minneapolis, Minnesota, uses "eco-networking" to both market her business and find products for her ethical wares boutique. She has never paid for advertising, yet her recognition is growing and growing.

Etsy.com, a favorite source, carries handmade artisan crafts sometimes made from recycled materials. Artists from all over the country make it an important resource for Charlotte to find beautiful merchandise for her store. Ecorazzi.com, a green gossip blog, refers her to the select, preferred products of her audience.

Cozzetto uses Meetup.com, Facebook.com, and her EthiqueNouveau.com blog to announce charitable events held in her store, such as disaster relief bake sales. Friends donate baked products to sell and the proceeds go to charity. The added benefit to opening her store as a venue for fundraising is that, "If you can get people into the store, they usually buy something," says Charlotte.

> **tip**
>
> To get more visibility for your efforts, link all of your accounts and website together so that the cross traffic will multiply your efforts.

What Is It Really all About?

Though the explosive potential of social media prompted Gary and his brother, A.J. Vaynerchuk, to create the innovative branding venture, VaynerMedia.com, his underlying sentiment is clear: Strengthening human connections are the ultimate goal. Social media is merely a conduit to help achieve it.

The uses for marketing using social networking are endless and evolving exponentially by the hour. It's a good idea to take at least one seminar annually to stay on top of the magnetic ways it can grow your business.

Customer Service

The century of the consumer has arrived. Customers have love-hate relationships with shopping, and they know they can make or break a business. If you recognize that it's your job to make shopping as pleasurable and painless as it can be, the odds of your succeeding in retail are good.

Paco Underhill of New York's Envirosell wrote a book called *What Women Want: The Global Market Turns Female Friendly* (Simon and Schuster, 2010). Envirosell is a human behavior-focused global research and consulting firm (PacoUnderhill.com). Retailers are heeding the wisdom offered in the pages of Paco's book, shaping marketing methods to women first. Because women are more demanding, designing for them first will satisfy the standards of both men and women. As they consider what Paco says they crave—cleanliness, control, safety, and consideration—they attract the powerful female dollar. You may have noticed from the social media stats that women lead in usage of those platforms on most of the major sites except for LinkedIn.

Customer-Centric Objectives

To distinguish yourself from the competition, you will have to offer something besides reasonable prices. That something could be as simple as a quick, easy, pleasant, or exciting shopping experience. Your goal must be your customer's goal. That means you must find out what the customer wants—not just profile the demographics of the customer you want. From store concept to order delivery, you want to weave the needs and wants of customers into your store's policies and procedures so that satisfying them is part of your business's DNA.

When the first person steps up to your cash register to make the first purchase, you'll begin learning who your customers are. Until then, who your store serves is just an educated guess. You want to learn why certain people buy from you, their likes and dislikes, and their interests and lifestyles. By keeping your fingers on the pulse of consumer preferences, you can plan your inventory and sales strategies to get the most from your relationships.

tip

Host your own online sales event around a holiday with lots of in store and social media hype pre-event. Comscore reported in 2014 a 32 percent jump in online sales on Thanksgiving Day, a 26 percent jump on Black Friday, and over $2 billion spent online on Cyber Monday.

Information Collection Is Key

There are several ways you can collect information to develop customer loyalty. One is by setting up shopping services and gathering personal information for creating cosmetics, travel, wardrobe, and technology profiles of your customers. You can also collect valuable information through warranty and service registration, and through continuity programs such as newsletters, order-replenishment programs, and reminder notices.

Two more ways of profiling customers are by conducting an online customer survey and having visitors sign a guest book in the store with their comments.

Getting to know your store regulars is relatively easy. These are the people who come in frequently and you get to know them through casual conversation and regular contact. You can strengthen these relationships by inviting them to invitation-only events like meet-the-author nights, special VIP sales, and previews of the new season's merchandise.

Since your goal is to convert shoppers to buyers and buyers to loyal customers, you want to increase not only the frequency of purchases but also the size of each transaction. Here is where your computer system can really help. It's your best tool for developing a detailed profile of each customer's purchasing activity. You can draw conclusions about your clientele, which will be helpful in developing one-on-one services as well as in merchandising.

Customer Relationship Management

Customer relationship management (CRM) is about building old-fashioned relationships using today's technology. CRM is shifting the business from being merchandise-oriented to being customer-centric. It changes your buying process from decision making based on historic results to looking at your best customers and understanding what they buy and why they buy it. CRM involves integrating marketing, sales, service, and other functional areas that affect your relationship with people. Instead of individual departments and salespeople keeping customer information to themselves, it is pooled in a common location.

CRM is growing in popularity because this integrated approach helps retailers discover what motivates shoppers and what items they're inclined to buy. This information can help you determine which shoppers are the most profitable, which are truly loyal, and which require additional attention.

Laying the groundwork for CRM begins by capturing data and using technology to access and massage the information. Basic information such as sales figures and customer names and addresses has value, but CRM takes your relationship with customers to a higher level. Whether the customer is a saver or a spender, how many children are at home, and where else he or she likes to shop are the nuances of the customer's character that lie at the heart of CRM. The more you know about your customers, the more personalized your service can be.

To accomplish the goal of personalized service, you need to apply the knowledge you have at various customer touch points—in-store visits, telephone calls, customer service, direct mail pieces, catalogs, your website, email, billings, off-site events, efaxes—to generate repeated positive experiences.

It is much easier and less costly to set up an information-gathering and analysis system from Day One than to try to do it later. Building positive experiences has to

Getting to Know You

Here are some quick and easy ways to find out what your customers are thinking, saying, and doing:

1. Read Yelp reviews of businesses like yours.

2. Ask front-line personnel (customer service representatives, cashiers, and salespeople) what shoppers are saying.

3. Budget for two sample offerings of your product to potential blogger promoters per month. Read what they write and watch their video blogs.

4. Use customer satisfaction surveys with lots of blank spaces for write-in comments. Prompt customers who shop your goods online to do this after a purchase. Keep it short or they won't complete it.

5. Interview customers who have recently given their business to another company.

6. Look at the Pinterest, Instagram, and Tumblr pages of your target audience, and your actual clients. Study what is important to them.

7. Interview recently lost prospects. Why did they not buy what you have to offer?

8. Use customer focus groups.

9. Read newspaper, magazine, and industry reports.

be imbedded in your company's culture. Whether you use one of the many CRM software packages on the market or a simpler contact management system, ensure that your operating procedures track customer value and profitability, identify risky and unprofitable customer groups, profile lost customers, and measure customer satisfaction.

Listen to the Right Customers

You cannot be all things to all people. Your programs and processes need to be designed with the paying customer in mind. This person is not always the most vocal. Combine high technology with the personal touch, and you'll get a more accurate picture of what customers are willing to pay you for.

Listen to the customer who receives value from your goods and services, who generates demand and a market for your business. Go beyond analyzing current customers and identify noncustomers who are members of market segments you want to capture. Technology makes it possible to do this. By taking a look at the characteristics of a profitable segment and seeing if another customer segment shares characteristics with this desirable group, you can identify potentially high-profit customers within your base.

In some cases, the cost of meeting a customer group's needs is too high. Sometimes the answer to a low-profit segment is to stop attracting that group by deleting the group from your mailing list, wording your advertisements differently, or advertising your promotions in narrowly targeted publications or locations.

You may also want to vary the level of service provided to different customer groups based on their profitability. One way to do that is to provide consistent levels of service to everyone, but vary the fees for that service based on the profitability of the customer. One example is home delivery. You could offer free home delivery based on order frequency or amount of goods ordered; customers who order infrequently or in small amounts could pay a nominal fee for delivery.

Another approach is to provide extraordinary service only to the most desirable customers. Low-value customers get only their basic must-have needs met while high-value customers get high-value services to attract, delight, and retain them. Frequent shoppers may collect points that entitle them to special events, limited offerings, or other benefits.

Promise Only What You Can Deliver

Your customers' expectations are often based on their experiences with other retailers, both brick-and-mortar and etailers. You must maintain a balance between what customers value and what you can actually deliver. That's a tall order. Exceeding those expectations is how the most successful retailers manage loyalty and attract a greater share of the market.

The approach you take depends on where you are and what you need to do. If your strategy is to be the low-cost provider and you want to compete on the basis of price as a commodity vendor, you may only need to meet minimum expectations. On the other hand, if you want to distinguish yourself as a high-service, premium provider, you will want to exceed expectations. Either way, you need to find out what expectations your customers have.

"I severely undercharged for the first house I built on contract," explains Jay Shafer of Four Lights Houses in California. "Luckily, the client saw what was involved and how hard I was working and paid me double what I had originally charged him. On the second house, I also underbid. On both of those projects I was pretty much just working for minimum wage and actually made more at my grocery store job.

▲

Born to Mobile Shop

Some shopaholics have crossed over to mobile use to satisfy the need to consume. Here are some useful facts about who is using throwing money at retail with their mobile devices from comScore's 2014 first quarter State of Retail Report:

❍ Men shop slightly less than women online

❍ Millennials spend more money online than any other age group: about $2000 per year.

❍ One in four mobile shoppers is over age 55

❍ More than half of ecommerce shoppers live in households with incomes over $75K and 40 percent are in households with over $100K

Thankfully, the second client also stepped in and offered a few extra thousand dollars to sustain my business."

Wine and social media guru, Gary Vaynerchuk, recognizes that though his infectious enthusiasm ripples positivity, he is also an over-promiser, through and through. "My intentions are so pure that I want to over-deliver for people." Vaynerchuk adds that he has since curtailed the negative effects of those kinds of actions.

You must align your service promises with your ability to deliver. For example, if you promise zero defects in the rooms you rent at your bed-and-breakfast, guests will expect you to deliver. That means you must set in place processes that guarantee there will be functioning TVs, clean bathrooms, and working air-conditioning before a guest checks in. Providing zero defects is the minimum expectation.

Loyalty and Retailing

Purchasing decisions are very much influenced by discounts and savings. The National Retail Federation research found that 65 to 95 percent of sales for some supermarkets are from loyalty member programs. Fifty-three percent of food retailers offer loyalty programs, 75 percent of their customers use them weekly, and 88 percent use them once a month.

You can use frequency marketing to identify, maintain, and increase the dollars spent by your best customers. If you identify those customers and methodically cultivate their loyalty, they'll give you their business repeatedly and refer others to you.

Services that Customers Value

Stephanie Covart Meyerring will continue to hold live shows with famous bands in her store and give a way tickets to random lucky customers. Jay Shafer is developing a tiny house village proposed to open in 2015, where the crowd who has many legal pitfalls to overcome to live in the wee homes can feel comfortable. Drawings of this special place show wholesome homes lined up neatly in rows, taking up very little footprint for the earth conscious. Utilities are hooked up just like at an RV park and each home would have a very tiny utility bills because they are so efficient. It's a way for people to spend money and time on the things that really matter.

How to Provide Exceptional Customer Service

It's fairly easy to get people to visit your store once. In Chapter 12, you learned a number of ways to attract consumers. This chapter focuses on how to keep their business. Exceptional customer service is what it takes to get them to come back again and again. Meeting this standard begins with friendly service. It is the most effective promotion your business will ever have. For some customers, you'll need to be a knowledgeable source of information. For others, you'll be a sounding board. Whatever your role, you'll want to be caring, concerned, reliable, and trustworthy.

tip

Customer service is more than personal selling. It's opening on time, making sure merchandise is easily accessible, having enough baskets and carts at the entrance, clearly labeling shelves and aisles, adequate staffing, and checking shoppers out quickly and efficiently.

A Warm Welcome

Customers will frequent your business if you make them feel important. Shoppers entering Electric Fetus in Minneapolis feel the love. "It's not always about the sale, but about your customer having a positive experience at your establishment," says Stephanie. "Listen to your customers, be creative, and create a community." Retailers suggest training your salespeople in the art of conversation and attentiveness. You want your employees to be able to answer questions about how to use or maintain a product, where it comes from, different things a customer can do with it, and what the warranty says. People with a positive attitude and the authority to do what is necessary to make the customer happy will help increase your sales.

Attentiveness

Look at customers when they enter your store and say hello, asking them if you can help them find something in particular. This will tell you what mission they are on. If they're "just browsing," smile and let them know you are there to answer any questions and continue your work. Since a lot of people like self-service, don't hover and interfere with the customer's shopping. Give him or her space and some time, and then approach them again to begin a conversation by making a comment on the merchandise they're handling or pointing out something interesting about the store.

Keith Covart remembers learning a customer service technique that he's now concentrating on implementing at Electric Fetus in Minneapolis. "I went to a Metro IBA seminar and heard about a very popular, tourist-oriented sandwich shop that requires its employees to keep eye-contact and conversation going the whole time they build the customer's sandwich. I started noticing that the clerks in my shop with the highest sales had lots of eye contact and conversations with customers. That also helps prevent shoplifting, so it's become something I'm trying to encourage more of in my employees."

Creature Comforts

Comfort is a service you can easily offer. Retail analysts have discovered that, with attention to a few important details, the dressing room area can be an effective closing tool. To encourage sales, make sure that the place where customers try on clothes has adjustable, flattering lighting and ample room to turn around in and to park a stroller. Remember that most consumers shop in pairs, so don't forget the companion. Have a chair or place for the adult or child to sit. When people have a chance to try something on and do not feel rushed, they are more inclined to buy, whether you're selling jewelry, makeup, shoes, or clothing.

tip

Think of customers as your guests. You want to make their time in your store as relaxing and enjoyable as possible. Studies show that the longer customers are in your store, the more they buy—provided that they have a basket or cart and a helpful salesperson ready to ring up purchases.

While children may not be your target audience, your prime customers with children appreciate the courtesies you provide for them. With the growth of single-parent and dual-earner, two-parent families, adults taking their children shopping is a frequent occurrence, so you'll want to address these people's needs. Have a kids' corner with some children's books and safe toys, maybe display monitor playing children's movies, or a storyteller at scheduled times. Many restaurants give crayons and coloring pages to little guests and then hang up the completed artwork by the cash register.

Waiting for a meal or in line is annoying for adults, but it's worse for children. When children go "ballistic" while shopping, they often take everyone on the launch pad with them, including other customers in line. Clever retailers have displays, balloons, puzzles, word games, coloring tools, activities, or toys available to distract, entertain, and calm the wee ones so the adults can finish their shopping in relative peace.

Warm, Fuzzy Policies

In a customer-friendly store, shoppers can pay by cash, check, credit card, or debit card. The store's website provides information and ordering opportunities to extend store hours to accommodate a shopper's schedule. The store is open at least one night a week, and hours are extended during busy holiday seasons. The dressing rooms and bathroom are clean, the store is well-lit, and the signage is readable and helpful. Shoppers can take their clothing purchases home on hangers. Gift certificates are presented in a box with a bow, and boxes are available for presents customers want to wrap themselves. Customers are kept informed about the status of their special orders, and rain checks are honored within 30 days. Items are held 24 hours for customers making up their minds about a purchase, and a layaway plan is available. All these policies and services will make customers want to buy from you.

High Value-to-Price Ratio

Employees at a durable-goods store need to provide a higher level of customer service than those at a convenience store. Computers, furniture, carpeting, cars, snowmobiles, and other infrequent purchases are carefully considered and researched by shoppers before they buy. The decision to buy from you will be heavily influenced by delivery and installation capabilities, warranty periods and conditions, credit options, training, and after-sales service. As a rule of thumb, the higher the price to be paid by customers, the more they will want to confirm that they are getting the best value for their investment.

Stillwell House Antiques in Red Bank, New Jersey, isn't one of those shops where you'll find dirty, old furniture of questionable value. Proprietors Ron Knox and Paul

Gallagher maintain an impeccable shop in a historic home, with each room holding merchandise that is properly evaluated and valued. "Our niche is French Country, and we work hard to maintain a fine collection in that area," says Knox. But in addition to its collection, the shop's service policies set them apart. Knox and Gallagher will let customers take a piece home for a few days to determine whether it works with their existing décor or not. They'll consult with buyers to educate them about the pieces and will deliver the piece to the customer's home at no charge. In addition, the store has a 100 percent buy-back guarantee—if the customer wants to sell an antique purchased from Stillwell House at any time, the store will take it back in exchange for 100 percent of the purchase price in store credit. "If the piece was good enough to be sold in our store the first time," says Knox, "we'll welcome it back."

Personalized Shopping

Those who are attracted to platinum-level customer service enjoy the "Personal Shoppers" feature offered at both Wine Library's brick-and-mortar location and website. Wine enthusiasts have the option of a personal appointment with a consultant, as well as informal conversations, to finely tune their purchases.

Saks Fifth Avenue, Nordstrom, and Neiman Marcus have formalized the approach to personalized service into personal shoppers. Independent stores can develop their own models. Invite your customers to sign up for this free service. Place ads, put signs in your store, and/or send a mailing to let people know that you can help them select personal or corporate gifts, furnish a new apartment, or pull together wardrobes for special occasions (a cruise or a honeymoon, for example). Invite an image consultant or savvy traveler to kick off the program with a demonstration of accessorizing a desk or wardrobe, or showing people how to pack. Have special business cards for employees skilled in personal shopping who will develop this special clientele.

fun fact

Stew Leonard's, the hugely successful dairy/grocery in Connecticut, has two basic laws of customer treatment set in stone in the front of his stores. Rule one is, "The customer is always right." Rule two is, "When you think the customer is wrong, refer back to rule one."

Delivery

Florists, dry cleaners, large appliance dealers, pizza outlets, and furniture retailers are usually expected to offer delivery services. However, in these time-scarce times, customers now expect home delivery of groceries, pharmaceuticals, videos—the list goes on. You can provide this customer service in many ways.

If you intend to buy a delivery vehicle, be sure that your truck or van is attractive and clean and advertises your business name, address, telephone number, and web address. Delivery personnel should be neatly dressed (perhaps even wear uniforms), have good driving records, and be trained in customer service. Employees need to know what to do if they are late making a delivery, the customer isn't home, or the customer refuses to accept the order. There is more to "service" than dropping off something on your way home. If you're going to offer delivery, do it right.

If your budget won't allow for buying commercial vehicles, you might use a local courier or taxi service. Or consider cooperating with a noncompeting store to share the cost of deliveries. Many retailers use UPS or an overnight carrier. The Wine Library in Springfield, New Jersey, uses insured UPS and FedEx shipping. Because state laws, weather conditions, and fragility affect perishable wine shipments, The Wine Library has specific, customer service-geared shipping policies, only using insured carriers. The store makes sure customers stay happy by shipping only Monday through Thursday, so that wine never sits on anyone's porch for an entire weekend if they aren't there to accept the package. They recommend express shipping and use a form-fitted, Styrofoam bottle package that protects the wine from weather and handling.

Gift Registry

Gift registries are increasingly popular customer service programs, and they are no longer just for brides. With today's gift registries, presents for any occasion can be bought off a gift registry in stores or online. Grandparents in particular appreciate guidance in selecting toys for children and gifts for hard-to-please teenagers.

Some retailers still use the traditional approach of walking people through their store and writing down the brand, make, model, size, color, or other description of the desired items. Other merchants have printed lists to work from. Some do telephone or videocall consultations and have toll-free phone and efax numbers, while others use a printed or efaxed catalog. The internet marries high technology and old-fashioned TLC with global online access and 24-hour ordering and shipping opportunities. Some other gift registry ideas include putting together a network of stores that offer a range of gift items, including travel packages, charitable donations, and escrow account deposits.

aha!

For gift items, prepare two receipts—one regular receipt for the customer and a second gift receipt with the date of purchase and coded price. Retailers also suggest putting a coded sticker on the inside of the gift box to make returns easy for everyone.

Gift Certificates

Other popular customer services are gift certificates and gift cards. The retailers we interviewed for this book all agreed that no store should be without them. They are an effective way to solve your customers' gift-giving dilemmas, and they bring new customers into your store or to your website. Many certificates are never redeemed, or recipients buy additional merchandise above the gift amount, making the certificates very profitable for retailers. Certificates help customers find "the perfect gift" so people can get exactly what they want.

Retailers advise you to number each gift certificate for tracking purposes. A sample gift certificate can be found below. To make your gift certificate extra special, have an artist create a unique design for your store, print it on card stock, and present it in a box or an elegant envelope.

In the case of gift cards, you can either work with a provider like QuickBooks or Teraco Inc. to purchase pre-printed, pre-programmed cards or you can invest in the equipment you need to produce them onsite. When purchasing the pre-paid cards, you

Gift Certificate

Susie's Fashions

gift certificate

1234 Style Parkway
Peoria, IL 12345
(555) 555-5555

$

To:

From:

Auth. #:

Message: _____

_____

_____

_____

www.susiesfashions.com

generally choose certain denominations and must have a card scanner and POS system programmed to deduct the amount of a customer's purchase from the card. Cards often run about $1 each, plus a monthly fee of $45 to $60 if the provider performs regular management of the program. If you're going to produce the cards onsite, you need a supply of gift cards and coding equipment, which will generally run about $600 to $800.

How to Handle Unhappy Customers

What happens if you don't concentrate on customer service? Research shows that people who have received poor customer service tell an average of 10 others about their bad experience, and 10 percent of those tell 20 other people. Unfortunately, good news does not travel as fast as bad news. Fewer people pass on the good news when they have been treated exceptionally well.

The poor handling of complaints can damage your reputation very quickly. Take everyone seriously, but look at them objectively. What can you learn about your market and your operation? Separate complaints into those about products and their performance and those about customer service. Complaints about products can alert you to vendor problems, advertising glitches, faulty delivery, or quality control problems. Do you have signs up that say, "One-hour photo processing," but rarely deliver in less than three? Are you getting frequent complaints about customers receiving incorrect change? Complaints about customer service should stimulate better training, hiring, and review practices.

Nearly every business encounters difficult customers. How these people are handled can make a big difference in the success or failure of a business. Remember that it takes months to gain a new customer but only seconds to lose one.

Listen and empathize, ask questions, and resolve the problem. Keep in mind that there is always room for improving your relationship with your customers. Always acknowledge the customer's concerns and clearly state how they will be addressed.

Sometimes you'll make mistakes, and at other times you'll encounter someone you can't please despite your best efforts. To resolve a problem, the most effective method is merely to ask the customer what you can do to make things "right." Surprisingly often, many don't want anything other than an apology or a sincere promise to do better next time.

Handling Returns

When a customer wants to return a purchase, you have the opportunity to demonstrate your commitment to customer satisfaction. Listen to the reason for the return,

▲

have a clearly defined policy, and then calmly and pleasantly tell your customer what you can (and in some circumstances, cannot) do for him or her. All three components of dealing with a potentially difficult situation must be present to build trust: Listen, stay calm, and be pleasant. You want your customer to feel confident that you treated him or her fairly and professionally.

Apologize to your customer and take back any defective merchandise sold in your store. Offer store credit when confronted with a questionable return. You'll find the majority of your customers will be honest. Tagging merchandise and the box with a store ID can help reduce incidents of people trying to return something to you that they didn't buy in your store.

For some clearance sales and second-quality merchandise, you may want to have a no-returns policy. For items you do accept back, it is customary to give the customer who purchased with a credit card either a credit card credit, a store credit slip (see page 225) or a merchandise exchange. For purchases of more than $100, pay refunds by check. Some stores have a no-exceptions policy requiring a receipt for large purchases.

You will encounter your share of people who will show up with an unfounded complaint or request for a refund or exchange when it is obvious the item has been used or worn. The retailers we interviewed expressed different ways of handling these inevitable situations.

If you get strong support from your suppliers and are confident that you can send the merchandise back to the source for full credit, you might feel comfortable having a "no questions asked" policy on refunds and exchanges. Small retailers usually aren't able to get that kind of cooperation from suppliers, particularly when they're new and haven't established their value to distributors and manufacturers. Your return policy should reflect the support available to you from your suppliers. Their warranties, service, and return policies are a significant part of how you serve your customers.

You should have a clearly stated policy posted by your checkout stand(s) and printed on the back of your receipts. This will help avoid customer dissatisfaction with the way you do business. Ten to 30-day returns with receipts are standard policies. If you sell or repair any kind of equipment, you may want to set up a loaner program while the customer's computer is being repaired in your shop.

Over time, you're bound to encounter some customers who intend to bully you into accepting an obviously mistreated, old, or worn item. Don't give the stage to dissatisfied customers intent on making a scene. Take them aside and listen politely to their complaint. Then address the facts, offer to do what you feel is fair (or whatever you are authorized to do), and be done with it. You can't please all the people all the time.

In all return situations, retailers say it's important to treat everyone with respect. Some customers you'll like, others you'll tolerate, and in rare circumstances, you will refuse to do business with someone.

Store Credit Slip

Customer name: _____

Address: _____

City: _____ State: _____ Zip: _____

Home phone: _____ Work phone: _____

Date of return: _____

Merchandise description: _____

Amount: _____

Received by: _____

Total credit: _____

Please note that store credits are valid for 12 months.

The Internet Raises Consumer Expectations

The internet gives consumers the power of information immediacy, so they now have greater control over what they buy, what they pay, and from whom they purchase. Customers can shop in many ways—through catalogs, stores, or websites, or all three in the same day. For a retailer to become and remain customer-centered requires constant vigilance. You must continually monitor changing customer and market perceptions.

The pressure for your company to stay in touch with potential customers will only increase as more and more consumers get used to doing business on the internet. In light of these realities, you have no choice but to hone your ability to understand customer needs. If you apply the lessons you learn to your daily business, you can be the leader who sets the standard others will have to meet.

The Customer Is Always Right

Fierce competition means that many of the products you offer will be of comparable quality, price, and value as the products of other local and online retailers. Therefore, the attention you give to the planning and delivery of consistently good levels of customer service will determine your level of success and profitability.

Customers are the final arbiters of your fate. Retailers who are successful over the long run are those that meet the true wants and needs of their customers. You have to deliver this message to every one of your new employees.

Unfortunately, many small retailers refuse to accept the premise that the customer is always right. We all know that the customer is not always right. However, if you want them to patronize your business, you need to treat them as if they are. This begins with you instilling in your employees a real concern for the customer. Get employees to consider how they can go the extra mile for their customers. These are the most effective ways of developing loyal customers. Consumers quickly recognize businesses that have well-trained employees who work together as a team, and they reward those businesses by spending money in those stores and referring others to them.

⦂∷ Risk
Management

Y our business operates every day with the possibility of damage, injury, or loss. Small businesses are generally less able than big businesses to absorb the expenses incurred from risk, so it's important that you understand the kinds of challenges you might encounter in your new business. Initially, there is the threat of disputes with partners, investors, landlords, and employees, and accumulation of debt. Add to that, heightened competition, merchandise shortages, theft, fines, bad debt, collection problems, and being underinsured.

Today's retailers must learn to anticipate legal and/or consumer action. Government agencies are ready to take action if you don't conform to the laws, and customers can turn to consumer groups or the media—or seek legal remedies—if they believe they have been mistreated. Therefore, you must be alert and sensitive to the perceptions and implications of your operation. All those concerned with retailing activities must be aware of federal, state, and local regulations concerning business activities. As with all legal matters, consulting a licensed attorney is advisable.

The Law

You may already be aware of a few basic rules governing retail trade. For example, you are not allowed to ship merchandise that has not been ordered to the consumer, and consumers are likewise not required to pay for items they do not order. Advertising out-of-stock items is forbidden. Retailers must have enough of the advertised item to meet a normal level of demand. Retailers selling items by mail must disclose how long it will take to deliver the items to the consumer. If you cannot deliver the merchandise by the stated time, the buyer can cancel the order. There are a few more regulations you should be familiar with in operating your business.

The Sherman Antitrust Act (1890), the Clayton Act (1914), and the Robinson-Patman Act (1936) were all designed to prevent businesses from engaging in activities that could injure the public or competition. Courts have ruled that retailers cannot pressure manufacturers to refuse to sell to competitors, acquire other firms if the intent is to lessen competition, or conspire to fix prices. Under the Robinson-Patman Act, retailers and manufacturers may face discrimination lawsuits if they charge different prices to different people on unequal terms.

The FTC is an independent administrative agency that determines what business methods, acts, and practices are deceptive or unfair. Most cases brought against businesses by the FTC deal with deceptive advertising and mislabeling of retail products. The agency requires door-to-door sellers to identify themselves as salespeople before entering a person's home, and to allow three days for the customer to decide if he or she wants to cancel an order.

Retailers are sensitive and vulnerable to charges of discrimination of many kinds. Bias because of race, color, creed, sex, national origin, and sometimes age are expressly forbidden by the Civil Rights Act of 1964.

When your business reaches a yearly gross business volume of $500,000, you are subject to the National Labor Relations Act of 1935. Under this law, employees have the right to organize and bargain collectively through a representative of their own choosing without interference from the retailer. The act also states that no employee and no one seeking employment shall be required as a condition of employment to join any company union or to refrain from joining, organizing, or assisting a labor organization of his or her own choosing.

There are several laws that affect your consumer credit policies and practices: the Consumer Credit Protection Act (Truth in Lending), Fair Credit Reporting Act, Fair Credit Billing Act, Equal Credit Opportunity Act, Consumer Leasing Act, and Fair Debt Collection Practices Act.

Insurance

Retailers have diverse needs that go beyond the average small business. Use the "Insurance Coverage Checklist" on page 230 to make sure you have sufficient insurance. Since you can never afford to insure your business 100 percent against all hazards, it's a good idea to think in terms of the two major categories of risk you face: those over which you have little or no control, and those you can control to some degree. Extended coverage covers the property against any direct loss or damage due to such things as explosions, riots, windstorms, hail, aircraft, vehicles, and smoke. Glass insurance protects against replacement of plate-glass windows accidentally or maliciously broken. Vandalism and malicious mischief insurance protects against losses caused by either of these possibilities. Sprinkler insurance covers against leakage, freezing, or breakage of sprinkler installations. Both building and contents should be insured. With the recent floods, hurricanes, and earthquakes many areas of the country have been experiencing, the added expense may be worth it. There is even coverage for rock throwing at windows or exterior signs.

Your business is liable for injuries to customers, employees, and others with whom you do business, either on or off your premises. A comprehensive general liability policy can include liability coverage for defects in merchandise that your business has sold, food poisoning from your restaurant, or bodily injury and property damage caused by an accident in the garage or on the parking lot of your business.

There are many types of crime insurance policies. Fidelity bonds insure against losses due to theft or

tip

Don't skimp on disability insurance. According to the National Association of Insurance and Financial Advisors, if you're between the ages of 35 and 65, your chances of becoming disabled are greater than your chances of dying.

other misappropriations of cash, inventory, or other business property by employees. Money and securities insurance covers losses that occur away from your firm's premises—for example, a robbery of daily receipts being transported to the bank. Robbery insurance covers loss of goods stolen where there is an assault or threat of an assault, as in a holdup. As you might expect, burglary insurance covers the loss of inventory, money, or equipment due to a break-in at your store. Losses of inventory, money, or equipment due to theft or shoplifting by employees, customers, and others can be covered. Surety bonds protect you from losses caused by the failure of others to produce on schedule. If your contractor does not complete your ski outlet in time for the snow season, you may recover your losses from the insurance company.

While insurance against burglary and robbery is available, there are so many restrictions and the cost is so great that most retailers do without it. This usually means that the result of merchandise losses due to such thefts must be passed on to the consumer in the form of higher prices. Higher prices put you at a competitive disadvantage, so see what you can do about safeguarding your store against pilferage. Many retailers buy sophisticated alarm systems, many of which are connected directly to police stations. Solid building construction, metal grids over windows, good outside lighting, and strong locks are also helpful in preventing burglary.

Insurance Coverage Checklist

Discuss your options for insurance coverage with an insurance agent who is familiar with your type of retail business. Checkmark the items you must have now to start up, "X" those you can get later when you have more money, and "O" the type(s) you don't need or that don't apply to your operation.

❑ Automobile	❑ Health
❑ Boiler and machinery	❑ Inventory
❑ Business interruption	❑ Key-person
❑ Business life	❑ Liability
❑ Crime	❑ Power plant
❑ Disability	❑ Property
❑ Earthquake	❑ Sprinkler
❑ Fidelity bonds	❑ Tradesmen's liability
❑ Fire	❑ Unemployment
❑ Flood	❑ Vandalism
❑ General liability	❑ Water damage
❑ Glass	❑ Workers' compensation

A standard fire insurance policy pays you only for losses directly due to fire. Business interruption insurance can reimburse you for loss of earnings that occur until normal business resumes. Things such as payroll costs for key employees, interest expense on a mortgage or rent, and other ongoing expenses can be covered for a specific period of time.

Consult with your insurance agent and get competitive bids for the insurance package that best suits your financial and business situation.

Product-Related Issues

Let's take a look at the goods you're selling. There are the risks associated with the conditions under which they're made, and there are those associated with how they're sold, shipped, handled, used, and presented.

Pricing

Make sure you price your goods honestly and fairly and avoid being guilty of deceptive pricing. There is nothing illegal about trading a customer up to a better quality item when they shop with you, but it is illegal to advertise an item that is not available in the store and to try to sell the customer a higher-priced item instead of the cheaper one promised. For example, if you advertise an AM radio for $19.95 (perhaps as a loss leader) in the hope that customers can be persuaded to purchase an AM/FM boom box at a much higher price, you will be subject to prosecution if you don't have the AM radio to sell to the customer who wants it.

Price comparisons must be honest and legal. If you feature an item in a promotional display at $8.99 claiming that it regularly sold at $14.99, you must have sold the identical merchandise at the $14.99 price in the past. Some department stores have been accused of marking merchandise up slowly and steadily in the months before a sale, at which point it was marked say, "30 percent off," right back to the original and true price. Making shoppers think they got a great deal isn't the same as giving them one and it's not ethical.

warning

Product tampering, whether by employees or others, is damaging to brand images, consumer confidence, and profits. Keep your eyes open for containers that look different from others of the same kind, wrapping or safety tabs that have been repositioned, nonuniform contents in a container, signs of tampering at the top or bottom of a tube, or unusual sediment or liquid around a product.

Many merchants have "half price," "buy one item and get another for one cent," and "two for one" sales. Most are honest representations. Be aware that inflating the price a few weeks before the sale in anticipation of the specials to be offered later is illegal.

Another practice that could get you unwanted attention is nonuniform pricing. Consumer groups are pushing for unit pricing—computing and showing the price per ounce or other standard unit—in addition to the total price to permit easier price comparisons. Pricing that varies from packages in different sizes and brand to brand irritates consumers.

Product Safety Information

Retailers should provide customers with adequate product safety information. If you fail to give adequate warning of possible injury that may result from the use of the product, you can be charged with negligence. The Consumer Product Safety Commission (CPSC) has the authority to take legal action against both the retailer and manufacturer who are found to be in violation of the Consumer Product Safety Act (CPSA) of 1972. The CPSC keeps close watch over products that have high frequencies of injury, such as bicycles, football helmets, power lawn mowers, space heaters, personal watercraft, spas, baby cribs, and swimming pools. Product liability insurance can protect you against injury suits. Stores that sell potentially hazardous goods such as recreational equipment and items for children are usually willing to pay the high premiums for this type of insurance.

The Consumer Product Safety Act requires retailers to report a product that they believe fails to comply with a voluntary standard or creates an unreasonable risk of serious injury or death. Call the Consumer Product Safety Commission at (301) 504-7923 or contact your state's consumer protection agency, which can be located in the government listings of your telephone book or online at cpsc.gov.

False Claims

A salesperson's verbal promise that a product will perform in a certain way is an express warranty and will often hold up in court if your customer files a lawsuit. Typical selling statements like, "These tires should last as long as you own the car" and "Your daughter will probably outgrow these shoes before they wear out" are considered sales talk. However, if a retailer claims that a suit "will not wear out for two years," the customer may have legal grounds for compensation if the suit wears out sooner. Remember that claims on your website need to be valid as well.

The best way to reduce product-related risk to your business is to inspect or test the merchandise you sell. Make sure that the claims made and promotional materials you give out are truthful. The retailers we interviewed for this book were quick to say that they only sell goods that come with adequate instruction booklets and labels. Read the fine-print terms in purchase orders and sales contracts for boilerplate disclaimers or indemnities, cautions a California store owner.

Packaging and Labeling

The Food and Drug Administration has established rules concerning labeling requirements and health claims for foods and nonprescription drugs. Small businesses can be dragged into product liability lawsuits when the goods they sell, service, manufacture or lease cause injury to someone. Failure to provide adequate warning labels and instructions as well as design or manufacturing flaws can have harsh financial consequences.

Warranties

The Federal Trade Commission's Rule on Pre-Sale Availability of Written Warranty Terms requires that manufacturers provide retailers of their products with the warranty materials they will need to meet FTC requirements. They can do this by providing you with copies of the warranty to be placed in a binder; providing warranty stickers, tags, signs, or posters; or printing the warranty on the product's packaging. As long as manufacturers provide you with the warranty materials needed to comply with the rule, manufacturers cannot be held legally responsible if the retailer fails to make warranties available.

You are required to make available the written warranties to consumers before they buy consumer products costing more than $15. You must do this with all written warranties of the products you sell—warranties from manufacturers as well as any written warranties you extend. You can do this by displaying warranties in close proximity to the warranted products or by furnishing them prior to sale and posting prominent signs to let customers know that warranties can be examined upon request. One appliance retailer, for example, suggests posting a refrigerator warranty on the front of the appliance. A retailer of small products, such as watches or tape recorders, might keep warranties indexed in a binder behind the counter or in the department.

Mail order companies who accept orders for warranted consumer products through the mail or by telephone must include either the warranty or a statement on how consumers can get a copy of the warranty in their catalogs or other advertising. This information should be near the product description or clearly noted on a separate page.

Door-to-door retailers must offer the customer copies of written warranties before the sale is completed. For more detailed information, go to ftc.gov and read the requirements for making warranties available prior to sale.

Sales Contracts

Have your attorney review all sales contracts before you have them printed. You must specify all the terms of agreement—price, quantity, method of delivery, time of arrival, time of payment, buyer inspection, and seller protection. There are many controlling laws and regulations regarding agents of a company and that company's liability for any laws violated by your buyer's actions.

Transfer of Title

It's important for you to know at what point the title of goods shipped to you is transferred because the owner of the merchandise is responsible for loss or damage before and during transport. FOB (free on board) is the most common shipping term to describe transfer of title. When merchandise is shipped to you "FOB destination," the seller pays the freight and other charges—including damages—until the goods reach the FOB point (your store). You're responsible for getting the merchandise into your store.

Customer-Related Issues

There are two sides to every customer: profitability and liability. You can't live without them, but sometimes you can't work with them. Accidents and mistakes are inevitable in this business, and regrettably so are problem customers. The majority of complaints can be solved amicably. For others, the customer is not worth keeping. To keep the peace and your piece of the action, be forewarned that there are risks involved in dealing with John Q. Public.

Physical Safety

When you invite customers into your place of business, you are to some extent responsible for their safety on your premises. You can be found negligent if you don't maintain your business or you fail to correct a situation that could lead to injury. An icy walkway, loose step, or wet floor could cause a customer to slip and fall. This injury could have probably been prevented by removing the ice, fixing the step, or mopping the floor. The store could be found negligent if a suit is filed. Performing an audit of potential risks can help you minimize the number of incidents as well as the amount of money you'll have to pay out to remedy problems. Here are four things you can do to identify potential risks:

1. Evaluate your liability risks from your customers' point of view by walking through your business, from curb to alley, noting various sources of possible danger:
   - Are the front of the store and sidewalk well maintained?
   - Is the parking lot uneven or poorly marked?
   - Do the entry and exit doors open easily?
   - Do the aisles, restrooms, and access meet Americans with Disabilities Act (ADA) standards?
   - Are the aisles wide enough?
   - Do lights shine in customers' eyes?
   - Are the edges of counters and displays safe?

tip

A guide to the legal and business requirements of buyers is available through the National Retail Federation (nrf.com) or you can order *Management of Retail Buying* (Wiley) by R. Patrick Cash, Chris Thomas, John W. Wingate, and Joseph S. Friedlander.

2. If you provide a service at a customer's home, evaluate your liability risks.

3. Walk through the store and look at things from an employee or delivery person's point of view:
   - Where are the cleaning materials stored?
   - What kinds of protective gear or procedures do you have for cleaning, repairing, or packing the store and inventory?
   - Are all the tools and equipment in good working order?
   - Are the loading dock, storage units, and utilities safe?

4. Go over your list of risks with your insurance agent to decide the best and most economical method of handling the risk of loss and protecting your business.

Customer Property Loss

To ensure the protection of a customer's personal property, advise them not to leave their briefcases, purses, cellular phones, and jackets unattended while shopping. Some stores have cubicles or coat racks near the checkout stands for customer convenience. Check with your insurance agent to see if an insurance rider is necessary and what security you are required to provide. Train your employees to keep a close eye on what customers arrive and leave with, and to report any irregularities or claims for lost items to you immediately.

Handling Bad Checks

Handling bad checks is a necessary evil for retailers. There are two ways you can combat this expensive aggravation: Have a rigorous policy on accepting checks that requires at least two pieces of identification, and use a check verification service such as TeleCheck (tele check.com) or XpressCheX (xpress-chex.com). These services electronically read the account data encoded on the check and reject any check reported lost or stolen, or from an account that has had overdraft problems. In most states, retailers can recover merchandise from customers who have paid with a bad check, but not always. Remember that not all bounced checks are criminal acts; some are honest mistakes, so use discretion and diplomacy to tell the difference.

Counterfeit Money and Merchandise

With the high quality of graphics programs and printers these days, counterfeit money is not always easy to spot. You will be relieved to know that your bank can give you an instruction sheet on how to identify a counterfeit bill. You can also buy pens to test the authenticity of cash received. These are available at most office supply stores.

Counterfeiting is an approximately $600 billion industry accounting for five to seven percent of world trade. Work only with established suppliers and ask your manufacturer's representative for ways to authenticate merchandise. The fraud unit of your local law enforcement agency can give you a briefing on counterfeit money and merchandise.

Extending Credit

It is not uncommon for retailers to extend credit to customers on expensive purchases such as furniture and major appliances. Often this financing is given simply on the credit worthiness of the buyer, but in other instances the seller or lender demands that the purchaser's promise to pay be backed with some security.

Before you offer financing to your customers, there are a few basic things you should know. Usually, the retailer asks for a conditional sales contract on the merchandise purchased, or a legal hold on the merchandise until full payment is made. If a customer fails to pay on an unsecured debt, you can collect the money owed only by suing. If he fails to pay on a secured debt, the retailer may repossess the security and sell it, or keep it, in full satisfaction of the debt.

The Truth in Lending law (Consumer Credit Protection Act of 1969) requires you to inform customers of the terms and conditions of your credit policies when a finance charge or other charges are assessed. When you let a customer buy a dining room set on an installment plan, you need to advise the buyer of the cash price for the merchandise, the down payment required, the amount of the contract to be financed, the annual percentage rate charged, and the amounts and due dates of payments. You should also know that customers have the right to change their minds (right of rescission) within three days of purchasing a "big ticket" item on an installment plan, and you must void the contract.

Organized Retail Crime

Retail stores report losing $30 billion a year to organized retail crime. The NRF identifies many types of ORC in its 2014 survey. "Boosters" hijack retail delivery trucks, "fence operators" steal merchandise and then convert it to cash and drugs, and "ticket switchers" use sophisticated methods to change pricing on merchandise.

There are 27 million shoplifters, or one in eleven people, in the United States today, reports the National Association for Shoplifting Prevention.

To combat this problem you can:

- Vigilantly scan for shoplifters by assigning employees zones to protect, hiring security guards, and using surveillance cameras with video analytics to detect suspicious activity and facial recognition software to track known thieves.

- Use cable, security bars, locking racks, and anti-push locking carts.

- Use electronic article surveillance (EAS) systems that attach special tags onto everything so that an alarm goes off if someone tries to walk out with merchandise without paying.

- Use mobile point of sale (mPOS), systems such as the (square.com) so employees can circulate with eyes on the floor rather than being captive behind the sales counter. Read about the top ten mPOS systems here: pos-systems-review. toptenreviews.com.

warning

According to National Loss Prevention Associates Inc., a licensed private investigative firm, employee theft accounts for 44 percent of all retail losses causing an annual loss of $13.2 billion in the United States.

EAS tagging is a labor-intensive but almost unbeatable anti-shoplifting tool. It is productive on items of any size, allowing retailers to display high-ticket merchandise on the floor, rather than in locked cases or behind the counter. Experts say theft can be reduced by 60 percent or more when a reliable EAS system is used.

There can be large differences in cost of an EAS system, depending on the system, the size of your store, and the amount of merchandise to be protected. Considering that store personnel will have more time to assist shoppers if they're not preoccupied with watching for potential thieves, experts estimate that a reliable EAS system can pay for itself within two years. Today, there is a push for a common industry standard and manufacturer-added EAS source tagging. With source tagging, an inexpensive label is integrated into the product or its packaging by the manufacturer.

Everyone in your business should be involved in controlling shoplifting. This takes training. Your local police or sheriff's department, mall security, or merchants association can help. Stay in touch with them and other retailers to be alert to illegal activities that may be going on in your area and to learn what you can do to avoid becoming a victim.

Here are a few preventative measures you should always take: Employees need to be aware of a customer's presence as soon as they enter your business. Making eye contact with every customer within 25 feet of you lets visitors know you are there. Even when talking to a customer, employees need to remain aware of other customer activity. Know where the vulnerable merchandise is in your store. Frequently raise your eyes from your work and look around. Train your employees to be alert for suspicious customers. Customers carrying open bags or wearing loose-fitting clothing in which merchandise can be easily concealed should be watched. People who appear nervous or apprehensive and are spending a long time browsing may be suspect.

Tact must be exercised at all times to avoid improper accusations or embarrassment. If a customer appears to be about to walk off with an item without paying for it, you might say "I can ring that up for you here if you like." When it is obvious that shoplifting is taking place, call security, dial 911, or activate a silent alarm. Do not attempt to apprehend a suspect by yourself.

To control losses from price tag switching, securely fasten all price tags or use tags that shred when tampered with. Double-mark major items with the price on one tag and a price code attached elsewhere. If the two do not match, you will know that the item's price tag has been switched.

stat fact

Merchandise valued between $1 and $50 accounts for nearly two-thirds of all merchandise stolen, while merchandise worth $100 or more makes up nearly 20 percent of all thefts, says Charles A. Sennewald, founder of the International Association of Professional Security Consultants.

The retailers we spoke with feel fortunate not to have had many problems with theft. They say a combination of employee vigilance, store layout, and tagged packaging assists their efforts to minimize loss. Having a buzzer or bell by the door and using mirrors are a couple of the strategies our retailers use.

When designing the layout of your store, try to eliminate blind spots that enable shoplifting. An open layout makes it easier for employees to see what's happening in various departments and aisles. Two-way and convex mirrors, closed-circuit TV, video cameras, and other surveillance devices may also deter would-be criminals.

Some stores employ uniformed guards as deterrents to shoplifting and robbery. Others have plainclothes security guards circulating throughout the store. At least one employee should be working in every department at all times, or have a manager circulate throughout the store.

To combat a common shoplifting technique of wearing one garment under another, many clothing stores require customers to use dressing rooms that employees need to unlock for them and/or check each garment with a designated employee. Employees should clear out the dressing room, look for torn-off tags, and count hangers after each customer leaves.

Bathrooms are another vulnerable area in your store since there are usually no monitoring devices there. Post signs on doors directing customers to leave carts and unpaid-for merchandise outside the bathrooms, and have an employee check the stalls periodically.

Watch Out!

Here are six things you must do before detaining a person for shoplifting:

1. See the person approach the merchandise.
2. See the suspect take possession of the merchandise.
3. See where the person conceals it.
4. Maintain uninterrupted surveillance to ensure that the person doesn't dispose of the merchandise.
5. See the person fail to pay for the merchandise before leaving the store.
6. Approach the person outside the store.

▲

Especially valuable or easily concealed merchandise can be displayed in locked cabinets or tethered atop tables. Electronics are attached to cables on tables at Best Buy so they can be examined but not removed. Employees retrieve identical inventory from the stock room should the customer decide to buy. Jewelry is displayed in glass cabinets and shown piece by piece with the supervised assistance of a salesperson. Additionally, oversized, stiff packaging for small items can deter theft as it is difficult to hide.

Posting signs from law enforcement that your premises are under surveillance and that you will prosecute under the full extent of the law will deter some amateur thieves.

Employee-Related Issues

When you think about staffing your business, give some thought to the legal consequences of how you fill those personnel needs. Areas where you might be vulnerable to lawsuits involve on-the-job injuries, family and medical leave conflicts, pay and privacy disputes, and discrimination charges.

Occupational Safety and Health Administration

If you have employees, you are probably covered by regulations set forth by the Occupational Safety and Health Administration (OSHA). If you are a sole proprietor with no employees, you generally aren't covered, but if you use independent contractors, the law still may cover you. Check with your local OSHA office—osha.gov—for a checklist of policies and procedures your business must follow. If you have fewer than ten employees, you are exempt from most of the injury- and illness-recording requirements. However, you must report any accident that results in one or more deaths or the hospitalization of three or more employees.

Retailers with any employees, regardless of the size of your business, must display posters that inform employees of their job safety rights. Spanish and English copies of these posters are available by contacting the OSHA office in your area.

Americans with Disabilities Act

The Americans with Disabilities Act (ADA) says that stores, day-care centers, hotels, theaters, pharmacies, and restaurants must have reasonable policies, practices, and procedures to avoid discrimination on the basis of disabilities. Be sure you provide an accessible path of travel throughout your business, including bathrooms, dressing rooms, telephones, drinking fountains, activity centers, and checkout stations.

Auxiliary aids and services must be provided to individuals with vision or hearing impairments and other individuals with disabilities, unless this would be particularly burdensome to you.

ADA accessibility requirements also apply to web pages. If you have a website, the information on your site must be presented in text format that is compatible with screen-reading devices. (People with visual impairments use these.) You can also provide accessible formats such as Braille, large-print or audiotaped information, or an electronic file on computer disk or an electronic bulletin board.

Employee Theft

It is sad but true: Pinkerton Investigative Services (pinkerton.com) reports from the US Chamber of Commerce that an estimated 75 percent of all employees steal from their employers. The five main categories of employee theft are:

1. Merchandise
2. Supplies
3. Cash from the register
4. Conspiracy with shoplifters
5. Conspiracy with delivery personnel

The incidence of employee theft is higher in retailing than in nonretail operations because employees have greater access to a wide range of consumer goods. The financial impact of employee theft on your business goes beyond the items stolen to the indirect costs of lost productivity, turnover, hiring, and other expenses.

Most retailers bond employees who handle large amounts of money. Through fidelity bonds, the retailer is reimbursed for losses up to the amount specified in the policy if an employee takes off with any of the retailer's funds.

One important way to avoid employee theft is to carefully screen all job applicants. When making key hiring decisions, there are eight basic areas to look into before entrusting someone with the keys to your store. These are: an applicant's driving history, criminal record, previous residences, prior employment, educational achievement, character references, credit check, and professional licenses and certificates. Omissions and inconsistencies on job applications should be questioned. References and past employers should be contacted by telephone.

Retailers are also very vulnerable to theft by delivery personnel. Some of these problems are short counts and merchandise removal. Some security procedures you can use to reduce supplier pilferage are:

- Establish a receiving area for all incoming merchandise and restrict access to the area to authorized store personnel only.

- Employ security officers to monitor the store and inspect packages.
- Employ outside security agencies to "shop" your store to detect dishonest employees who may be conspiring with suppliers to remove merchandise under the guise of legitimate transactions.
- Require employees to store their handbags and backpacks in lockers before beginning work, or use clear plastic bags.
- Use video cameras.
- Install mirrors.

Combatting Shrinkage

Shrinkage is the loss of merchandise for unaccountable reasons. Some results from: vendor fraud, employee theft, external theft, clerical mistakes, or bookkeeping errors. Losses can be caused by unrecorded markdowns, unrecorded allowances, unrecorded breakage, and mistakes in pricing or charging the wrong price. To minimize such shortages, take the following measures:

- Catalog merchandise upon arrival at the store.
- Properly mark, price, and identify merchandise before transfer to the selling floor.
- Record all price changes.
- Record each transaction at the computer terminal or cash register.
- Change records before transferring merchandise from one branch store to another.

warning

Mercedes Gonzales of Global Purchasing Group (globalpurchasinggroup. com) says tip offs a theft may be about to occur include persons who wear overly baggy clothing, move items from one area to another, wear coats on warm days, waving items in the air, and are alone but keep looking at other customers.

Shrinkage from all causes has become more and more of a problem. Today, a 2 percent loss in sales volume is considered acceptable in the industry, although many stores experience heavier losses. Shrinkage losses cut deeply into net profit. For example, 2 percent shrinkage for a store doing $5 million in annual sales means an actual loss of $100,000 per year.

Tighten Store Security

Here are six simple things you can do to tighten security in your store:

1. Equip your store or warehouse with a security alarm system hooked up to a central service company.

2. Use locked trash bins to decrease the risk of merchandise being thrown into the bins to be retrieved later.

3. Do not permit personnel to park near docks or exit doors. A long walk to stash or transport items can be a deterrent to theft.

4. Strictly enforce inventory-control and tracking procedures.

5. Follow up on all references when hiring any new employee, including relatives and friends of friends.

6. Implement an anonymous tip program that motivates employees to report theft, drug abuse, and other business abuses by co-workers and outsiders.

Emergency Preparedness

Take advantage of the free or low-cost services offered by the Red Cross and your local police and fire departments to train you to cope with natural disasters and accidents. They will show you what to do in case of fire, hurricanes, tornadoes, earthquakes, floods, and lightning. Learn what actions to take and who to call in case someone gets sick in your store or falls on your sidewalk, or a car runs into your store. What will you do if there's a gas leak, power failure, or hazardous waste situation? Find out ahead of time—the things we're talking about here are not for on-the-job-training. You don't want people to panic and cause more problems.

A number of the risks discussed in this chapter can be reduced or controlled by taking precautions and using common sense. Being aware of what could happen—and learning what to do if the unthinkable occurs—can minimize damage to the reputation and operation of your business.

Planning
for the Future

I n the next few years, what can you expect to see in retailing that you can capitalize on to grow your business? Let's drag out the crystal ball and see what lies ahead.

The demand for a quality experience, price value, and time savings will continue. You always need to look for ways to improve your retail environment. Some of the retailers we interviewed for this book gave us these seven "must dos":

▲

1. Make sure your store is easy to navigate.
2. Make the merchandise accessible.
3. Have product information readily available.
4. Ensure that sales associates are focused on providing personal assistance.
5. Find and keep good employees.
6. Help customers help themselves in your store.
7. Offer 24/7 shopping convenience online.

Also, don't forget to educate your customers in every way possible—through signage, personal selling, videos, web links, newsletters, and so forth. Give them information about products, fashions, trends, solutions to problems, safety, and usage tips.

Change Is an Everyday Challenge

The life spans of retail stores and retail concepts keep getting shorter and shorter. One of the things being heavily looked at in the 21st century is the extent to which the internet liberates retail. Industry watchers predict that most consumers will go back and forth between the web and local stores. The lines will blur between who does what in terms of service, purchasing, delivery, returns, and information.

No formula lasts forever. Customer needs and preferences change constantly. The good news is that in the United States, there is an average of 76 people per square mile, with disposable income to spend on goods and services. The bad news is that there are more outlets selling more products to the same 76 people per square mile. Be ready to reinvent yourself and your company to survive and thrive.

Here are five guidelines to follow:

1. Clearly define what success looks like, and make sure that everyone on your team understands and focuses on that definition.
2. Do not be complacent no matter how well things seem to be going. A false sense of superiority makes it easy to ignore encroaching competitors. To stay relevant, stay alert.
3. If you are a new brand, you need to advertise that fact heavily and provide clear evidence that you offer something unique. Innovate.
4. Leverage technology to collect information about consumers; then act on that information. Analyze and apply demographic and psychographic data to improve customer service.
5. Cultivate loyal relationships with employees, suppliers, and customers through regular interactions, innovative programs, and fair practices.

Every attempt to reinvent the company must begin with a total approach to doing everything better. The Japanese call it kaizen. Initiate vitality in everything from store planning and design to assortment, service, and marketing. Approach every day with fresh eyes: What does your signage say about you? Your customers? Community involvement? Pricing strategy? Your promotions? Your salespeople? Your displays, colors, hours—everything talks to your bottom line. What messages are you sending, and who do you need to reach to remain in business?

stat fact

According to a recent report by A.T. Kearney, brick and mortar stores are still the foundation of retail, capturing 90 percent of all U.S. retail sales.

Rethink the Rules

Retailers are becoming quite creative when it comes to integrating the various channels they do business in. Starbucks and computer giant Hewlett Packard put a deal together where Starbucks stores are promoting HP's computer recycling program, which fits in with Starbucks' earth-friendly philosophy. Use your imagination to come up with new ways to deliver goods to the consumer quickly and economically. Capture the magic of retailing by thinking of new ways to leverage the physical properties of your business—the look, feel, smell, and ambiance of your environment and tactile sensations of experiencing the merchandise.

Encore?

What do the retailers we interviewed see in their futures? Would they do it all over again? What advice do they have for you?

Keith Covart, age 69, of Electric Fetus in Minneapolis, Minnesota, is glad his daughter is taking over the business for several reasons. When his employees expressed gratitude that he kept the business in the family, instead of retiring and selling it, he realized how they consider it a home of sorts. Some of his employees have been with him for 39 years. Though he feels a little more "out of the scene" now with his hearing too damaged from continual rock concerts to advise customers on new music, he likes overseeing while his daughter takes over. "I really need her. She's doing a lot of the things I can't do anymore."

Keith says it never felt like work because listening to music and sharing it is what he loves to do, and that's important because the road to making a successful business can be long. He adds, "You'd better be in it for the long haul, because there are a lot of ups and downs—just stay calm."

New York designer Matt Murphy continues to see his client base expand into new industries and with more comprehensive creative offerings. What began as a brand consultancy in the second stage of his career has now grown to encompass multiple touch points throughout the life of his client's brands. Beyond developing effective identity solutions, his studio also creates their physical and online environments, as well as their marketing and communications strategies. Murphy says "I believe we will only see an increase in category and lifestyle cross-over. And, I believe retailers and agencies that address the 'everything is everything' ethos—a multidisciplinary approach—will maintain their relevance."

Christine Ward of Patina wistfully remembers a recent venture that burned to the ground, a green store called Shoppe Local. "We were only open three months when it happened. We were paired with some great local designers and manufacturers at the time and instead of disconnecting with them, we made room in our other stores for their work so we could stay connected. Whether you view it as green or smart, it's economical to adjust to changes internally. People are aware of where their products come from. I personally want to keep my own dollars within my community." She foresees recreating the short-lived but successful Shoppe Local venture, soon.

Jay Shafer continues to "create a contagious model for responsible, affordable, desirable housing" by working through zoning issues with Sonoma County for his tiny house village. It will host 16 to 22 houses per acre, each no more than 400 square feet, and be governed by co-op style community decisions.

Stephanie Covart Meyerring reflects, "We've been at our current location since the 1970s. It is a destination. People come to our store because of our customer service and

Top Ten Causes of Retail Failure

Ever wonder why retail businesses go under? Take a look at the top ten reasons, listed below:

1. Economic factors
2. Management incompetence/lack of experience
3. Poor sales
4. Heavy expenses
5. Neglect
6. Disaster
7. Capital problems
8. Fraud
9. Customer problems
10. Overexpansion

community we've built. There are not many businesses in our immediate area. We have a unique demographic and feel fortunate because of that. My Dad used to always call our Minneapolis location the worst location in town. But we are centrally located and have worked hard to consistently provide a positive experience and offer what our customer wants. This has allowed us to win many awards and be voted best store because of what we have created."

The Future of Retailing

The basic premise of successful retailing is to know your merchandise, give your business a recognizable personality, maximize product presentation, and make the purchase easy for the shopper. While few people believe that virtual retailing will make shops obsolete, retailers will need to justify and adapt their physical presence to remain profitable. Some retail experts believe that retail's street presence will become more about building an emotional bond with the consumer than about buying. Whether online or offline, the dividing line between retailers that survive and those that don't will be brand strength—offering visitors more than the simple purchase of a product and creating a memorable brand experience.

Down the road, you may be incorporating LED touch screens, virtual reality experiences, and multimedia sensory stimulation into your store's interior. In the future, stores will be less utilitarian and more of an emotional experience. Destination purchases are price-sensitive, but impulse purchases are not. To win over customers in a market saturated by sameness of merchandise, retailers will offer customers gathering places that are hard to duplicate. Stores are experimenting with various forms of entertainment, such as jazzy piano bars, esoteric coffee clubs, and kiddie play lands. They are also reaching out to an aging population with seating areas, easy-to-read tags and signs, and easy access to merchandise. Some say that in the future retail experiences will provide an oasis in the middle of an overburdened world. Retail will be the conduit of fantasy in a 3-D, physical space choreographed to stimulate shoppers' senses.

Know Your Customers

Baby boomers, those people born between 1946 and 1964, represent a large pool of older, richer, well-educated consumers spending their earned and inherited incomes. Seventy-eight-million strong, the eldest of their group turned 60 in 2006. The youngest households today belong to the "Echo Boom" generation, also called Generation Y (or GenY). These are the nearly 80 million people born between 1982 and 1995. This generation is currently forming first households. Householders under the age of 25 claim less than 4 percent of all household spending in the United States, but their influence is growing in several markets. They account for more than 5 percent of the market for men's apparel, women's apparel, and footwear, and they claim more than 10 percent of spending on infant clothing. Also very noteworthy: This generation of highly educated shoppers is embracing ecommerce.

tip

Add social media sharing buttons to your email signature and website and your click-through rate will increase by 158 percent, according to a 2014 study by We Are Social.

Thanks to the many retailers who took time out of their busy schedules to speak with us and offer their advice—you are starting off on sound footing with the wisdom of experienced entrepreneurs. Plan well, choose something you love, work hard, and reap the rewards of retailing. This is an exciting business. The one thing we can guarantee is that no two days will ever be the same. Enjoy!

Appendix

Retail Store Resources

They say you can never be too rich or too thin. While these can be argued, we believe you can never have too many resources. Therefore, we present for your consideration a wealth of sources for you to check into, check out, and harness for your own personal information blitz. These sources will get you started on your research. They are by no means the only sources out there. We have done our research, but businesses tend to move, change, fold, and expand. As we have repeatedly stressed, do your homework. Get out and start investigating.

Associations

Alliance of Professional Tattooists, (816) 979-1300, safe-tattoos. com

American Amusement Machine Association, (847) 290-9088, coin-op.org

American Booksellers Association, (800) 637-0037, (914) 406-7500, bookweb.org

▲

American Disc Jockey Association, (888) 723-5776, adja.org

Association for Wedding Planners Intl., (916) 392-5000, afwpi.com

Center for Total Quality Franchising, (800) 733-9858, aafd.org

Food Marketing Institute, (202) 452-8444, fmi.org

International Association of Professional Security Consultants, Charles A. Sennewald & Associates, (415) 536-0288, iapsc.org

International Franchise Association, (202) 628-8000, franchise.org

Music Business Association, (856) 596-2221, musicbiz.org

National Association of Chain Drug Stores, (703) 549-3001, nacds.org

National Association of College Stores, (800) 622-7498, nacs.org

National Association for Convenience and Refueling, (703) 684-3600, nacsonline.com

National Community Pharmacists Association, (703) 683-8200, ncpanet.org

National Home Furnishings Association, (800) 422-3778, nahfa.org

National Retail Federation, (800) 673-4692, (202) 783-7971, nrf.com

North American Retail Hardware Association, (800) 772-4424, (317) 275-9400, nrha.org

National Shoe Retailers Association, (800) 673-8446, (520) 209-1710, nsra.org

National Trust for Historic Preservation, (800) 944-6847, preservationnation.org

Personal Care Products Council, (202) 331-1770, personalcarecouncil.org

Books

Brand Against the Machine: How to Build Your Brand, Cut Through the Marketing Noise, and Stand Out from the Competition, John Morgan, John Wiley and Sons, Inc.

Chase's Calendar of Events, 2015, McGraw-Hill

Contagious: Why Things Catch On, Jonah Berger, Simon & Schuster

Crush It!, Gary Vaynerchuk, HarperCollins

Encyclopedia of Associations, Gale Cengage Learning, gale.cengage.com

Epic Content Marketing: How to Tell a Different Story, Break through the Clutter, and Win More Customers by Marketing Less, Joe Pulizzi, McGraw-Hill

E-Service: 24 Ways to Keep Your Customers When the Competition Is Just a Click Away, Ron Zemke and Thomas Connellan, AMACOM

Delivering Happiness: A Path to Passion, Profits and Purpose, Tony Hsieh, Business Plus, Hachette Book Group

Dot Boom: Marketing to Baby Boomers Through Meaningful Online Engagement, David Weigelt and Jonathan Boehman, LINX

Entrepreneur Magazine's Franchise Bible, 7th Edition, Erwin J. Keup and Peter Keup

Jab, Jab, Jab, Right Hook: How to Tell Your Story in a Noisy Social World, Gary Vaynerchuk, HarperCollins Publishers

Retail Superstar: Inside the 25 Best Independent Stores in America, George Whalin, Penguin Books

The New Rules of Marketing and PR: How to Use Social Media, Blogs, News Releases, Online Video, and Viral Marketing to Reach Buyers Directly, 4th Edition, David Meerman Scott, John Wiley and Sons, Inc.

The Small House Book, Jay Shafer, Tumbleweed Tiny House Company

Shoplifters vs. Retailers: The Rights of Both, Charles A. Sennewald, New Century Press

The Tao of Twitter, Mark W. Schaefer, McGraw-Hill

Consulting Services

48 Days, Dan Miller, (888) 373-7771, (615) 373-7771, 48days.net, customerservice@48days.com

Dionco, Inc., James Dion, 312.527.9790, info@dionco.com

Karp Resources, Karen Karp, (631) 765-9406, karpresources.com, karen@karpresources.com

Fitch, (212) 260-1070, fitch.com

Merchandise Concepts, Anne Obarski, (614) 389-3248, merchandiseconcepts.com, anne@merchandiseconcepts.com

Dave Ratner, Dave's Soda & Pet City, (888) 763-2738, daveratner.com, dave@daveratner.com

Pinkerton Investigative Services, (800) 724-1616, pinkerton.com, pinkerton.info@pinkerton.com

The Prouty Project, Jeff Prouty, (952) 942-2922 proutyproject.com, jeff.prouty@proutyproject.com

The Robin Report, Robin Lewis, (212) 750.5405, therobinreport.com

Consumer Research

eMarketer, (800) 405-0844, eMarketer.com

Envirosell, Paco Underhill, (212) 673-9100, envirosell.com

Faith Popcorn's Brain Reserve (212) 772-7778, faithpopcorn.com, info@faithpopcorn.com

Forrester Research, (866) 367-7378, (617) 613-5730, forrester.com

Google Trends, google.com/trends

Google AdWords, adwords.google.com

Marketing Charts, (646) 233-0126, marketingcharts.com

Mintel, (212) 796 5710, mintel.com

Pingdom, (212) 796-6890, pingdom.com

Trends Research Institute, (845) 331-3500, trendsresearch.com

Specialty Retail Report, (800) 936-6297, specialtyretail.com

Equipment

Checkpoint Systems, (800) 257-5540, checkpointsystems.com

National Cash Register, (800) 225-5627, ncr.com

POS World, (888) 801-7282, posworld.com

WordStock P.O.S. and Inventory Control, (800) 753-9673, wordstock.com

Merchandise and Visual Display

Retail Design Institute, retaildesigninstitute.org, (513) 751-5815

Risk Management Resources

Business Security Publications, (858) 755-2931, employeetheft.com

Loss Prevention Associates, Inc., (888) 688-2405, lpassociates.com

Threat Analysis Group, (281) 494-1515, threatanalysis.com

Social Responsibility

Charity: Water, (646) 688-2323, charitywater.org

Coalition for Consumer Information on Cosmetics, (888) 546-CCIC, leapingbunny.org

Fair Trade Federation, (302) 655-5203, fairtradefederation.org

Forest Stewardship Council, (612) 353-4511, fscus.org

Oceanic Preservation Society, (303) 444-2454, opsociety.org

Software

Acclivity (formerly M.Y.O.B. US Inc.), (800) 322-6962, accountedge.com

Cheftec, Culinary Software Services, Inc., (303) 447-3334, culinarysoftware.com

LabelCalc, Nutritional Analysis for Food Manufacturers, (888) 804-0001, labelcalc.com

Peachtree, Sage Software, (770) 724-4000, na.sage.com

QuickBooks, Intuit, quickbooks.com

Mix & Burn Systems, Mix and Burn LLC, (651) 209-1500, fye.playanywhere.com

Prism POS, Merchant Technologies, (800) 395-8324 merchanttechnologies.com

Successful Retail Business Owners

Amy Dubin, Janam Indian Tea, (503) 820-8036, janamtea.com, info@janamtea.com

Beverly Calder, Bella Main Street Market, (866) 663-9469, bigmerlot.com, cooking. com/bellamarkets, bella@bakervalley.net

Charlotte Cozzetto, Ethique Nouveau, (612) 822-6161, ethiquenouveau.com, info@ ethiquenouveau.com

Christine Ward, Rick Haase, Patina, (866) 877-9995, patinastores.com, customer service@patinastores.com

Deve Wolfe, Tempting Teal Boutique, (541) 432-WOLF (9653), temptingteal boutique.com, wolfefleece@gmail.com

Dan Dye and Mark Beckloff, Three Dog Bakery, (800) 487-3287, threedog.com, threedog@threedog.com

Erik Ekman, Outside Van, (800) 971-8830, www.outsidevan.com, info@outsidevan.com

Gary Vaynerchuk, Wine Library, (888) 980-WINE (9463), winelibrary.com, info@ winelibrary.com, vaynermedia.com, gary@vaynermedia.com, tv.winelibrary.com

Jennifer and John Valente, Dollar Card Marketing, (619) 234-6567, triptychonline.com

Keith Covart and Stephanie Covart, Meyerring, Electric Fetus, (612) 870-9300, electricfetus.com

Matt Murphy, Matt Murphy Designs, (917) 534-3053, mattmurphy.com, services@ mattmurphy.com

Ron Knox and Paul Gallagher, Stillwell House Antiques, (732) 972-6454, stillwell houseantiques.com, stillwellhouse@aol.com

Trade Publications

California Apparel News, (213) 627-3737, apparelnews.net

Chain Store Age, chainstoreage.com

Retailing Today, (813)-627-6946, retailingtoday.com

In-Store Marketing, Path to Purchase Institute, (773) 992-4450, shoppermarketingmag.com

Progressive Grocer, (800) 422-2681, progressivegrocer.com

Websites

dealtime.com: a site for comparing products, prices, and stores

ebay.com: an online marketplace

facebook.com: social networking

48days.net: small business ideas, coaching, and community

gordonbrothers.com: overstocks, closeouts, wholesale appraisals

imediaconnection.com: connection site for the marketing community

linkedin.com: professional and social networking

meetup.com: social and professional group events

mysimon.com: a pricing and comparison service

myspace.com: social networking

priceline.com: an ecommerce site where you name your own price *shutterfly.com*: photo hosting

toptenwholesale.com: wholesale shopping and advertising

twitter.com: social networking, information feed

wordpress.com: information exchange, written word hosting

Glossary

Above-market pricing: Pricing above the normal market value for trendy or scarce products or services.

Advisory board: A cross-section of community citizens appointed by a retailer to offer advice and counsel to management on a variety of issues.

Aggregation: An approach to target market selection whereby customers' traits, responses, needs, and wants are grouped and examined by similarity, rather than individual detail.

Anchor tenants: The major tenants in a shopping center that serve as the primary attraction.

Assignment: The transfer of title, right, and interest in certain real property; the document used to convey a leasehold is called an "assignment of lease" rather than a deed.

At-the-market pricing: When retailers set prices that are about the same as competitors'.

Balanced tenancy: The types of stores in a planned shopping center chosen to meet all of the consumers' shopping needs in the trading area.

Base rent: Minimum monthly rent payments, as set forth in a retail lease, excluding pass-throughs, percentage rents, and other additional charges.

Base year: The year in a lease term used as a standard in a rent escalation clause; operating costs in the next year are compared with costs in the base year, and tenant's rent is adjusted either up or down.

Basic stock: The amount and assortment of merchandise sufficient to accommodate normal sales levels.

Below-the-competition pricing: Setting prices lower than competitors' prices.

Boutique department: Small specialty shops within a larger store that feature a narrow range of exclusive, fashionable merchandise in an attractive atmosphere; a boutique layout approach is adopted by many department stores as a variation on conventional departmental layouts.

Breadth: The width of a merchandise assortment; the number of different styles, colors, sizes, and other variants a retailer carries.

Brick-and-mortar merchants: Traditional retailing in physical businesses as opposed to virtual retailing, which is conducted online without a physical headquarters customers can visit.

Bulk marking: A merchandise marking practice (used for items that sell at very low prices and are subject to rapid price changes) whereby items are not marked until placed on the selling floor.

Buying groups: Organizations that coordinate or pool the buying resources of many small businesses into larger orders with major manufacturers or suppliers.

Cashwrap: Cash register or checkout stand.

Category management: Emerging practice that brings suppliers and sellers together to determine the right product mix within a specific product category; the goal is an efficient assortment of profitable products.

Chain: A retail organization consisting of two or more centrally owned units that handle similar lines of merchandise.

Channel: The medium through which a message-sender communicates with and sells to an audience.

Checking: A phase of the physical handling process that involves matching the store buyer's purchase order with the supplier's invoice (bill), opening the packages, removing the items, sorting them, and comparing the quality and quantity of the shipment with what was ordered.

Circular: A store promotion printed on one page and distributed by third-class mail, newspapers, or by hand.

Classification dominance: Displaying and arranging merchandise in such a way that psychologically the consumer is convinced the firm has a larger assortment of merchandise in the category than competitors.

Clayton Act: Declares certain practices illegal even if they do not actually restrain trade or do not constitute a monopoly or an attempt to monopolize.

Click-and-mortar strategy: A strategy of physical businesses to incorporate the internet in buying and selling.

Cluster anchors: A group of small stores that sell similar or complementary merchandise and operate in the place of the traditional anchor tenant in certain specialty centers.

Come-on item: An item that a retailer sells at a loss (below cost) to draw customers into the store; also known as a loss leader.

Community shopping center: A shopping center in which the leading tenant is a category killer, variety store, or department store.

Comparison goods: Merchandise that consumers will usually shop for at several stores before buying.

Consignment: A situation in which suppliers guarantee the sale of items and will take merchandise back if it does not sell; the store does not pay for the inventory, but rather keeps a percentage of the receipts from each sale.

Consumer Credit Protection Act: Requires retailers to explain in easily understood language the finance charge and annual percentage rate on the merchandise they finance.

Consumer Leasing Act: Requires a leasing company to make an accurate and detailed disclosure of all terms and costs in leasing contracts.

Convenience center: A small shopping center anchored by a quick-stop food store and occupied by other service-oriented tenants.

Convenience goods/products: Frequently purchased items for which consumers do not engage in comparison shopping before making a purchase decision.

Cooperative advertising: Promotional programs in which wholesalers or manufacturers pay a portion of the retailer's advertising cost under specified conditions.

Core service: The primary benefit customers seek from a service firm.

Debt service: Regular payment made on a loan.

Depth: The number of pieces stocked of the different styles, colors, sizes, and other variants in each line a retailer carries.

Developer: The individual or entity that invests in building a retail property and is responsible for construction, marketing, and leasing; this person may also be the owner of the land.

Dual distribution: A situation in which wholesalers also operate retail outlets.

Ecommerce: Buying and selling over the internet.

Effective space: The amount of retail space in a given trade area that is capable of drawing consumers.

Electronic cash register (ECR): A point-of-sale register that uses electronic light beams to enter information at a very high rate of speed.

Electronic data interchange (EDI): A computer network that links manufacturers, distributors, and retailers for streamlined ordering.

Electronic funds transfer system (EFTS): A system for the automatic transfer of cash from a customer's account to a retailer's account.

Endcap: A display set up at the end of a store aisle; always well-stocked and changed frequently.

Equal Credit Opportunity Act: Prohibits discrimination on the basis of race, color, religion, national origin, age, sex, marital status, and receipt of income in any aspect of a credit transaction.

Experience qualities: Attributes, such as taste, that can only be discerned after purchase or during consumption.

Express warranties: Written warranties for products or services.

Fair Credit Billing Act: Legislation establishing a billing dispute settlement procedure for "open-end" credit; also imposes certain other requirements on retailers to assure fair and accurate handling of credit accounts.

Fair Credit Reporting Act: Protects the consumer's right to an accurate, up-to-date, and confidential credit report.

Fair Debt Collection Practices Act: Designed to eliminate abusive debt collection practices and to protect the consumer from harassment and unfair collection procedures.

Federal Trade Commission: A government agency responsible for enforcing the Clayton Act and other antitrust laws, as well as laws pertaining to advertising and trade.

Federal Trade Commission Act: Legislation passed in 1914 to create the FTC.

Fixed-payment lease: A rental agreement in which rent is based on a fixed payment per month.

Food court: An area in a shopping center, usually in an enclosed mall, where different kinds of food are available from individual vendors selling from separate stalls.

Franchise: An exclusive right to sell a product or perform a service; in retailing, an individual will purchase this right from a chain store or other type of a parent corporation and operate the store according to the rules and regulations of the franchisor.

Free-standing retail space: A store that is not an integral part of a shopping center, enclosed mall, or mixed-use development; also called pad space; many downtown department stores are free-standing.

Frontage: The section of a store that faces the street or the pedestrian walkway in a mall; also refers to window display area and entrance.

Generic merchandise: Merchandise that is unbranded and which is typically somewhat lower in quality than brand-name merchandise.

Implied warranty: A provision of the Uniform Commercial Code that requires that all merchandise sold be fit for the purpose for which it is intended.

Impulse items: Items purchased on impulse when they are seen by a shopper without prior intent to buy.

Independent retailer: A local, nonchain store owned by a single individual or family.

Industrial shopping center: A type of specialty center based around stores and services having to do with plumbing fixtures, hardware items, or the care of automobiles.

Initial markup: In pricing merchandise, the first markup of a new item after purchasing it wholesale.

Keystone: A standard apparel markup that sets a selling price for merchandise at double its cost (a 100 percent markup).

Kiosk: A booth or stall set up in a shopping center, sometimes on a temporary basis, to sell goods such as tobacco, newspapers, magazines, seasonal merchandise, candy, keys, and other small impulse-purchasing items; also, a multimedia electronic selling or information tool set up inside stores or malls.

▲

Layaway: Customer service in which the shopper makes a down payment on an article, pays the balance due in installments, and the retailer retains ownership until the customer has paid in full.

Lifestyle presentation: Arranging merchandise in such a way that it is compatible with the consumer's activities, interests, and outlook on life.

Loss leader: A product intentionally sold at a loss to attract customers; also known as a come-on item.

Manufacturer's brand: A brand, often referred to as a national brand, owned by a manufacturer who may sell to anyone who wants to buy the brand.

Maintained markup: The average markup of an item sustained over a period of time, allowing for future markdowns and other reductions in selling price.

Margin: Refers to the amount of profit a retailer makes from a certain item; it is always expressed as a percentage of the sales price.

Markdown: A reduction in the original selling price of an item.

Market development: A strategy that focuses either on attracting new consumer segments or completely changing the customer base.

Marketing fund: An account controlled by the landlord that is specifically for funding shopping center promotions and advertising, and to which all merchants in the center must contribute based on a predetermined amount stated in their leases.

Market price: The amount actually paid for a property.

Market rent: The rent a retail site could command under prevailing market conditions.

Market share: That portion of consumer dollars spent on a particular merchandise category that a given retailer can capture.

Merchandise distribution: An aspect of merchandise management in multiunit organizations related to getting merchandise from consolidation points/distribution centers to the individual stores.

Merchandising: The management of stock in a retail setting, including how it's displayed, point-of-sale materials used to promote it, and the quantity that's stocked.

Merchant wholesalers: Wholesalers who take title to the goods they sell.

Merchants association: An organization formed in shopping centers and controlled by the tenants to plan promotions and advertisements for the good of the center as a whole; usually all tenants are required to participate, and both tenants and landlord pay dues.

Minimum rent: The rent that will always be due each month in a tenant's lease term, regardless of sales volume and exclusive of any additional charges; often used in conjunction with a percentage rent arrangement and sometimes called fixed minimum rent.

Mom-and-pops: Small stores, generally operated by members of a family with limited capital; typically locally owned and operated; can be three-or-four-store chain if the owners are involved on a daily basis at each store.

Nonmarking: The practice of not price-marking individual merchandise items; usually the display fixture will indicate prices.

Off-price retailers: Outlets offering well-known brands of merchandise at substantial discounts compared to conventional stores handling the same products.

Order point: The level of stock below which merchandise is automatically reordered.

Original retail price: The first price at which an item is offered for sale.

Outlet center: A type of specialty center comprised of at least 50 percent factory outlet stores offering name-brand goods at discounted wholesale prices; the manufacturer will usually operate the store, eliminating the retail markup.

Power retailers: Merchants with sufficient financial strength, marketing skill, and price/value relationship to enter a market, however saturated, and make a profit.

Price discrimination: Varying the prices charged to different retailers for identical merchandise without an economic justification for doing so.

Price line: A limited number of prices that reflect varying levels of merchandise quality; price lining may occur either in the context of rigid price points or price zones.

Price point: A small number of different prices; for example, a merchant might price all "good suits" at $175, all "better suits" at $225, and "best suits" at $350.

Price-sensitive: The tendency of the price for an item or service to vary based on demand, availability, and competitor pricing.

Price zones: A pricing strategy in which a merchant establishes a range of prices for merchandise of different quality; for example, prices for general kitchen items might be $10 to $200 lower than prices for gourmet kitchen versions.

Private brands/labels: Brands owned by a retail or a wholesale firm rather than by a manufacturer.

Promotion: Any form of paid communication or marketing from the retailer to the consumer.

Quantity discount: A reduction in unit cost based on the size of an order.

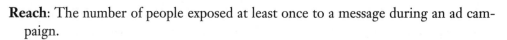
Reach: The number of people exposed at least once to a message during an ad campaign.

Receiving: A phase of the physical handling process that involves taking possession of the goods and then moving them to the next phase of the process.

Regional dominance: A location strategy whereby a retailer decides to compete within one geographic region.

Remarking: The practice of changing the prices marked on merchandise to reflect price changes.

Retail decision support system: The structure of people, equipment, and procedures that gathers, analyzes, and distributes the data that management requires for decision making.

Retail marketing mix: Those variables—product, price, presentation, promotion, personal selling, and customer services—that can be used as part of a positioning strategy for competing in chosen markets.

Retail saturation: The extent to which a trading area is filled with competing stores.

Robinson-Patman Act: Says that manufacturers must sell the same quantities of the same goods at the same price; they cannot discriminate regardless of the buyer.

Sales promotion: Marketing activities other than direct selling, advertising, and publicity that stimulate consumer purchasing; examples include displays, sales, exhibits, and demonstrations.

Sales retail price: The final selling price or the amount the customer pays for the merchandise.

Same-store retail sales: Anniversary (annual) comparison of sales from the same store at the same period from year to year to measure business health and growth.

Scanner: A permanently fixed device that emits a laser beam for scanning the bar codes on merchandise and that can provide automatic price readouts, automatic updates of inventory, and similar features.

Seasonal discount: A special discount given to retailers who place orders for seasonal merchandise in advance of the normal buying period.

Seasonal merchandise: Merchandise in demand only at certain times of the year.

Shelf space: Amount of point-of-purchase space occupied by food products in a grocery store, as measured by square feet, linear feet, or number of facings.

Sherman Antitrust Act: Federal legislation declaring that price-fixing is illegal.

Shopping goods/products: Merchandise for which consumers engage in a price- and quality-comparison process before making a purchase decision.

Showing: A term that describes the way in which outdoor advertising space is bought or sold; a 100 showing in a market means that advertising space was purchased on enough posters to reach 100 percent of the audience in an area at least once each month.

Shrinkage: Stock shortage determined by discrepancies between book and actual inventory values.

Single-price policy: All merchandise in a store is sold at the same price.

Site plan: A drawing of the retail site as it will look when it is completed, including individual tenant spaces, common areas, elevators, escalators, food courts, service areas, parking, and access routes.

Slotting fee: Fee that food manufacturers pay retailers for shelf space and/or to have products promoted in the highest-profile slots.

Source marking: The practice of the vendor, rather than the retailer, marking the goods.

Specialty goods/products: Products that consumers know they want and that they are willing to make a special effort to acquire.

Stock turnover: The rate at which inventory is sold in a retail store, normally expressed in turns per year; also called stock turn.

Stock-keeping unit (SKU): Specific measure of an item of merchandise for inventory purposes; SKUs can refer to anything from the size of a bottle of aspirin to the type of photo film.

Strip center: A type of shopping center designed in a single, unenclosed strip facing the street.

Super regional center: A shopping center anchored by at least three full-line department stores.

Target market: The specific group of consumers whom the retailer wishes to attract.

Tenant mix: The combination of retailers and service vendors leasing space in a shopping center.

Trade area: The geographic area from which a shopping center will obtain most of its customers; size depends on the type of center, location of competition, and other factors.

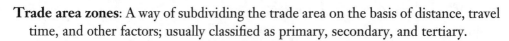
Trade area zones: A way of subdividing the trade area on the basis of distance, travel time, and other factors; usually classified as primary, secondary, and tertiary.

Trade discount: A reduction off the seller's list price that is granted to a retailer who performs functions normally the responsibility of the vendor.

Universal product code (UPC): A standardized form of product marking for electronic reading of price and other information that is used for food and health-and-beauty aids.

Upscale retailer: A retailer specializing in goods at the high end of the scale in price, quality, and consumer served.

Wand: An electronic device that can be passed over merchandise for reading machine-coded information.

Index